What people are saying about the movie documentary "Big Men," directed by Emmy Award-nominated director Rachel Boynton, Executive-Produced by Brad Pitt, and featuring some of George Owusu's story . . .

"Astonishing! This cool and incisive snapshot of global capitalism at work is as remarkable for its access as for its refusal to judge."
—Jeannette Catsoulis, *The New York Times, Critic's Pick*

"A great one. Richly detailed. First Rate."
—Alan Scherstuhl, *Village Voice*

"Unforgettable!"
—Kenneth Turan, *The Los Angeles Times*

"Brilliant! If you want to see how the world works . . . you need to see 'Big Men,' a remarkable new investigative documentary about oil, money, Africa and America . . . Vivid, compassionate, unstinting."
—Andrew O'Hehir, *Salon.com, Pick of the Week*

IN PURSUIT OF
JUBILEE

IN PURSUIT OF
JUBILEE

A TRUE STORY OF THE FIRST MAJOR
OIL DISCOVERY IN GHANA

GEORGE YAW OWUSU

with M. Rutledge McCall

Library of Congress Cataloging-in-Publication Data

IN PURSUIT OF JUBILEE, A True Story of the First Major Oil Discovery in Ghana

ISBN:
Hardback 978-0-9973519-6-5
Paperback 978-0-9973519-7-2

Includes bibliographical references and index
1. Oil and Gas Industry   2. International Business   3. Ghana   I. Title

This work depicts actual events in the life of the author as truthfully as recollection permits and/or can be verified by research. All persons within are actual individuals; there are no composite characters.

The author has made every effort to ensure that the information in this book is accurate. The author and publisher do not assume, and hereby disclaim, any liability to any party for any loss, damage, or disruption caused by errors or omissions, whether such errors or omissions result from negligence, accident, or any other cause.

First Edition
Printed in the United States of America
2017938652

Rights for publishing this work outside the United States of America or in non-English languages are administered by Avenue Lane Press.

Dedicated to my wife Angelina Owusu,
my father Opanin Yaw Owusu, mother Madam Margaret Afia Mansa
and grandfather Reverend Yaw Adu-Badu

FOREWORD

In Pursuit of Jubilee tells the story of a man's courage, conviction, patriotism and resilience, a man whose unique story serves as a source of inspiration to all who seek to help transform their communities in particular, and humanity in general in the face of unrelenting challenges, intrigues, sabotage and skepticism.

Not surprisingly, the announcement of the Jubilee Field oil discovery was met with some skepticism and disbelief in certain political and industry circles in Ghana. Against the backdrop of earlier discoveries not having turned out to be "major hits," perhaps the skepticism and disbelief were understandable. Parliamentary proceedings as captured in *The Ghanaian Hansard* of June 19, 2007 provide ample manifestation of this.

As if that weren't enough, rumors began to surface relative to the role of the EO Group and the interest of its principals in the persons of Mr. George Yaw Owusu and Dr. Kwame Bawuah–Edusei in the Petroleum Agreement, which constituted the basis for the exploration and undertakings of the Jubilee Partners in the West Cape Three Points Block.

The two gentlemen were tagged "NPP"—a political party in Ghana. Their EO Group was projected as fronting for President Kufuor and his party, the NPP, and, driven by lack of knowledge and in some cases by a combination of sheer ignorance, mischief and malice, some politically motivated circles began to question their equity of 3.5% in the share-holding structure of Jubilee Field Partners.

The author of this book has done great justice to the specifics of the nightmare of protracted harassment he and his group went through to the extent that it will serve no useful purpose to recount the details here. But suffice it to say that the state-sponsored harassment reached a crescendo when the Attorney-General prepared a charge sheet of twenty-five (25) counts against the EO Group with the significant exclusion of its partner, Kosmos Energy and officials of GNPC and the erstwhile Kufuor Administration.

This is indeed a narration of courage, resilience, endurance and fortitude. A true life story of a patriot who loves his motherland and refuses to give up on her because of the intrigues and mischief of his fellow citizens.

Hopefully, *In Pursuit of Jubilee* will inspire the same spirit of fortitude and patriotism in those who read it and digest its lasting lessons for the benefit of humanity and nation building.

It is a must-read for all who seek the truth, and only the truth about the role of George Yaw Owusu and the EO Group in the historic discovery of oil in commercial quantities offshore in Ghana's West Cape Three Points Block in the year of the country's Golden Jubilee as an Independent nation.

Truth always wins. And fortitude endures.

— Abdul Malik Kweku Baako
Editor-In-Chief, *The New Crusading Guide*

ACKNOWLEDGEMENTS

I have had the good fortune of meeting many incredible people whose stories might not have found the light of day, had I not taken the time to document their journey alongside mine, and to take the opportunity to thank them for traveling this incredible road with me.

Several brilliant men, women and businesspeople in Ghana and across many parts of the world were instrumental in my work in Jubilee Field. I owe it to these people to tell my story. I did not set out to write a book that would assault the character of those who leveled spurious charges against me, nor to disparage their decisions to do so. However, this story stands as a cautionary lesson for all of us, that in each situation we find ourselves, we must understand the repercussions of every smile, every handshake, every word and every promise given.

In the years of my involvement in the creation of Jubilee Field, my name was subjected to many attacks, but none left permanent scars. I walked away with countless business and life lessons, most of which confirmed the fundamental virtues of humility, integrity and discipline, which I had learned long before I had the opportunity to join many great people in doing something great for our country. These key virtues never wavered, in spite of the struggles, challenges, triumphs and disappointments we encountered during our efforts in leading Ghana into oil and gas exploration successes.

A special note of thanks to M. Rutledge McCall for his outstanding professionalism and diligence on this project, and his invaluable help which kept me going through the years of writing. My gratitude to Jim Barnes, a man who worked tirelessly, often without any monetary compensation, simply because of his belief in the truth and my innocence; I cannot thank you enough. It is through a journey as challenging as this that I get to truly appreciate, even more, the extraordinary leadership and tremendous inspiration of Asantehene Otumfuo Osei Tutu II. I owe a huge debt of gratitude for having been a beneficiary of your generosity and prudent counsel.

I am truly thankful also to Akenten Appiah-Menka, a visionary whose unflagging support and optimism guides people like me in venturing into opportunities around the world. I am grateful to have worked with lawyer Phil Inglima with Crowell and Moring, for his diligence for the truth and a willingness to uncover the facts of my case. You have a rare combination of integrity and perseverance.

My thanks to the lawyers I met in the United States: Adrian Mebane and Femi-Dekula Thomas also with the Crowell and Moring Law Firm. To the team at McGuire Woods Law Firm, in the U.K. — thank you.

To my lawyer, Kwabena Addo-Atuah, for your relentless work over three years, and for the work of my lawyers in Ghana: Sampson Obeng, Yaw Eshun, Abdallah Ali-Nakyea and Leo Kyeremateng for their local understanding of the legal implications of this case.

I owe Joseph Owusu a debt of gratitude for his loyalty and friendship, especially with the Tullow negotiation in London. Thank you for standing by me through my trails and challenges during my decade-long ordeal. To Dai Jones, Alex Bruks, Yaw Afoakwa, Kwabena Sarpong, Kwabena Kwakye, Egbert Faibille, Kwabena Owusu-Akyaw, Kwami Sefa Kayi, Ibrahim Mahama and Joojo Aboagye-Atta, thank you for your praiseworthy efforts. Kweku Baako, your relentless pursuit of truth and respect for journalistic integrity is something that the Ghana natives will be truly grateful for in the years to come.

To Jack and Diane Webb, I am incredibly thankful for what I found to be their genuine kindness and remarkable support to the economic progress in Ghana. Very few people are as noble, humble and forward-looking as both of them, and the Ghanaian community - especially in the city of Houston and across the United States - have had the benefit of their service through the years.

To those whose support and encouragement during this journey were critical and on whose shoulders I stood: Ernestina Owusu, Rebecca Aidoo (Mama), Adelaide Appiah, Gifty Osei-Tutu, Geophysicist Alex Ababio, the late Moses Oduro Boateng, Theophilus Ahwireng, and Kojo Quainoo, I am truly thankful for all your work. To Ransford Boateng, who worked with me through some of the most challenging days, I pray for God's blessing on your life for the reassuring person you had been for me. The Honorable Kwame Pianim and Honorable Kwesi Botchwey have both been a ray of hope for me, and I am very thankful for their wisdom and encouragement.

To President John Agyekum Kufuor and President John Mahama, your country, both now and in the future, will remain thankful for your diligent work and rare courage in leadership to ensure that this golden moment of oil exploration did not elude the nation. For many Ghanaians who would never have had the chance to see the persistent work of people like Honorable Albert Kan-Dapaah, Honorable Paa Kwesi Nduom, Honorable Aaron Mike Oquaye, Honorable Joseph Kofi Addah, Honorable Felix Owusu-Agyapong, Honorable K.T. Hammond, Honorable Joe Oteng-Adjei, Honorable Kofi Buah, and Dr. Valerie Sawyer, – your service leaves a great legacy for the future of generations to come. I thank you all for your work.

I had the good fortune of meeting Yaw Appiah-Nuamah, Opanin Kwesi Owusu and the late Naval Captain Amos Yaw Mensah, all of whom showed me much generosity and offered the sound counsel that I needed the most. It is men like you, of character, integrity and excellence that encourage people like me to keep on forging ahead. I am grateful for your generosity and friendship. My gratitude to Mr. Steven Sekyere-Abankwa for an unrivalled objectivity and honesty, and for your unpretentious love for Ghana in doing whatever it took for its success.

My friends in Houston, Yaw Mensah and Kwame Acheampong who trusted in the opportunity to make a difference and worked to organize the first conference that led to the discovery of Jubilee Field. Okyeame

Essah-Mensah, Lawrence Frimpong, Jermaine Nkrumah, Dr. Sannie Reagan and Ben Asante have all been instrumental business thinkers and to all of them I owe debt of gratitude beyond words. Nanette Putterman, Jaleen Akuoko and John Hauser, I cannot thank you all enough for everything you do, and with such grace and brilliance. My gratitude also to E. Obeng-Amoako Edmonds for his own tireless pursuit of excellence that drives him to add value to every work.

I cannot recount my journey on to the Jubilee Field without a special thank you to Dr. Kwame Bawuah-Edusei. You have been a great advocate for entrepreneurial success in Ghana, and I sincerely thank you for your own commitment to making a difference for your country.

There are many more people I may have missed, both individuals and organizations, whom I had the benefit to know. I thank you all for your contribution to my life and the work of Ghana's oil discovery that I am humbled to have been a part of. There are many people in Ghana I would never have the chance to meet but who I hope might appreciate the sacrifice and ingenuity of people who stood and challenged themselves to put forth diligent efforts in the face of incredible odds for the good of all. For my fellow Ghanaians, I trust that the lessons gleaned from my experience might become a template, a blueprint, of what occurs not only in the energy exploration and development business, but also when a person sets out to accomplish his goals and dreams in life.

My journey is that of one person. My prayer is that many more entrepreneurs will dare to seek opportunities and take risks that will someday make a difference for Ghana and the world at large. This book is written for our sons and daughters, who may one day be faced with a decision about whether to respond to the call and add their talent, experience and efforts in continuing to improve their nation. It is answering that call that makes the pain of the journey worthwhile.

—George Yaw Owusu

CONTENTS

INTRODUCTION

Ghana, a small African country located on the beautiful Atlantic coast-line just north of the Equator, was called the "Gold Coast" until 1957, when she gained her independence from Great Britain. There was good reason for the name: the country's gold deposits were among the world's largest, putting her in a league with South Africa. And, as in South Africa, the billions of dollars earned from Ghana's gold deposits did not improve the lives of her indigenous people. Yet, another hope for prosperity was on the distant horizon.

By the end of the 20th century, things had changed for Ghana. Times had become leaner, her natural resources less plentiful, her economy more precarious than ever. Her neighbors, Nigeria, Ivory Coast, Equatorial Guinea, and Gabon had been pumping crude oil in impressive quantities for decades. So, it would be natural to assume that oil must also exist in Ghana. Yet, from the late 1800s through the late 1900s, as many as 100 exploratory oil wells had been drilled off the coast of Ghana by multinational oil firms such as Amoco, Texaco, Phillips and others, and not one had discovered and produced com-mercial quantities of petroleum. It was as if Ghana was an empty hole surrounded by oil-producing nations.

What was Ghana's problem? Was the country technologically in-capable of discovering a new natural resource with the potential to lift the nation out of poverty and provide a better standard of living for her citizens? Were Ghana's leaders satisfied with her gold reserves and cocoa production, to the point where there was little motivation to invest in searching for a natural resource that experts believed was there, given the numerous regional energy discoveries? Whatever the reason—politics, money, technology—fate seemed rigged against the beautiful country nestled on balmy shores reminiscent of a Caribbean paradise.

And so, near the dawn of the new millennium, during his campaign for the Presidency of Ghana, a challenge was given by John Agyekum Kufuor: "Find oil in Ghana."

In Pursuit of Jubilee: A True Story of the First Major Oil Discovery in Ghana is about a businessman who was born, raised and educated in Ghana, and who rose to the challenge and initiated an effort that would result in one of the largest discoveries of premium grade oil on the African continent.

Initially, the Ghanaian government would hail George Yaw Owusu as a hero for a find that potentially put the nation shoulder-to-shoulder with the region's biggest oil producers, holding up the possibility of raising Ghana from a beautiful African curiosity to setting the nation on a path to what could become economic parity with First World countries. It was the opportunity of a lifetime.

Yet, even before a drop of oil could be produced, a firestorm would ensue when the new government of Ghana launched a criminal investigation of Mr. Owusu, bringing the nation's emerging oil industry to the brink of chaos and plunging his life into a nightmare that would last for years and subject him to repeated police interrogations, accusations in the news media, attacks by powerful politicians, insinuations by his own business partners, and shady players determined to bring him down.

The nation's then-former President, John Kufuor, would be swept into the foray, causing him to declare, "I am almost tempted to believe it when people say that oil finds are a curse."[1]

Where did the truth lie? In his book, *Africa: Altered States, Ordinary Miracles*, author Richard Dowden wrote, "Maybe we should weep for Ghana—and insist that occasionally principles and people matter as

---

[1] John Agyekum Kufuor (President of Ghana from 2001 to 2009), as quoted in an October 25, 2010, *Financial Times* article by London correspondent William Wallis, titled "Curse of Oil Follows Ghana's Former President."

much as petroleum."[2] Did George Owusu help pull off the nation's most breathtaking achievement in its modern history through criminal acts, bribery and corruption? Had top government officials been involved, perhaps even the nation's President?

This riveting story answers those questions and tells why, during a time when economies around the world were collapsing, the government of Ghana relentlessly went after one of her own sons, a man upon whom the nation had bestowed its most coveted award, for his efforts in helping to catapult Ghana onto the world stage.

Read these pages and learn their lessons well: as often as not in life, good deeds, honesty and hard work aren't always met with joy.

—M. Rutledge McCall

[2] Richard Dowden, *Africa: Altered States, Ordinary Miracles*; Public Affairs, 2010 (p.538).

CHAPTER

1

AN EXPLOSIVE BEGINNING

After waiting nearly two hours in a small, nondescript room at the Criminal Investigation Department (CID) headquarters in Accra, a group of uniformed and plainclothes police officials entered and escorted me and my lawyer to another room, where several dozen more police officers were waiting. One of the investigators informed me that, as part of their inquiry into various activities involving my company's acquisition of offshore oil exploration rights in Ghana five years earlier, the court had issued search warrants for my home and my office. They were to be served immediately.

Numb and disbelieving, I was escorted across town to my office in a convoy of police cars and a bus filled with armed, uniformed officers, with blue lights flashing and sirens wailing all the way.

As we sped through the sweltering streets, Accra's perpetual crowds of street beggars peered in through the windows, trying to get a glimpse of the criminal in the back seat.

I was ordered to wait outside while investigators descended en masse into my office, to the confused looks of my staff members. My lawyer's objections were ignored as officers confiscated files, computer hard drives, and countless documents.

When they had taken what they wanted from my office, the speeding police convoy took me all the way down the Tema Motorway to my house, where my wife and our young grandson watched, frightened and helpless, as a phalanx of armed, uniformed officers and plainclothes detectives stormed in. Every room was searched, personal items pawed through, more computer drives taken, other documents seized, and every item photographed.

It was embarrassing and degrading. I protested, of course, as any innocent man would who was being victimized by his own government. But it was no use.

The day had not started out this way.

* * *

Tuesday, June 16, 2009, had been a seasonably humid day in Accra. I had just entered my lawyer's office when his phone started ringing. He waved me to a chair and answered the phone. I sat down.

As he listened to the caller, a look came over his face that I'd seen enough times recently to know who it was.

I mouthed the words, *the CID?*

He nodded to me and said into the phone, "No, inspector. Mr. Owusu cannot come in again. Not today."

I felt my blood pressure begin to rise. I had just returned from an appointment with my doctor and here these guys were again, requesting another interrogation. I had been through a grueling session with the

CID just the previous day. And the week before. These officers weren't giving up.

My lawyer listened again, then said to the investigator, "No. I told you. Mr. Owusu is on medication for high blood pressure and is under doctor's orders to rest."

He covered the mouthpiece and whispered to me, "It's about a form you forgot to sign after they questioned you yesterday. A minor matter. He says it will only take you a minute to drop by and sign it."

I shook my head and muttered something in Twi, my native Akan language. In Ghana, a country where the police is perceived to be corrupt, nothing was a minor matter when the CID was involved.

The officer on the phone was probably one of the same ones who had interrogated me several times during the past few days—sessions that had driven my blood pressure to deadly levels. They had questioned me over and over, about things I hadn't done, supposed crimes that had never happened, rumors I knew nothing about, and false accusations having to do with the efforts I had initiated five years earlier that resulted in the largest oil discovery in the history of Ghana.

A discovery worth billions of dollars.

Fittingly, as frightening as it was to be ordered in for interrogation by the police in relation to a series of felonies I was being accused of, the start of my career in the oil business had been even more terrifying.

Nearly two decades earlier and thousands of miles away, an explosion ripped through the Atlantic Richfield Company plant in Channelview, Texas. I was there and saw it all.

It happened on Thursday, July 5, 1990, at 11:15 p.m. during my shift at the ARCO plant. I had stopped to talk to another worker for a few minutes. While we were chatting, I received a call on my walkie-talkie from my supervisor.

"George Owusu," my radio squawked. "Come in, please. Over."

I grabbed my radio, clicked it on, said, "This is George. Over."

"I need you to check a valve on a tower on the plant grounds. Over."

While I received instructions on which tower and valve I had to go check on, the man I had been talking to got in his van and drove away.

I pedaled over to the tower on my bike.

No sooner had I climbed to the top of the tower and put my hand on the valve, when the plant erupted in a violent explosion and a fireball lit up the night sky. The plant looked as if a bomb had been dropped on it. Flames and thick plumes of smoke shot a hundred feet into the dark sky. Warped steel and wreckage was strewn all over the grounds. The explosion was felt several miles away, shattering windows in nearby houses and blowing out street lights. Neighbors a mile away reported a "flash like an atomic bomb."[3]

The man I had been talking with just moments before the blast had arrived faster at his area because he was driving. As soon as he had gotten there, the explosion occurred. It would take days to find all of his body parts.

I watched from the top of the tower a couple of hundred feet in the air as the horrific scene played out, terrified, not knowing what had happened. Trembling and stunned at the devastation around me, I somehow made it down the tower and got to the office, where I was warned that the explosion could be followed by a violent chain reaction. So we waited to make sure there wouldn't be any more blasts before we evacuated the plant.

The plant's fire brigade quickly arrived and began fighting the blaze. Hazardous Materials Units began arriving from the nearby Shell Oil Refinery. Harris County fire trucks were all over the place. Firefighters, ambulances, and police cars were pouring into the plant.

Four dozen people had been on shift at the plant that night. The initial death toll was reported as 14. The total body count would reach 17, and would include several contract workers, and a tanker truck driver

---

[3] See: http://www.chron.com/news/article/July-5-1990-ARCO-refinery-explosion-fire-kill-157969php

who burned to death in the cab of his vehicle as he tried to flee the scene. Five other people were badly injured, as well. Two cooling towers, a steam generation facility, a pipe rack, and two tanks were damaged.

When I finally arrived home, my wife was waiting in the driveway. I fell into her arms and sobbed. I was diagnosed with post traumatic stress disorder and was admitted to therapy. It would be a year before I would be ready to return to work.

The incident had literally been the explosive start of my new career in the oil business. The start of a nearly two-decade journey that would lead to police investigations thousands of miles away in Ghana, inquiries by the U.S. Department of Justice (DOJ), charges of fraud, multiple interrogations by the CID, and half a decade of fighting for my very life and freedom.

For me, the ARCO explosion was the beginning of one hell of a career.

And now, 19 years later, with the police in Accra hauling me in for questioning again, the explosive end to my career had begun. My life was about to enter a long and bizarre battle as the new government of Ghana bore down on me, determined to see me behind bars, unfazed by the fact that I was also an American citizen.

I suspected a couple of people who were probably behind the government's relentless pursuit of me. People whose motives were not difficult to discern. One hundred and sixty billion dollars worth of premium grade crude oil was a powerful incentive.

But what was surreal about what was happening to me now was that just six months prior to start of the CID interrogations, I had been basking in the euphoric glow of being fêted as a national hero. Just the previous year, I had been awarded the coveted Order of the Volta, an honor bestowed on me by the government of Ghana for outstanding service performed for my country.

As the police investigators pawed through my family's personal belongings on that fateful June day in 2009, a hopeless feeling of government oppression settled over me at the realization that my own father had experienced something similar, when a previous Ghanaian government had destroyed his life exactly fifty years ago that month.

CHAPTER

2

WARRIOR KING

Appropriately, the name Ghana means Warrior King. So maybe it made sense that the country's history was thick with intrigue, internal battles and strife, including more than three centuries of foreign influence, wars, fighting and subjection by outside overlords.

And now, it seemed that both Ghana's tumultuous history and that of my own family was coming back to haunt me.

I was born on February 24, 1949, in Ash-town, a suburb of Kumasi, the second-largest city in Ghana, back when the nation was still ruled by the British. I was the middle child of the seven children of successful businessman Opanin Yaw Owusu, who had been born in Ajumakase-kese, near Kumasi. A prominent and recognizable figure in the Kumasi area, my father was sought after by the townspeople for his wisdom and business acumen. My mother, Margaret Afia Mansah came from Akyawkrom, also near Kumasi. My mother was a member of the Church of Pentecost and was active in the women's fellowship.

Our large family lived a comfortable life in a 19-room house filled with all the comforts a young boy could imagine, including many furnishings imported from Britain. We owned a restaurant, a cocoa farm, and my father and uncle owned four Shell petrol stations in Kumasi. We also owned a restaurant and another petrol station in Yeji, a town on the western edge of Lake Volta.

We had old gas pumps with a giant glass receptacle on top, which held the gasoline. My father or uncle would prop me up on their shoulders and I would operate the hand crank to pump the petrol from the storage tank in the ground up and into the glass bottle. Then a hose would be inserted into the vehicle's tank and I would watch the yellow liquid drain out of the glass container and into the gas tank. You could say the petroleum business had been in my blood from a very young age.

When I was six years old, I was sent to Wesley College Practice School, a primary school attached to the prestigious Wesley College in Kumasi. Life was peaceful, almost idyllic, for the Owusu family.

Then, in early 1957, after the British colonial government had left Ghana, a rapid decline followed for businessmen who refused to side with Ghana's first president, Kwame Nkrumah, a 46 year-old grassroots organizer and self-described "African Lenin" communist from the Gold Coast.

Being a highly regarded, wealthy, traditionalist African who strongly disagreed with the communist leanings of Nkrumah, my father became an ideal target for the government's Preventive Detention Act, a law that allowed the government to imprison anyone perceived to be a threat or a potential enemy of the State. The situation had deteriorated to such an extent that if someone had a grudge against you, all they had to do was accuse you of insulting the President, and that was enough to land you in jail without trial and with no way of proving you hadn't made the alleged remark.

In June of 1959, as Nkrumah continued to consolidate his grip on the nation, my father was warned by a friend that the authorities were looking for him. My father's choices were stark: prison without a trial, or life without his family. He headed west, into Ivory Coast, losing everything to the Nkrumah government—his business, his livelihood, all of his assets and property.

And I was about to experience the first of many radical life shifts I would go through over the next several decades.

I was 10 years old when I was sent to live with my grandfather, Reverend Yaw Adu-Badu, a Methodist minister and traveling preacher who lived in a mission house in Enchi, in the Western Region of Ghana. He took me with him on his visits to dozens of towns, preaching to the people and all the while teaching me about Christianity and God. My father had laid within me a foundation of the Asante culture, customs, traditions and the history of Ghana. My grandfather had built within me a foundation of spiritual faith and a moral compass, with rules and guidelines that would prepare me for the challenges of life.

In 1960, I was sent to visit my father. It was a traumatic experience for me to see him living in exile and near destitution in Ivory Coast. Later that year, my parents divorced, and my mother, brothers, sisters and I moved into a one-bedroom house. At night, my brothers and I would spread blankets on the floor of the tiny veranda and sleep huddled together for comfort. It was a different life than I had lived during my first decade. In many ways, the new experience was an adventure. Yet, there was no escaping the reality that my family was now poverty-stricken, along with the vast majority of Ghanaians.

In February of 1966, during a trip to China, a military and police coup d'etat nicknamed "Operation Cold Chop" had been staged in Ghana, and Nkrumah was deposed. At last, my father was able to return home. But it would not be a triumphant homecoming. During his seven years of forced exile, hard times had set in for the once prosperous businessman. His days of wealth and influence were over. The military rulers were firmly in command.

The following year, 1967, I graduated from Swedru Secondary School and enrolled in Wesley College in Kumasi to begin my education as a school teacher.

How I longed for those tranquil days as a fresh-faced 20-something teacher, long before fate intervened and set me on the twisting path that now lay before me as a suspect accused of crimes against the nation of my birth.

CHAPTER

3

WELCOME TO AMERICA

I graduated from Wesley College in 1969 with a teaching certificate and was assigned to a primary school in Kumasi. On August 29 of that year, Dr. Kofi Busia, a sociology professor, was elected as Prime Minister of Ghana in an era that came to be known as Ghana's Second Republic. It was three years after the overthrow of Kwame Nkrumah's government, and the Busia government had been struggling to rejuvenate the anemic economy and get the nation's nearly 50% unemployment rate down.

In 1970, the nation was elated when the AGIP oil company discovered oil in the shallow waters offshore Saltpond. Named the "Saltpond Oil Field," the resource was desperately needed, yet it produced less than 5,000 barrels per day at its peak before dribbling down to 550.[4]

---

[4] The peak of 550 barrels per day was reached in 1984.

That would come to characterize Ghana: blips of initial excitement, quickly followed by the reality of life in a country whose politicians are perceived to have more of their own interests at heart than those of the people.

On January 13, 1972, while Prime Minister Busia was in Great Britain undergoing medical treatment, Ghana's military stepped in and took over the government, under the leadership of Army Colonel Ignatius Kutu Acheampong.

On January 6, 1974, I left Ghana for the United States. The odd new country was a culture shock for me. The idyllic splendor of Ghana, where temperatures rarely deviated from 80° Fahrenheit, had been replaced with snow, frigid temperatures, and the unique New York "attitude." Still, I was hooked. It was months before I saw green grass, but by the time the spring thaw had arrived, I knew I had found a new home in America.

My first roadblock to building a successful life was that neither my high school certificate nor my teaching diploma from Ghana counted in America. If I wanted a shot at a decent job, I would have to go to college all over again and earn a U.S. degree. And if I wanted to go to college, I would first need to pass my high school equivalency exam and earn my General Education Diploma (GED).

After moving to Chicago in 1975, I got busy.

In 1978, after acing the GED, I enrolled in a local community college. I used my credit card to pay tuition, and took five full-time courses each semester while working at a local hospital. I was up at 4:45 every morning so I could make it to my job by six o'clock. I took two different buses to get to work, carrying a suitcase of books and studying every minute on the way. Between meals, when the dishes were done and before the lunch rush, I would go into the bathroom, close the door, and do my studying and homework.

"This African boy must have some kind of a problem," my coworkers would tease me. "He's always in the bathroom!"

They had no idea that I was hunkered down in that little bathroom stall at Schwab Rehabilitation Hospital in Chicago through the late 1970s, studying during every chance I got. I earned straight A's. I was a resourceful 27 year-old kid, busily building a future in America, so I might one day return home to Ghana. Maybe even as a hero.

By 1980, I had enough community college credits to transfer to a university, and in 1982, I graduated from Illinois State University with a degree in Agribusiness. But Bloomington was a small town and jobs were scarce. It was time for a change, so I moved to Houston, Texas, the "oil capital of the world."

Meanwhile, back in Ghana, oil was also on the mind of the nation's new leader, Jerry John Rawlings. It was odd to have neighboring countries producing world-class quantities of crude while Ghana hadn't found commercial quantities of petroleum in a hundred years of searching. Even the government's Ministry of Mines and Energy, with a mandate to explore for oil, had produced no results.

To try to get in the race, in 1983, Rawlings formed the Ghana National Petroleum Corporation (GNPC) to replace the agency that had been responsible for the importation of crude oil and petroleum products. He established the GNPC as a government-owned company, backed by Provisional National Defense Council (PNDC) Laws 64 and 84, with a mandate to engage in the exploration and production of oil, and to ensure that Ghana benefited the most from the development of the country's petroleum resources.[5] Rawlings appointed a lawyer named Tsatsu Tsikata[6] as the GNPC's first Chief Executive Officer.

---

[5] See: "About GNPC"; www.gnpcghana.com
[6] He served a 12-year tenure as head of the GNPC.

CHAPTER

4

EARLY DAYS

In 1985, as I was looking for work in the greater Houston area, I received a job offer in Pasadena, Texas, at a Montgomery Ward retail store. My friends tried to warn me off, advising me that Pasadena was not a town widely known for its pleasantness toward black people. Some even pointed out that, until very recently, there had been a Ku Klux Klan book store on Red Bluff Road in Pasadena.

I needed the work, so I ignored their warnings and took the job. It paid $1,000 per month, the most money I'd ever made in my life. I did well at Montgomery Ward. I made many friends, and never experienced the racism people had tried to warn me about in Pasadena.

The following year I was moved to a Ward store in Baytown, Texas, and promoted to Manager of the Lawn and Garden department. I was now earning $19,000 per year—more than a 50% pay hike. Still, it wasn't easy to support a family and save money on a pre-tax income of less than $1,600 per month. I kept my eyes open for better opportunities, and joined a group of local Ghanaian Asante expatriates.

I made an interesting observation while managing the Lawn and Garden department at the Baytown Montgomery Ward: customers who didn't appear to be particularly wealthy were paying up to $1,000 in cash to buy fancy equipment like home lawn mowers. I became curious about what so many people were doing for a living that they could afford to pay cash for such luxury items.

I began my conversations with each customer with the question, "So . . . where do you work?"

The answer would play a pivotal role in shaping the rest of my life.

"I work in a chemical plant," my seemingly well-paid Montgomery Ward customers told me.

"Really? A chemical plant?" I responded. "What do you do at the chemical plant?"

"We make chemicals."

"What kind of a degree do you need to make chemicals?"

"Degree? We don't need a degree."

"How much do they pay at the chemical plant?"

"Oh, they pay quite a bit."

No one would be specific as to exactly how much money they were making at the chemical plant, but I concluded that it had to be a lot—definitely more than I was earning as a department manager at a national dry goods chain store, because I couldn't pay $1,000 in cash for a lawn mower in the mid-1980s.

It was time to look into another career change.

Determined to do whatever it took to get a job in that business, in 1988 I went to the ARCO Chemical plant in Channelview, Texas, and took an employment test. And I aced it.

The day I was offered a job at ARCO, I took off my Montgomery Wards jacket, never to work in retail again. My salary increased from $19,000 to $48,000—250% of what I had been making as a Ward department manager. I could buy a pretty fancy lawn mower now, if I wanted to. It felt like the sky was the limit.

The 564-acre ARCO Chemical complex was located in the area of Houston known as the Ship Channel. In operation since 1977, it had been acquired by ARCO in 1980 and employed more than 400 workers.

The job was not difficult. It required mechanical skills, critical thinking, and working with my hands. I was a quick learner. Around midnight, we would collect various samples from different areas of the plant and take them to the lab to be analyzed to make sure they met certain specifications—correct temperature, pressure, and other levels—to arrive at the precise composition needed to make each chemical compound. The compounds went through machines and into the various reactors. After the reactions took place, the chemicals then went to pipes, and from pipes into the distillation columns, and then into large storage tanks.

The plant was hot, even at midnight. We used bicycles to make our rounds, checking the machines to make sure they were functioning properly, and checking various lines, gauges, temperatures, levels, and volumes. It was almost like a factory where we never saw the product, but we knew it was in there.

I worked four days on and four off, and was allowed to put in up to two days of overtime each week. I was finally making serious money. But I had a lot to learn in the "black gold" business of Texas. And the lessons would serve me well.

During my second week of work at ARCO Chemical, I received heartbreaking news. My father had passed away in Kumasi, Ghana. I hadn't saved up enough money to make a trip home, but as a son, it was my responsibility to be there to help lay my father to rest. I went to the ARCO credit union to apply for a $1,000 loan to travel to Ghana. I was turned down because I was so new to the company. I wrote a letter to the credit union, telling them all about my father, what he had accomplished during his lifetime in Ghana, what he had endured, what he had lost. What an amazing man he was. I went to the credit union to give them the letter and to reconsider my application for a loan. They showed mercy and lent me the money.

That loan was precious to me. I couldn't have lived with myself if I had missed his funeral. Several of his children put our money together and gave him a farewell that honored his memory. To this day, whenever I drive past that ARCO credit union, I am filled with gratitude.

By the close of the decade, I'd had a great job with a company with a global presence, I was happily married, I had a beautiful wife and daughter. And I would be starting the process of building a house on the land I had purchased in Ghana a few years earlier. What more could a man ask for?

I had it all.

And then, just one day after July 4th, 1990, came the infamous explosion at the ARCO plant during my night shift, launching the real beginning of my experiences in the oil business.

A year after that horrific incident, after I had gotten over the post-traumatic stress, an old dilemma reared its head again: accept an offer at another firm for bigger money and high danger, or go elsewhere for lower pay and safer work.

I tried to land somewhere in between and accepted a position at Eltex Chemical as their Environmental Director, overseeing company compliance with EPA and OSHA rules and regulations. It was a perfect fit, considering what I had experienced.

Over the next seven years, from 1991 to 1998, I focused on my work at Eltex, absorbing as much as I could about the petrochemical industry, learning about its processes and protocols, working in corporate middle management, and on fully recovering from the trauma of the violent event at the ARCO plant.

By 1998, I had experienced a relatively peaceful seven years at Eltex. That year, I was installed as the Asantefuohene (Chief of the Asantes) of Houston. I also left the job at Eltex to take a position at Shell Oil as an Environmental Representative, overseeing waste management and traveling throughout the Midwestern U.S. The job entailed a lot of travel. I visited most of the Shell retail, distribution, and some pipeline facilities in each state on a rotating basis, making sure they were in compliance with U.S. EPA laws, rules and regulations, verifying that they hadn't spilled any gasoline or chemicals into the ground or contaminated groundwater. If there was any waste, I saw to it that they disposed of it properly and in appropriate hazardous waste landfills (or in non-hazardous waste material landfills, depending on the type of substances involved), and that all waste was correctly classified, to avoid the improper disposal of hazardous waste materials.

The salary was good and the sacrifices were manageable. I was learning entirely new activities pertaining to managing far-flung operations, including how to deal with different types of personalities, in diverse cities across the Midwest for one of the world's largest oil firms.

As head of the Asante group in Houston, I would often travel to various gatherings of Asante groups across the country, making new friends and acquaintances, some of whom would one day play important roles in my life.[7] In 1999, during a Ghanaian Asante diaspora organization meeting in Toronto, Canada, I met and soon became friends with Dr. Kwame Bawuah-Edusei, a physician trained in Ghana who had a family medicine practice in Washington, D.C., and was a friend and supporter of former Ghanaian presidential candidate John Kufuor. Bawuah-

---

[7] In addition to getting together to sing Ghanaian songs, eat Ghanaian food, enjoy one another's company, speak our native language, and collect money to help people in Ghana, the organization's main goal was to keep our way of life alive, and to make sure that our customs, culture, and traditions were not lost among our children who were born in America.

Edusei and I initiated a job creation venture to help reduce poverty and increase education by distributing equipment, books, and furniture to youth programs in Ghana.[8]

In 2000, I was promoted to the position of Commodity Manager at Shell, with authority to negotiate environmental waste disposal contracts worth millions of dollars. As the executive in charge of contract negotiations, any company wanting to do business with Shell that involved waste product disposal was required to submit a contract offer to me.

The broad experience I had been gaining in my 15 years in the petroleum industry was preparing me to step into a role that, in less than 48 months, would become my last formal job ever.

Meanwhile, the situation in Ghana was keeping pace with my busy life in Houston in interesting ways. By the end of the final year of the last decade of the century, another historic election was brewing in my homeland. The timing of related events would pave the way to my destiny. I was about to take the wildest ride a man could ever imagine.

---

[8] With two other men, we also formed a company called E-link, to use satellite technology to transfer data between West Africa and United States. The venture would fold in 2001.

CHAPTER

5

Opportunity Knocks

In 1998, Nuevo Energy Corporation explored for oil in Ghana. They found nothing. In 1999, Dana Oil, Fusion Oil and Gas, and Hunt Oil[9] explored for oil and they too came up empty. In 2000, Santa Fe Oil explored for the elusive black gold, but it was another unsuccessful effort. In fact, since 1896, nearly 100 exploratory wells had been drilled in the waters off the coast of Ghana. Not one had been able to find oil in commercial quantities.

The worldwide oil industry had come to regard Ghana as an exploration "graveyard." Its basins were yet to be derisked. Adding to the challenge, there was the general perception that the Ghana's petroleum

---

[9] Hunt had even drilled wells near the same West Cape Three Point Block that would one day yield a gusher of historic proportions, yet they had found nothing.

agreements could have the effect of discouraging capital intensive oil exploration activities. The petroleum business in Ghana was simply not an investor-friendly endeavor, compared to neighboring countries.

By 2000, Ghana's economy was in worse shape than before. Ghanaians were scraping out a pitiful existence. That year, Ghanaian presidential candidate and New Patriotic Party (NPP) opposition party leader John Kufuor traveled to Texas to sell his message of hope to the Ghanaian community in Houston. Things had only become more dire, since military coup leader Flight Lieutenant Jerry Rawlings had muscled his way into power nearly twenty years earlier. Kufuor was determined to change things—whether he won the election or not.

I did not know Kufuor personally. I had seen him on television and knew of him, of course, and I admired his courage as a leader in a country struggling to emerge onto the African stage and hopefully contribute to the global economic landscape. I could only hope his enthusiasm for the nation would transform into success.

John Kufuor stood nearly six feet four inches tall. He spoke in a thoughtful cadence in a deep voice, had a warm smile, a keen intellect, and possessed the calm, assured demeanor of a natural leader. Kufuor came across as a "big picture" thinker, yet possessed a keen grasp for detail. Rather than be involved in the minutiae of various issues, he preferred to set the agenda, state the goal, and then let his team do their job while he provided the requisite leadership.

In Houston, Kufuor told his fellow Ghanaians, "You live here in the oil capital of the world. If you are not managing to get a competent oil exploring company to come to Ghana and find oil for us . . . Nigeria has oil and they are less than 300 miles east of Ghana. Our next-door neighbor, Côte d'Ivoire, also has oil. Ghana sits in between. So I challenge every one of you: find an oil company and bring it to Ghana so we can strike oil, too."

I had left Ghana in January of 1974. In the years since then, I would hear of political and economic development from news outlets and friends who had returned to the U.S. from Ghana. My extended family still lived in Ghana, so it had always been a modest and very rewarding aspiration for me that maybe someday I would be able to contribute to the country in some small way. Any achievement for Ghana would hopefully impact the lives of all Ghanaians, including my own family.

As the chief of the Asante community in Houston, and as a manager at one of the world's largest oil companies, I took it as a personal challenge to do something for my country. All the better if presidential candidate John Kufuor won the election and reclaimed the Castle for the people. That was a long shot, of course. The political bloodline of Ghana's decades of dictators seemed to have a permanent grip on the government. Even the man Kufuor was running against, John Mills, former Vice President of Ghana, had been hand-picked by the nation's previous President, Jerry John Rawlings, who had controlled the country for almost two decades.

It would take a miracle.

That miracle was delivered on December 7, 2000, when John Agyekum Kufuor was elected as President of Ghana.

The following September, Yaw Mensah, one of my Ghanaian friends in Houston, called me.

"Albert Kan Dapaah, the Minister of Energy for Ghana, is coming to Houston," Mensah said. "He wants to meet investors."

Dapaah's responsibility as Minister of Energy was to help Ghana develop her energy resources. He had been sent to Houston to find oil and gas investors for Ghana.

Mensah asked me if I could help Dapaah get in touch with a few CEO's of major oil firms in Houston. Opportunity was knocking from 6,333 miles away. I wanted to say yes immediately, but I didn't want to promise something I couldn't deliver.

In my capacity as chief of the Houston Asante Association[10] I contacted my friend Joseph Owusu, a geologist and petroleum economist in the Commercial Development Group at Texaco Oil in Houston. I got in touch with the president of the Ghana Association, Dr. Benjamin Asante. I contacted Kwame Acheampong, a well-connected resource and friend. I told every experienced and respected oil industry contact I had that the Energy Minister of my country was coming to Houston and wanted to meet with energy industry experts, executives, and representatives to make them a pitch. I approached a Vice President of Shell, who agreed to put me in touch with a few key people. I contacted Chris Wilmot, a businessman with the Greater Houston Partnership (an organization dedicated to the promotion of business between Houston-based companies and the rest of the world). I reached out to everyone I could think of in the energy sector.

Our efforts to attract industry heavyweights began paying off. What had begun as an attempt to gather a few people to meet with the Minister soon grew into an important petroleum industry conference that would enable Ghana's energy experts from the GNPC to address major oil firms on the offshore hydrocarbon potential of Ghana. International oil firms—Texaco, Chevron, Exxon, Hess, Ocean Energy, and many others—made commitments to attend the conference.

At the time the Kufuor administration had taken office in Ghana in January of 2001, there had been only three companies prospecting for oil in the country. None had come anywhere near finding commercial quantities of oil. Virtually no companies were interested in searching for oil in Ghana. Her entire coastline was nearly bare.

In addressing the convention, Ghana's Energy Minister got right to the point:

"Ghana is actively looking for oil," Dapaah announced. "I believe there is oil in Ghana. It just hasn't been found."

---

[10] In Houston, there is an Asante association, as well as a Ghanaian association comprised of all Ghanaian ethnic groups.

The Minister strongly encouraged investors and oil firms to give it a try. At least, continue to investigate the potential of finding oil in Ghana, considering the finds in neighboring countries, he implored. I invited Alfred J. Boulos, the founder of the European Petroleum Negotiators Group, to address the gathering.

The consensus of the professionals was a repeat of what we had heard before: there was a possibility of offshore oil in Ghana, but for decades the GNPC itself had been keeping their requirements too high by copying the existing agreements of surrounding countries—which already had proven oil deposits. But the GNPC had steadfastly refused to heed the experts, and interest in the nation's petroleum possibilities faded. Ghana was simply asking too much from a company to even begin exploration, particularly since oil had never been discovered in Ghana in any significant quantities. Unless that changed, the experts agreed, no CEO of a major company would drill for oil in Ghana at a cost of up to a million dollars a day—and as much as $80 million—just to explore an unproven high-risk basin in Ghana when they could go to nearby countries and be assured of higher possibilities of success.

If Ghana would offer pragmatic entry requirements, one industry expert stated, the country could become a major league player, like Nigeria. That got my attention. Nigeria was the New York Yankees of the big leagues in the African oil game.

During the Jerry Rawlings regime in Ghana, a company called Vanco Energy (now Van Dyke Energy) had expressed interest in searching for oil in the country, but had been unsuccessful in securing an agreement with the GNPC. When Gene Van Dyke, the CEO of Vanco, heard about the conference I had been putting together, and that we would be hosting Ghana's Minister of Energy, he had Vanco's chief geologist, John Craven, call me to ask for an invitation to attend. At the end of the conference, Craven asked me if I would bring Minister Dapaah to the Vanco offices the next day. He explained to me that Vanco wanted to try again in Ghana, now that there was a new administration.

"Of course," I told Craven, eager to assist. "That's why the Minister came to Houston. To find investors."

The following day I met Gene Van Dyke.

"George," he said, "Will you help us look into getting a block to explore oil in Ghana?"

To be asked by Gene Van Dyke, the single largest holder of African oil licenses in the world at the time, to assist his firm in obtaining a block to explore for oil in Ghana was an exciting opportunity for me. The man had more deepwater drilling rights in Africa than ExxonMobil. From his humble start in discovering Louisiana gas fields in the 1960s, Van Dyke had gone on to lease blocks in Ivory Coast, Senegal, Gabon, Equatorial Guinea, Namibia, and Madagascar.

Three years earlier, in 1998, Unocal, Kerr-McGee (acquired by Anadarko in 2006), Royal Dutch/Shell, and TotalFinaElf paid Van Dyke a reported $50 million dollars for 78% of his Gabon lease, which he had acquired one year prior to that for a little over $2 million.[11] Within just five years, by 2006, he would hold more oil acreage rights than British Petroleum, Shell, and ExxonMobil combined. To say that 70 year-old Gene Van Dyke was a "player" would be like saying Michael Jackson had a couple of hit songs. The man was legendary.

I set up the meeting with the Energy Minister and the Vanco team. The next morning we met at the Vanco offices with Minister Dapaah and representatives from Ghana's GNPC. During the meeting, Gene Van Dyke took out a map of Ghana and circled a large, deep water area approximately 30 miles offshore, for which Vanco wanted exclusive rights. It was massive, equivalent to 10,000 square kilometers in the Gulf of Guinea. Nobody else wanted it because, at the time, there was no interest in exploring for oil in Ghana. When Van Dyke expressed interest in licensing this area for exploration, the Minister became very

---

[11] His partners covered the cost to drill four exploratory wells. Van Dyke kept 11% of all oil they discovered. See: http://www.forbes.com/forbes/2001/1224/112.html

excited. It was just what he had come to America for: to secure investment in Ghana's virtually deserted oil industry.

During 2001 and 2002, I became Vanco's unofficial consultant. Whenever Van Dyke was unable to get in touch with Minister Dapaah, he would call me and I would track down the Minister for him. Anything Vanco wanted to know about Ghana, I was there for them, guiding them through the maze of Ghana's governmental bureaucracy and cultural protocol. I opened up a whole new world of business possibilities for Vanco.

Things started stepping up when I was asked to accompany Vanco to Ghana later that year so Van Dyke could meet with President John Kufuor. I helped set it all up with GNPC Chairman Steven Sekyere-Abankwa, arranging for them to meet the executives, the decision-makers and the President.

Vanco's corporate emblem was an image of an elephant.

"We are searching for elephant-sized oil fields in Africa," Van Dyke said, explaining his firm's logo to President Kufuor.

Kufuor loved it. Coincidentally, the elephant was the symbol of his political party, the NPP. The two men hit it off. My efforts were paying off. Vanco applied for the rights to the enormous block. Because they were the first to apply, and nobody else had pursued the opportunity, they got it. We were on our way to acquiring the largest oil exploration block in all of Ghana. I was euphoric.

Vanco was awarded their block in July of 2002. I approached Gene Van Dyke to discuss the terms of my involvement in procuring and developing the field.

"What I want," I told him, "is a fair share for helping set all this up. I would like to be the Country Manager for Vanco in Ghana, coordinating and overseeing ground operations."

"No problem, George," came the reply.

At the time, I was too naïve to even consider asking for an ownership share in exchange for doing so much work to help Vanco get set up in Ghana. Yet, I was elated. My life was about to take a major turn—and return me to my homeland in grand style.

As I began to wind down my affairs in the U.S. in preparation to move to Ghana, Gene Van Dyke called me.

"George," he said, "let's go have lunch."

Something was a little off about the way he said it. But I brushed it aside as nerves and excitement about the major accomplishment we had just achieved.

When I arrived at the restaurant, Van Dyke was not there. Some of his staff members were waiting for me. They explained that Gene couldn't make it. I understood, of course. It's a big job to get ready to initiate a multimillion-dollar oil exploration effort thousands of miles away.

Then the bomb dropped.

"George," I was told, "we're sorry, but we cannot let you go to Ghana."

Apparently, it had been an internal policy decision.

Before I was shown the door, I was told, "If you have any costs, let us know and we'll pay you off."

Van Dyke never called me. I was left to surmise that the sacrifice I had made with my own career and leaving my family behind as I had sought to help make Vanco's dream come true was of little value to the firm.

I couldn't even begin to express the slam of emotions that hit me at being so unceremoniously kicked out of a deal I had been instrumental in helping put together. I was furious. I was crushed. I vented to my wife. I cried. I yelled.

When the time came for Vanco to go to Ghana for the official signing ceremony, they didn't invite me. I pressed them, asking them how they could so callously dump me, the man who had helped them through the process to secure the block, then not even take me to Ghana for the signing. They finally relented and allowed me to attend the ceremony. But they made it clear that I was no longer part of the team. They had gotten from me what they wanted. I was shunned and ignored while they celebrated and signed their papers and partied over their history-making event.

They paid me $15,000—$196 per week. Less than minimum wage for my eighteen months of efforts on their behalf. And they would go on to reap millions.

I was determined never to be taken advantage of again. The petroleum gods must have laughed at that. Because the oily part of the business wasn't finished with me. Not by a long shot.

CHAPTER

6

FIRST DEAL

On our way back to Houston after the Vanco signing ceremony in Ghana, during a stopover in Amsterdam, John Craven, Chief Geologist for Vanco, pulled me aside.

"George, you're so good at what you do," he said. "I saw what they did to you. Why don't you and I go and get our own block to explore?"

Craven had been Chief Geologist of two oil companies in Ghana, including Dana Petroleum, which had acquired a license in August of 1997. That effort had gone nowhere, and Craven quit Dana. Craven knew the geology of this area better than anyone. Through his work at Dana and having gained experience in Ghana, he had been instrumental in convincing Vanco to consider Ghana in the first place. He knew the terrain. He had helped negotiate the deal for Dana. He had been closely involved in the successful negotiation between Vanco and the GNPC. And his geophysicist, Jim Fox, was one of the best in the business.

Craven's proposal to partner with me made perfect sense. At that time, the Energy Minister's new mandate for the GNPC was to bring in exploration and development companies to invest in Ghana. We had helped Vanco get a block. We knew all the parties. We were familiar with the process involved in blocks being granted. I had been born, raised, and educated in Ghana. And Craven had worked in Ghana for several years. When the time came to negotiate for our block, it would be his third time in the process.

It was an easy decision to make.

"There's only one problem," I told Craven. "I don't have enough money to explore an oil block in Ghana."

"Don't worry about it," Craven said. "We can get the money. I already have an energy exploration company set up, in Ireland. It's called Ennex. We can do this, George."

His words were soothing balm to my battered spirit. I agreed.

But this time I would be wiser. With Vanco, I had gone in with my good name, reputation and honest work history, all on just the word of Gene Van Dyke, a savvy multimillionaire powerhouse and Texas oilman. I hadn't signed anything up front. And Vanco kicked me out the minute they got what they wanted. Lesson learned.

"This time," I told Craven, "we sign an agreement and go in as partners."

"Agreed," he said. "We'll bring your company into it, too."

That would work perfectly. In the latter months of 2002, we registered EO Group as a Ghanaian firm. In September of that same year, when I had been preparing to get involved in Ghana with my ill-fated plans to work with Vanco, I had formed a company with Dr. Kwame Bawuah-Edusei, which we named EO Group (E for Edusei, O for Owusu) and became equal partners. The original purpose of EO Group was to engage in business ventures in Ghana, primarily related to the importation of medical supplies and educational materials. We later agreed to amend the company purpose to include oil and gas exploration and related services.

By late 2002, John Craven and I had negotiated a partnership deal, and Ennex Energy and EO Group were ready to submit our application for a license to explore for oil in Ghana.

The block we applied for was named West Cape Three Points (WCTP). Craven chose the area because he was familiar with it from his work with Dana and Vanco. His interpretation of the seismic data had convinced him something was there, and when EO Group and Ennex partnered, he selected that block again. As a geologist, he had worked the area and knew the terrain well. It was in deep water, although not as deep as the Vanco block and only one-eighth the size of theirs.

In Ghana, when a company wanted to acquire a block for oil exploration and production, they would first approach the Ministry of Energy and purchase an application. The GNPC would inquire into the financial capability of the applicant to undertake the project, as well as ascertain their level of technical knowledge pertaining to oil exploration, development and production. This step would assure the government that a company would not sit on the block idle while they looked for some other party to flip the license to.

After we had passed the technical and financial capabilities tests, the government and our group then negotiated and signed a Memorandum of Understanding (MOU) with the government of Ghana. The MOU preceded negotiation of the full Petroleum Agreement. It spelled out the ownership structure, the work program, the fiscal regime, and the proposed benchmarks and completion timeframes. The MOU was the foundation, its terms the pillars, upon which the entire Petroleum Agreement was built. It was to be signed by the Minister of Energy, Chairman of the Board of the GNPC, the Managing Director of the GNPC, and the contractor.

The Petroleum Agreement itself was divided into three sections, each of which delineated exploration activities and related timeframes. If an agreement covered a term of seven years, for example, the first three years may comprise the company's plan to conduct and acquire seismic data and drill one well. The second two years would be for drilling a second exploratory well. And the final two years for drilling another exploratory well.

The oil company would first make their presentation to the GNPC, explaining how the firm planned to carry out those activities. If the GNPC was satisfied with the presentation, the parties would then negotiate the terms and sign the MOU, after which the Minister of Energy would invite the firm to negotiate the terms of the Petroleum Agreement with the government of Ghana. All negotiations would be conducted in accordance with GNPC's model Petroleum Agreement.

There were five key areas to be negotiated:

1. The Fiscal Terms: These elements could vary, depending upon the overall perceived risk profile of the block, which was determined by: whether the block was in shallow or deep waters, the perceived challenges of the geological formations, and the quality and quantity of existing geological and geophysical seismic data on the block. The elements of the fiscal terms to be negotiated were:

   (a) Royalty.

   (b) GNPC's participation, carried interest.

   (c) GNPC's additional participation, paid interest.

   (d) Additional oil entitlement after the contractor has achieved the agreed/negotiated internal rate of return.

   (e) Corporate income tax rate.

2. The Proposed Work Program.

3. Decommissioning Requirements and Funding.

4. Relinquishment Requirement.

5. The Development Program for any commercial gas discovery, etc.

The government's negotiating team consisted of representatives from the Internal Revenue Service, the Attorney General's department, and legal, financial and technical experts from the GNPC.[12]

It was a lengthy, technical, fairly intense process. Negotiations could be as short as two months or could take up to two years to complete, depending on how quickly the parties were able to work through the various issues and negotiate a mutually acceptable agreement.

In early 2003, John Craven and I submitted our formal application to Moses O. Boateng, Managing Director of the GNPC, and paid the $7,500 fee. We then negotiated an MOU with the GNPC to explore the West Cape Three Points block, including delineating the details of the ownership terms (EO Group 15% interest, Ennex 75%, and the government of Ghana 10% carried interest). All that remained was for the Ministry of Energy, through GNPC, to write up the finalized MOU for all parties to sign and we'd be in business. We had managed to fast-track the process because Craven had been involved in the Vanco negotiation, which allowed us to leverage his experience with developing previous MOU and Petroleum Agreement terms and processes as our knowledge base, making adjustments as necessary.

The GNPC was impressed with the credentials of geologist John Craven and geophysicist Jim Fox, who had gained extensive experience in the Tano and the Cape Three Points areas when he worked for Dana Petroleum, Vanco Energy, and Philips Petroleum.

The GNPC Board reviewed the Ennex/EO Group application. They

---

[12] After 2007, representatives from the office of the Attorney General were added to the government's team.

expressed some concern about our lack of an assured source of exploration and development funding and a technical partner with strong capabilities in deep-water exploration. We assured them we could attract a qualified technical partner as well as sufficient funding. The Minister of Energy and the GNPC agreed to sign the MOU with the understanding that Ennex/EO Group would be required to procure the funding source and technical partner, or the application could be declined.[13] We agreed, and on February 27, 2003, the government prepared the MOU, detailing the terms upon which the block would be awarded to Ennex/EO Group.

Not long after Craven and I had left Ghana and returned to Houston, the GNPC informed me that they had finished writing up the final MOU. It had been approved and signed by the Minister of Energy, by GNPC Chairman Sekyere-Abankwa, and by Managing Director Moses Boateng. The document was ready to be picked up for Ennex and EO Group to sign.

At last, I was on my way. I wasn't a middleman, wasn't a facilitator, wasn't a door opener. I was a partner in an oil exploration venture with a highly experienced geologist and the government of Ghana.

John Craven was busy at the time, so he asked me to go to Accra and retrieve the MOU for us to sign and return to the GNPC. I went to Ghana, picked up the MOU, and flew home to Houston on cloud nine, eager to get started on our oil exploration venture.

When I returned to Texas, I took the MOU to John Craven for our signatures.

"John," I said excitedly, "Let's sign this and get going."

Craven said no.

---

[13] Steven Sekyere-Abankwa, former Chairman of the GNPC, in a statement made to the Ghana Police, CID Station, on March 29, 2010, concerning the details of the negotiations between the government of Ghana, the GNPC, and EO Group/Kosmos Energy, which resulted in the granting of an oil exploration license and the signing of the parties' Petroleum Agreement in May of 2004; and to George Owusu and M. Rutledge McCall during an interview on Thursday, June 6, 2013.

It was as if he had slugged me in the gut. I was speechless.

Craven's plan had been for us to involve a major investor to finance the venture for a share of our ownership percentages. At the time, the price of oil had been drifting downward. He felt that, given the low, declining, and unsteady oil prices, we would not be able to get anyone to invest in it.

"Look, if I sign this," Craven told me, "I'll be obligated to spend that kind of money to drill these wells."

He was concerned that if he signed the MOU, he would be on the financial hook, with only three years to conduct seismic acquisition, processing and interpretation, and to drill an exploratory well. It would cost tens of millions just to drill exploratory wells and—hopefully—strike oil. With oil prices sinking, he felt that time and the cost-benefit analysis was working against us and that the project had become even more challenging .

"With the worldwide oil business going down," he said, "it would be very difficult for us to find the required investors to bring into this deal."

In the oil business, you could drill an exploration well, and after several assessments, you might discover that a find was not viable, for several different reasons. For example, you may have found what appeared to be a possible field in a certain water depth, but when you looked at the price of oil at the time, and the technology available and calculated what it would cost to bring the oil to the surface, it might not make economic sense to continue.

When the earlier exploratory wells were being drilled in Ghana, the technology wasn't the best and the price of oil wasn't high enough to make the investment financially feasible, particularly in the very deep-water areas. In cases like those, even if oil was found and was in sufficient commercial quantities and of acceptable quality, the find would have been abandoned. But ten years down the line, when technology had improved and the price of oil had risen, it might become a good investment, depending on the size of the field and the quality of the crude oil it contained.

"Can you lower your share to five percent?" Craven asked me. "So we can have more shares available for prospective investors?"

Although Craven was in at seventy-five percent, Bawuah-Edusei and I agreed. We lowered EO Group's share by two-thirds to just five percent.

Craven tried to find investors at that adjustment but was still unable to attract any.

And then, after all of the work we had done, after passing all of the tests and meeting all of the requirements set by the GNPC, Craven decided not to sign our MOU with Ghana.

He apologized and abandoned the deal.

I was stunned.

CHAPTER

7

REGROUP

After Craven backed out, I was left with an MOU signed by all of the relevant Ghanaian government officials, a proposed exploration, development and production timeframe schedule. And no proven exploration entity attached to close the deal. It was a highly unusual position to be in, to put it mildly. It was like hitting what had appeared to be an in-park home run at the bottom of the ninth, only to be tagged out at home. It was almost as bad as when I had been mugged by Vanco.

I had spent months of effort, and money. I had dipped precariously into my financial reserves, all on what ultimately amounted to a wild goose chase, with no deal closed. I was scoring 0 for 2. Discouraged didn't even begin to describe my state of mind.

As I was scrambling to figure out what to do next, I was informed that GNPC Deputy Managing Director Amankroahene had passed away, and that there had been a cabinet shuffle in the Kufuor administration. Energy Minister Albert Kan-Dapaah was being moved over to Minister of Communications and Technology, and Dr. Paa Kwesi Nduom would be replacing him as Minister of Energy. A little time would be needed for the new appointees to settle into their positions, and that provided me a little time space.

It wasn't the first time God stepped in to give me some much-needed breathing space. And it wouldn't be the last. The clock was ticking.

John Craven may have had too much to lose by making the move in pushing ahead with our deal. But I had nothing to lose. I believed in what I had. Besides, oil prices always tended to fluctuate, and technology always improved. I had faith that they would both increase. I just didn't know how long it would take.

That August I called one of the geologists in the exploration department at Shell and told him I had an oil block in Ghana.

"Would Shell be interested?" I asked him.

"In Ghana?" he replied. "Is there even oil in Ghana?"

I took it to a company called Vaalco Energy.

"Where? Did you say Ghana?"

They too said no thanks.

I took it to Occidental Petroleum. They kept my paperwork for two and a half months before telling me no.

I contacted Hess.

Bawuah-Edusei contacted the China National Offshore Oil Company (CNOOC).

Everybody we took the deal to rejected it. Some even told me, "Mr. Owusu, if you get a block in Nigeria, call us. But Ghana? No thanks."

After going to more than a dozen companies throughout August and into September, my friend, Joseph Owusu, who worked in the Commercial Development department at Texaco, recommended that I talk to Texaco to see if they might be interested. He told me to bring the paperwork to him at Texaco.

Joseph had been instrumental in helping me get the petroleum industry convention set up the previous year in Houston with Minister Kan Dapaah, and had been encouraging and supportive after my Vanco disappointment. He had been there when then-Presidential candidate John Kufuor had come to Houston in 2000. And when Ghana's Minister of Energy had come a few months later. He had gone over the seismic data. He had been there for me when I was pitching the other firms after John Craven and Ennex Energy had backed out. Joseph Owusu was a man I could count on.

Joseph made a lunchtime appointment with a Senior Vice President in Oil Exploration at Texaco for us to talk about my possible West Africa exploration opportunity. At the time, Joseph's office was at a satellite office 20 miles away from my downtown Houston office. I made the drive across town during my lunch hour and waited in the lobby while Joseph went to tell the executive of my arrival.

I waited. And waited.

I figured it was taking time because the executive's office was up on the fifth floor, and Joseph had to go up there from his office.

I waited some more.

Joseph finally showed up.

"He said we are so busy in Nigeria and Angola that we don't have time to take a look at Ghana," he said apologetically.

He explained that Texaco had made a huge discovery in Nigeria and didn't even want to think about a country that nobody had ever heard of.

After similar experiences with all of the other big oil companies that had told me to get lost, I started to wonder if going after oil in Ghana was like tilting at windmills. If all these major petroleum firms were saying there's no oil in Ghana, who was I to contradict their combined centuries of expertise? There was just one problem: me. If I was anything, I was driven. Four letter words like quit weren't in my vocabulary.

I set out to give it one more shot.

I recalled that when Ennex Oil had backed out of our deal, just before we had parted ways, John Craven had mentioned a man from Dallas who had recently sold an oil company and was starting a new one.

"His name is 'Muscle man' or 'Musslemin'. Something like that," Craven had told me. "He's forming a new oil exploration business."

"What's the company's name?" I had asked.

"I don't know."

"What's the guy's first name?"

"I don't remember."

"Do you have his phone number?"

"No, I don't. All I know is, he's in Dallas."

Great. No address. No phone number. No name, really. Nothing but "muscle man" and "Dallas."

I was desperate—nobody wanted my deal with Ghana. It was my last chance. How do I find this man? I lived in Houston; he was supposedly in Dallas. I rummaged through my notes and managed to dig up a scrap of paper with the odd name written on it. Musselman. Dallas. I dialed the Dallas telephone directory for information.

To my surprise, there were many Musselmans in Dallas.

I took out a pen and a piece of paper and asked the operator for the number of every Musselman in Dallas. Alan Musselman. Bill Musselman. Carl Musselman.

In those days, directory assistance phone calls cost fifty cents to obtain three names and they would only give you three at a time. I would dial the information operator. They would give me three names. I would write down the three names. They would charge me fifty cents. I would call again. The operator would give me the same first three names. I would tell her I already had those three and ask her to please give me the next three names.

Don Musselman. Edward Musselman. Harry Musselman.

And on and on, until I had gotten the number of every Musselman in the Dallas phone book. Then I compiled my list and I started cold-calling them. Each and every one. Almost.

"Hello. Are you the Musselman in the oil business?"

"No."

"Sorry to bother you."

"Hello. Are you the Musselman in the oil business?"

"What is this, a prank call?"

"Sorry to bother you."

And so forth.

A dozen or more calls later, 10:30 at night, a girl answered.

"Hello. May I talk to your dad, please?"

I waited. A man came on the line.

"Hello. Are you the Musselman in the oil business?"

"Yes. This is Jim Musselman."

Pay dirt.

He confirmed that he was that James Musselman. He said he was the former CEO of Triton Energy, which had made a major oil discovery in Equatorial Guinea in 1999, and had recently sold the firm's assets to Hess Oil. He had just formed a brand new company named Kosmos Energy.

It was late. He was going to bed. I had two minutes to give him my pitch. I told him who I was and what I had.

He said, "Okay. Tomorrow, call this man. His name is Brian Maxted. He's my Chief Technology Officer and is a geologist. He might be able to do something with it."

He gave me the number.

Why wait until tomorrow, I thought to myself.

I dialed the number. The guy answered.

"Mr. Musselman says you need to see me," I told Maxted.

Unbeknown to me, Musselman had called Maxted right after our brief chat and told him about me, and the two men had decided they should meet with me.

"Okay," Maxted replied. "When can you come to Dallas?"

We settled on the following day. The timing was perfect. That same week, the Society of Exploration Geophysicists was holding their annual conference in Dallas. The attendees happened to include some GNPC officials from Ghana, one of whom was Thomas Manu,[14] Director of Operations of the GNPC. I knew him from my two previous experiences with the GNPC.

I would leave no stone unturned. I called my friend Alex Ababio, a geophysicist who had worked for the GNPC for a decade before moving to Houston and who also knew Manu. Alex now worked as a geophysicist at GX Technology, a seismic processing company that acquired and processed seismic data and sold it to oil companies. Alex was familiar with the WCTP block. He recalled from his experience that the area was in the sweet spot of the rich Tano basin with much potential. He put together a technical summary on the block, which I presented to Brian Maxted, Chief Geologist of the newly formed Kosmos Energy in Dallas. Musselman wasn't able to attend that first meeting, so I sat down in a Dallas hotel room with Maxted and a Kosmos geophysicist and engineer named Kenny Goh.

Brian Maxted, who was just a few years younger than me, was from a town in England called Stoke-on-Trent, 30 miles from Liverpool. Maxted had worked for BP for 17 years before leaving the firm in 1994 to go to Malaysia to work for Jim Musselman at Triton Energy. After Triton's discovery in Equatorial Guinea, Maxted was moved to the company's headquarters in Dallas. When Musselman sold Triton to Hess Corporation, Maxted stayed with Hess until 2001.

I told him my story.

"Okay," Maxted said when I finished, "but who are you? "

---

[14] Thomas Manu was a holdover from the Rawlings administration and had served under Tsatsu Tsikata, former Chairman of the GNPC, who was then being tried for financial crimes against the State.

I suddenly realized that he probably thought I was one of those "4-1-9 scam artists" (as fly-by-night operators were referred to in some African countries), so I gave him my business card.

"I work in the industry. For Shell Oil," I told him. "I'm a Commodities Manager. I'm a U.S. citizen and I was born and raised in Ghana. I've worked for several petroleum firms."

I sensed that Maxted wasn't quite convinced. In fact, I sensed he either didn't trust me or didn't like me. At the time, I couldn't tell which.

"I'd like to bring in someone else," I told him.

I called Thomas Manu, who was in the hotel, and asked him to join us. He confirmed that EO Group was legitimate and was trying to bring oil and gas investors to Ghana, and that we had recently presented an application and negotiated an MOU with the government. Maxted became convinced.

He told his boss, Jim Musselman, that they should take a serious look at what I was bringing to Kosmos. After all, little Kosmos Energy had nothing else going in September of 2003.

I was there to change all that.

During October and November of 2003, EO Group put together a comprehensive package for a meeting with Kosmos Energy. As we were making our formal presentation to their team in Dallas in November, a Kosmos lawyer expressed skepticism that the two-man EO Group could even negotiate an MOU. I reminded them that the MOU had already been negotiated—and approved and signed by all of the required Ghanaian government officials. The only signature missing was that of an exploration and production partner, because the original contractor, Ennex Energy, had gotten cold feet and declined to sign the document.

The essential groundwork had been completed. We had already paid the license application fee to the Ministry of Energy. I had established legitimate business relationships with the key Ghanaian officials. I had a negotiated MOU. I had good working relationships with the necessary government officials having built credibility with the GNPC when I helped Vanco Energy to secure their block a year earlier.

All that was needed was for Kosmos to be approved as a credible and capable contractor by the government of Ghana, their name and pertinent signatures affixed to the MOU, and they would be onboard. Then we could proceed to the Petroleum Agreement negotiation phase with GNPC. For Kosmos, the opportunity was a no-brainer. It was an offer I imagined not many oil exploration and production companies would refuse, though many had. The deal would not only put Kosmos instantly into the game, it potentially represented the relatively new firm's entire future. In fact, they would be in the driver's seat on the project, as the Operator.

I did not know it then, that I was probably handing Jim Musselman and Kosmos Energy a golden goose. For EO Group, Musselman's oil exploration experience and success on the African continent, along with his current negotiations to close a financing deal with international investment banking firm Goldman Sachs to back Kosmos in their oil exploration activities, would be the perfect golden knife to carve that goose.

Kosmos agreed to join EO Group in the oil exploration business in Ghana.

The timing couldn't have been more perfect. It was all coming together—again. Still, I was cautious. I had been to this dance before, with Vanco and then with Ennex. And I had been left bitterly disappointed in each situation. I could only pray it wouldn't happen a third time.

Yet, sure enough, later in November, Musselman unexpectedly passed on my offer.

I was numb. I had struck out again.

"It's too early for Kosmos," Musselman explained to me. "Our financing isn't quite together yet."

Unknown to me at the time, Kosmos had been experiencing a bumpy start in setting up financing through one of their original funding entities, Goldman Sachs, who had pulled out. Kosmos was scrambling to secure a funding partner so they could move forward as an oil exploration firm. They were a brand new company, just weeks old, and weren't quite ready to take the plunge and pick up any projects just yet. They were talking with Blackstone Group, but it could be months before that deal could be finalized.

In a last ditch effort to salvage the deal, I requested more time from the government of Ghana to replace one of the parties in the MOU I had negotiated earlier with the GNPC. I was given a time limit, after which, the deal would be canceled.

As Thanksgiving of 2003 loomed, one of the few things I had to give thanks for was that signed MOU with the GNPC. But even that was contingent upon my finding a partner capable of footing up to a million dollars a day for exploration costs. EO Group couldn't afford a thousand a day, much less a million, and oil companies around the world had already declined to partner with me to move the GNPC deal from provisional to active.

The end of the road was approaching. I had no prospects and had racked up a sizable dent in my family's savings with my wild goose chase for a partner for the black gold exploration venture.

Happy Thanksgiving, George.

I started thinking about winding down EO Group and getting on with my life as Commodities Manager for Shell. After all my intensive business activities over the past three years, my wife would be happy to have me back. Even if it would take me awhile to get the oil fever out of my system.

As December approached, the cheerfulness of the Christmas season was lacking. And yet, like an addict who cannot stay away from his drug of choice, I picked up the phone once again.

I made phone call to Jim Musselman, for one last try.

We talked. About life. About the oil business. About Ghana. Then suddenly, a ray of hope.

"In order for Kosmos to do this, George," he told me at last, "first, we will have to go to Ghana."

"Of course," I replied, feeling a gush of adrenaline. "No problem."

"Let's go in December," he suggested.

December was days away.

"I think December might be a bad time to go to Ghana," I responded cautiously. "It's Christmas time and people will be thinking about shopping and family. Why don't we wait until January? We'll have more time to prepare."

It was a little risky to say no to his suggestion, but scheduling would be difficult on such a short notice during the holiday season, and trying to squeeze in a sudden trip to Ghana could sour things.

To my relief, he agreed.

Dare I hope again? I was 55 years old. I had traveled an impossibly long distance from Kumasi, Ghana, to Houston, Texas. Do dreams come true for a man approaching his sixth decade on Earth? Time would tell.

We made plans to go to Ghana in January of 2004.

My life in America was over as I had known it.

So was my life in Ghana.

CHAPTER

8

LAST SHOT

It had been more than three years since Mr. John Kufuor had visited Houston and as a candidate for the Presidency of Ghana had made his challenge to us Ghanaians in the petroleum industry to help find oil in our country.

On January 12, 2004, the Kosmos team, including Paul Daily and Ken Goh, accompanied me to Ghana. Kosmos didn't pay my airfare, because it was a speculative situation for them and they didn't know if they were going to move forward with a deal. Although Bawuah-Edusei was a friend of President Kufuor, neither he nor I were card-carrying members of Kufuor's NPP party, nor were we connected with the Ghanaian government. We were merely private citizens who happened to live in America and were driven by a genuine desire to contribute to the future of Ghana.

EO Group later introduced Musselman and his Kosmos team to President Kufuor in his office. Kufuor smiled at my description of Musselman and his team as "some of the smartest geoscientists in the industry."

"If anybody can find oil in Ghana, Mr. President," I said, "it is these men. I am confident that if given the chance, we will be successful."

We told the President that Musselman's previous company had been the first to strike oil in Equatorial Guinea, and we were going to do the same in Ghana.

Jim Musselman was a big, friendly, bear of a guy. He had the charisma of John Wayne and the larger-than-life demeanor of a classic oil baron. He also wore his heart on his sleeve and didn't hide his emotions. His moods could shift between calm and analytical, to effusive and impatient. He was a Texas titan, a typical self-made man, a natural leader.

Thus began four years of exciting, exhausting work, impossibly long days, and great challenges to overcome. Only to be followed by another four years of heartbreak and distress, near total ruin, and cruel attacks from all sides.

As was their custom, the GNPC made their presentation to the EO Group/Kosmos Energy team to convince us that Ghana had potential for a meaningful oil discovery. We were instructed to assemble our technical experts, explain what we knew about Ghana, assess our chances of finding oil, and tell them what we had accomplished in the oil business. It would be my second time being involved in making such a presentation for the GNPC, and my second time as a partner in an oil exploration venture.

EO Group and Kosmos' technical and geological teams gathered in Ghana, and by March we were reviewing seismic and other

April 15, 2004

James C. Musselman
President, CEO &
Founding Partner

Minister of Energy
Ministry of Energy
The Ministry's Area
Accra, Ghana

Dear Sir:

Please find attached an application by Kosmos Energy, LLC and EO Group to take out an exploration license over the Western Cape Three Points Block, offshore Ghana. Kosmos is of the view that considerable potential remains offshore Ghana and that we have the human and financial resources to quickly and thoroughly explore this acreage for the benefit of Ghana, GNPC and our respective companies. We will be happy to provide any additional material required by the Ministry in evaluating our application. We would like to come to Ghana to discuss our application at your convenience.

Sincerely,

James C. Musselman

JCM/hs

EO Group/Kosmos cover letter for updated oil exploration application

petroleum-related data[15] and laying the groundwork for our presentation to the GNPC and negotiations for a Petroleum Agreement with the government of Ghana.

While the presentation was being prepared, EO Group and Kosmos Energy began negotiating our partnership agreement. Bawuah-Edusei and I asked for 15%, the same amount we had negotiated under the original deal with Ennex Energy. Kosmos balked. After uneasy discussions through March and into April of 2004, we finalized our deal. Kosmos wrangled us down to a 3.5% equity stake in the block—even less than the 5% we had renegotiated under the Ennex deal. However, they agreed to pay EO Group $250,000 as part of the sweat equity to help get Kosmos set up in Ghana.

Kosmos would be getting a fair deal for partnering in our WCTP license. We had brought them a promising block to explore. And they didn't even pay us a signing bonus.

Bawuah-Edusei and I agreed to the deal. We were giving Kosmos something of great value, including all of the groundwork I had laid during the previous two years, gaining important contacts, and securing a signed MOU. And we needed an oil exploration partner with a proven track record in order to move ahead. It was a win-win for both parties.

On April 15, 2004, we submitted our official joint application to the Ministry of Energy for a license to explore the WCTP deep-water block offshore. We were almost there.

The EO/Kosmos team was smart and tight. The GNPC had conducted their own due diligence and came away satisfied. They already knew me from my previous application. Jim Musselman's team had a track record of finding oil in Equatorial Guinea with his company, Triton Energy. Kosmos Energy had the financial backing of two of the largest private equity firms in the world. And the Kosmos technical personnel

---

[15] The best seismological data on hand at the time was 2-D seismic data which had been produced by a petroleum firm that had been unsuccessful in finding oil around the same block that EO Group and Ennex had chosen earlier.

were considered among the best in the business: Dr. Paul Daily, with a degree from Oxford University, Jim Musselman, educated at Duke University, Greg Dunlevy, trained at Harvard University, Ken Goh, an expert in tropical terrain from Malaysia, and Brian Maxted, a geologist and international expert in oil and gas with previous experience at BP.

During this time, two other companies, Africa Petroleum and Sahara Petroleum, had submitted applications to the GNPC for the same WCTP block we had filed for. Determined to make certain that the best possible deal was obtained for Ghana from among the most qualified candidates, the GNPC conducted an open, rigorous, and fair competition among the three applicants.

In the end, the GNPC and the Ministry of Energy approved our application over the others. Now, the hardball negotiation, to hammer out the terms of the Petroleum Agreement, could begin.[16]

Yet, before the EO Group/Kosmos Energy team could even begin to negotiate with the multi-agency team representing the government of Ghana, Energy Minister Dr. Paa Kwesi Nduom informed Moses O. Boateng, Managing Director of the GNPC, that he didn't feel comfortable with the transfer of the signed MOU from EO/Ennex to EO/Kosmos. Nduom stated that the deal had been between EO Group and Ennex Energy, and that if a new partner was to be brought in or replaced, then the process should begin all over again.

Boateng, who had 25 years of experience in finance and banking and was an authority on financial analysis and negotiation, took Nduom's concerns to GNPC Board Chairman Steven Sekyere-Abankwa.

Sekyere-Abankwa, who had been appointed Chairman of GNPC on March 26, 2002, was no pushover. He was a recipient of the distinguished Hubert Humphrey Fellowship, a professional development program in

---

[16] The basic fiscal terms of Ghana's Petroleum Agreements evolved over time and were based on: Agreements signed before the "M-Plaza Workshop" (agreement negotiations) in January of 2003, Agreements signed after the M-Plaza Workshop but before June of 2007, and Agreements signed after the summer of 2007.

corporate finance, financial markets and financial institutions in the U.S., where he was attached to the American University in Washington D.C. A career banker and Project Financial Analyst, Sekyere-Abankwa had a Bachelor of Science Degree in Business Administration, an MBA, and his previous stints included positions at the Capital Investments Board, the National Investment Bank, and as Managing Partner of J.S. Addo Consultants, which had established Prudential Bank Ltd.

Part of Sekyere-Abankwa's job as Chairman of the GNPC was to look out for the interest of Ghana in awarding oil exploration licenses to foreign companies coming into the country to explore and produce the natural resource. Sekyere-Abankwa, who looked like a chairman—trim, neat, impeccably dressed—sounded like a university professor when he spoke. He was precise and sure when explaining an issue, highly intelligent, and could quote obscure laws verbatim at the drop of a hat. He also had the focus of a machine and tolerated no interruptions when he was speaking. It would be easier to get a rolling train off a railroad track than move Sekyere-Abankwa from a position he knew to be correct, lawful, and expedient to the issue at hand.

Chairman Sekyere-Abankwa and Managing Director Boateng explained to Minister Nduom that it was not unusual to have a partner in an agreement replaced, so long as the other parties, including the government, agreed to the replacement and were satisfied with the terms of the agreement. The Chairman was satisfied. Boateng was satisfied. EO Group was, too. So was Kosmos Energy. In fact, the Chairman told the Minister, Kosmos was a much stronger candidate for the partnership than Ennex had been, particularly given that Ennex had abandoned the deal at the last minute.

After a bit of quibbling and positioning, the Chairman convinced the Minister that transferring the MOU was not an issue, and announced that negotiations could commence.

So far, so good. We were halfway home.

Then, Kosmos changed their position. One of their geologists had dissected all of the technical data and as a result, Kosmos announced to the GNPC that they wanted to extend the boundaries of the block to be licensed. It was an interesting turnabout from their original back-and-forth as to whether they wanted to get involved with me and Ghana in the first place. Now Kosmos was wanting more than I had brought to them.

The GNPC declined the request.

Kosmos was adamant—they wanted an increase in the acreage of the license.

The GNPC was equally adamant in denying the request.

Kosmos dug in.

The Chairman wouldn't budge.

"You are going to get only what EO and Ennex had already picked," Kosmos was told. "The agreement is only for what had been previously negotiated before Ennex backed out."

Sekyere-Abankwa explained that the EO/Kosmos agreement would be basically stepping into the shoes of the Ennex/EO agreement with the GNPC. Redoing the boundaries would require the entire deal to be scrapped and the process started all over again—MOU, approvals, negotiating, everything.

Kosmos didn't want to back down.

Chairman Sekyere-Abankwa's team was strong, experienced, and capable. He understood that the oil companies hired consultants specializing in petroleum negotiations to make presentations to his team, and he had assembled an equally qualified team to respond.

Kosmos pointed out that no oil had been discovered in Ghana and that they were taking all the financial risk.

It was a standoff.

Managing Director Boateng was aware that this was Ghana's opportunity to drill more wells and to do so, they needed to be pragmatic. They had to negotiate a good deal for Ghana, but there weren't many companies breaking down the door to come drill in Ghana. It might not be wise to expect the moon. If oil was found, then they could be in a stronger negotiation position in subsequent deals with other oil firms.[17]

Boateng questioned Kosmos further on their work plan, their schedule, how they would handle various possible scenarios and challenges that might occur during the course of exploring for oil in the deep waters off the coast of Ghana.

I was starting to get nervous. These Ghanaians were good. Very good.

A final point to come to terms with was that the available seismic data was all in 2-D rendering. Boateng decided that, as part of the agreement, we would be required to acquire a 3-D data in our block within a certain timeframe.

We agreed.

Then we went back and hashed out the fiscal terms and other issues. In the end, the numbers were not more favorable to us than they had been in previous GNPC deals with other companies—Dana Petroleum, Hess Corporation, Devon Energy, Vanco Energy and Ennex Energy/ EO Group. Kosmos Energy would receive 90% (with EO Group's 3.5% coming out of Kosmos' share, leaving Kosmos with 86.5% of the deal) and the government of Ghana would receive a carried interest of 10%, a royalty rate of 5%, and an option to acquire an additional paid interest of 2.5% at their discretion. Each party was satisfied.[18]

---

[17] During the negotiations, the government of Ghana agreed, in order to become competitive, to reduce the existing rates of Royalty, Carried Interest, Additional Paid Interest and Additional Oil Entitlement. The strategy on the part of the government was that lower rates would be negotiated until a commercial discovery of oil and gas was made, after which the rates would be revised upwards in line with those in oil-producing countries in the sub-region and elsewhere in the world. The guideline was that the State's take of the net oil should fall between 50% and 55%, instead of the existing 55% and 65% (GNPC adopted and applied this policy between 2003 and June 2007). The rates were revised upward after June of 2007. SOURCE: Steven Sekyere-Abankwa, former Chairman of the GNPC, in a statement he made to the Ghana Police, CID Station, on March 29, 2010, concerning the details of the negotiations between the government of Ghana, the GNPC, and EO Group/Kosmos Energy, which resulted in the granting of an oil exploration license and the signing of the parties' Petroleum Agreement in May of 2004.

[18] Hess Corporation's lower royalty rate of 4% (July 2006) had been based on the fact that their block was in ultra-deep water where operations are relatively more risky and costly. The GNPC

NAME OF COMPANY	DATE OF AGREEMENT/ NEGOTIATION	DEEPWATER	ROYALTY	GNPC CARRIED INTEREST	GNPC ADDITIONAL PAID INTEREST	PETROLEUM INCOME TAX	ADDITIONAL OIL ENTITLEMENT	WORK PROGRAM SEISMIC ACQUISITION
BEFORE M-PLAZA WORKSHOP								
DANA PETROLEUM	August 1997	Deepwater	5%	10%	10%	35%	NIL.	Acquire both 2D and 3D Seismic Data
DEVON & ENCANA	August 2002	Deepwater	10%	10%	15%	35%	ROR of 14% →12% ROR of 18% →16% ROR of 23% → 22%	Acquire 3D Seismic Data
VANCO ENERGY	July 2002	Ultra Deepwater	5%	15%	NIL.	35%	NIL.	Acquire 2D and 3D Seismic Data
AFTER M-PLAZA WORKSHOP BUT BEFORE COMMERCIAL DISCOVERY OF OIL IN JUNE 2007								
ENNEX & EO GROUP	April 2003	Deep water	5%	10%	2½%	35%	ROR of 22.5% →7% ROR of 25% → 15% ROR of 30% → 20%	Acquire 1000 sq km 3D Seismic Data
KOSMOS/EO GROUP	July 2004	Deepwater	5%	10%	2½%	35%	ROR of 25% →7½% ROR of 30% → 15% ROR of 40% → 25%	Acquire 3D Seismic Data
TULLOW , SABRE OIL ANADARKO & KOSMOS	July 2006	Deepwater	5%	10%	5%	35%	ROR of 19% → 5% ROR of 20% → 10% ROR of 25% → 15%	Reprocess Existing 3D Seismic Data
HESS CORPORATION	July 2006	Deep & Ultra Deep	4%	10%	3%	35%	ROR of 12½% → 5% ROR of 17½ % → 10% ROR of 22½% → 15%	Acquire 3D Seismic Data
VITOL UPSTREAM	March 2006	Deepwater	7½%	10%	5%	35%	ROR of 12% → 10% ROR of 17% → 12½% ROR of 22% → 16%	Acquire 3D Seismic Data
GASOP OIL (GH) LTD	July 2006	Deepwater	5%	10%	10%	35%	ROR of 12% → 10% ROR of 17½ → 12% ROR of 22½ → 17½	Acquire 3D Seismic Data
DEVON ENERGY	Amendment	Deepwater	5%	5%	15%	35%	ROR of 22½ → 15% ROR of 25% → 20% ROR of 28% → 25%	To enable them drill a second well in a marginal prospect.
AFTER DISCOVERY OF OIL IN COMMERCIAL QUANTITITIES IN JUNE 2007								
AFREN PLC	August 2008	Deepwater	10%	10%	15%	35%	ROR of 14% → 12% ROR of 18% → 18% ROR of 23% → 22%	Drill a well
AKER ASA	Nov. 2008	Ultra Deep	10%	10%	15%	35%	ROR of 12½% → 10% ROR of 17½% → 12½% ROR of 22% → 20%	Acquire 3D Seismic Data

Financial Terms of Ghanaian Deepwater Petroleum Agreements

compensated for their relatively lower Royalty rate with a 3% additional paid interest, which was higher than Kosmos' 2.5%. The GNPC always negotiated on a risk return trade-off basis. The fiscals in all the agreements signed after the M-Plaza Workshop but before June of 2007, yielded for the State between 50% and 55% of the net oil, which met the criterion set by GNPC after the downward review of the fiscals in February of 2003. SOURCE: Steven Sekyere-Abankwa, former Chairman of the GNPC, in a statement he made to the Ghana Police, CID Station, on March 29, 2010, concerning the details of the negotiations between the government of Ghana, the GNPC, and EO Group/Kosmos Energy, which resulted in the granting of an oil exploration license and the signing of the parties' Petroleum Agreement in May of 2004.

At last, on May 14, 2004, EO Group and Kosmos Energy, the GNPC, and the Government of Ghana represented by the Minister of Energy, entered into a Petroleum Agreement for exploration and development rights to the WCTP block. The agreement was approved by the Board of the GNPC, the Ministry of Energy, and the Cabinet of Ghana. Once the Cabinet approved it, the agreement was sent to Parliament and was referred to the Parliamentary Select Committee on Energy, which comprised members of both the NPP and NDC parties,[19] who spent days reviewing the agreement to make sure that the terms and conditions of the agreement met the aspirations of the country.

The parties signed the agreement on May 22, 2004.

On July 19, 2004, on the recommendation of Ghana's Parliamentary Select Committee and the multi-agency Negotiating Committee representing the government of Ghana, the full House of Parliament unanimously and without opposition approved the EO Group/Kosmos Energy agreement, opening 483,600 acres for exploration.[20]

The clock had started ticking. It was time to hunt for oil. If we didn't start drilling by mid-2007, we would be in breach of the agreement. And we didn't even have a drilling rig.

On July 19 of that year, Parliament approved our Petroleum Agreement and my new job was about to begin.

[19] These included Honorable Doe Ajaho, Moses Asaga, Haruna Iddrisu, Kwame Ampofo and Alhaji Amadu Sorogho, as well as other prominent members of Parliament. However, there were subsequent complaints from the NDC party that the negotiation had been rushed and that our Petroleum Agreement had been granted too quickly. However, every necessary step had been covered, every law and regulation followed, and every approval and signature had been acquired.
[20] It was both ironic and highly political that many of the same Members of Parliament who had approved the Petroleum Agreement in the first place would later turn around and publicly criticize it.

CHAPTER

9

On Our Way At Last

By the end of the middle of 2004, we were reprocessing and evaluating the old 2-D seismic data and would soon be shooting all new 3-D.

Later that year, I prepared to move to Ghana to begin my new position as Country Manager for the EO Group/Kosmos Energy partnership at a monthly income of $3,000—less than a third of my previous salary. I explained to Kosmos that $3,000 per month wouldn't cut it for paying living expenses in Ghana and taking care of my family in Texas. They responded that since there were no guarantees that we would discover oil, the managing partners didn't want to risk spending too much money in the interim. I would have to buckle down and stretch my $692 weekly income as best as I could. It wouldn't be easy. I would be sending $2,000 per month to Houston to support my family, leaving me only around $1,000 to live on.

My wife and friends thought I was crazy to accept such a huge pay cut to take on far more work in a little developing nation thousands of miles away. I hadn't lived in Ghana for over thirty years and had become used to the American way of life. It would be a challenge to live like a local, but I was resourceful and knew how to navigate life the Ghanaian way. You learn to be a problem solver. You learn to pivot.

My share of the cash payment made to EO Group as part of the Kosmos Energy partnership deal would come in handy. I was still in the process of building a house in Kumasi, in the hopes that my family would someday join me in Ghana. My wife and daughter weren't thrilled that I was moving there, but they recognized the great opportunity the sacrifice would afford the family. If it paid off.

I arrived in Accra in November of 2004. I had left Ghana as a teacher, and returned as an oil explorer. There was a lot of work to do. I was filled with hope, energy, and excitement. I had no office, no telephone, and only a laptop computer. I found an Internet café called Busy Internet, where I would be able to get my work done and communicate back and forth with Dallas, Houston, Accra, Takoradi, and Kumasi. I would need a proper office soon, but for now, I would make it work.

Among my many tasks was to oversee logistics, health and safety, transportation systems, accommodations and shipping. I was also the liaison between Kosmos Ghana office, the GNPC, the Ministry of Trade, Ministry of Energy, Customs and Immigration, as well as the go-between for the parties and companies traveling back and forth between Accra and Dallas. I was at the beck and call of Kosmos Energy during their study of the block to verify its potential, and I would soon be the one sending data and reports to Texas. I would be retrieving, discussing with the team, and delivering various documents involving the GNPC geologists, and geophysicists. And I would be making the long and arduous trip back and forth from Accra to Takoradi on what was then a rugged road that was still under construction. The 120-mile journey often took four hours to drive.

The GNPC monitored everything we did. I attended the periodic meetings with the GNPC, as well as some of the meetings with the partners in Dallas and London, and with others in Ghana.

I was working 60 hours per week. And I loved it.

I later had my Toyota 4-Runner shipped from Houston. Kosmos provided a Toyota Sequoia as my business vehicle. To supplement my meager income, I rented out my 4-Runner.

* * *

(Source: Author Records) Takoradi Port, Western Region

Dating back to 2002 and into 2003, when John Craven and I had been going through the process of applying for the WCTP block, whenever I was around certain GNPC staff members, I sensed that they held me in low regard. It was an uncomfortable feeling that I couldn't pin any specific reason on. I conjectured that it may have been because the GNPC's efforts to find oil in Ghana had been unsuccessful for so long, that they thought I was just another big talker who would end up like all the others before me—drilling wells with no commercial quantities. The feeling was immensely discouraging. Yet I received a lot of encouragement from some of the GNPC personnel.

Particularly, one day, a geologist named Lawrence Apaalse, pulled me aside and said, "George, who knows if you and Kosmos will be successful. I don't know. But don't give up, because you never know." He constantly encouraged me, telling me things like "George, don't worry, keep going. Who knows? This might be it."

During those days when I would be exhausted, frustrated, lonely or upset, his words would ring in my mind.

Don't quit.

Who knows?

His encouragement fed my persistence and fueled my hope. During the dark days that lay ahead, his words would become a source of much-needed inspiration.

More encouragement came that December when John Kufuor was re-elected President of Ghana. By January, the EO Group/Kosmos operation was nearly ready to start shooting 3-D seismic data on the block.[21]

The start of the deepwater exploration drilling phase was almost upon us. And there was still no budget for an office or staff. I did a lot

---

[21] The seismology system for searching for geologic areas on the ocean with the potential of containing oil is done by creating shock waves that travel through the water and beneath the surface of the earth and are reflected back by the various rock or sediment layers. The seismic responses are then interpreted by geologists and seismologists for indications of petroleum and natural gas traps. Once a potential oil pool is found, the location is marked using GPS coordinates. See: http://science.howstuffworks.com/environmental/energy/oil-drilling2.htm

of work in the Busy Internet café, my hotel room, and the front seats of my rental vehicle. It wouldn't be until the following year that I would receive a raise to $4,000 per month—one-sixth the standard salary for a petroleum industry Country Manager.

I slogged forward, telling myself it would all pay off some day.

Still, I couldn't survive on the paltry salary I was receiving. So, before things got too far ahead, I asked Kosmos for a pay advance so I could set up a car rental business, an activity that would one day come back to haunt me. My plan was that as we began to increase staff and operational activities grew, we would be able to rent cars to our crew, staff, management, and other oil industry personnel we would be dealing with. Most of the personnel who would be coming to work or performing other functions for us would be going from Accra to Takoradi, where most of the ship and crew operations would take place.[22] Kosmos agreed to give me an advance. I used the money to purchase two vehicles to use as rentals. I negotiated and signed a fair market-based business agreement with Kosmos for their employees to use my vehicles. I named the car rental company Newbridge Hospitality Service. In business, you learn to pivot.

Throughout the last quarter of 2004, as our seismic acquisition preparation efforts got underway, the car rental business grew. I acquired a couple more vehicles through friends and acquaintances who agreed to lease their personal automobiles to Newbridge and receive a portion of our rental income.

On February 11, 2005, around the time Professor Mike Oquaye took over as Minister of Energy from Dr. Paa Kwesi Nduom, the news media discussed our progress . . .

---

[22] The port of Takoradi handles the majority of Ghana's national export activity. Takoradi is the sister port city of Sekondi, and is the capital of the Sekondi-Takoradi Metropolitan District of the Western Region of Ghana.

"US FIRM INVESTS IN OIL EXPLORATION"

"Kosmos Energy and EO Group begin oil exploration by acquiring seismic data offshore at Cape Three Points in the Western Region, for analysis as a first step of an intensive oil exploration venture in Ghana, following the government's vision of making Ghana self-sufficient in oil and gas and as a net exporter of these products in the near future. Seismic firm Veritas DGC is contracted to undertake the project, using a seismic vessel called the Seisquest. Moses O. Boateng, Managing Director of the GNPC, says the acquisition of the data is expected to last for a month. Cost of the seismic data acquisition will total $6 million, with the entire exploration exercise to total $30 million in all. The effort is backed by Blackstone Capital Partners (the largest private equity firm in the world) and by Warburg Pincus (a privately-owned private equity firm)."

—*Daily Graphic,* February 11, 2005[23]

Not all newspapers would prove to be as accurate in their reporting in the years that lay ahead.

But it was official. We were on our way.

* * *

When a petroleum company does an initial seismic study and their data indicates evidence of the existence of an oil prospect, they give the prospect a name by which to identify it. When we first identified the initial prospect in WCTP, Kosmos asked me to submit names for it that were indigenous to Ghana. These names would then be submitted to GNPC for approval before application to any well.

---

[23] Daily Graphic, in a Feb. 11, 2005, article by Mabel Aku Baneseh, titled "US Firm Invests in Oil Exploration."

Initially, I decided to submit typical female Akan names. In Ghana, when Akan parents name their children, they often give them at least one name that corresponds with the day of the week they were born. For example, the name Yaw is given to a male child born on "Thursday" (my middle name is Yaw; I was born on a Thursday). Kwame is the name given to a male child born on "Saturday" (my partner Kwame Bawuah-Edusei was born on a Saturday). Kofi Atta Annan, former Secretary-General of the United Nations, was born on a Friday, thus his first name Kofi is the name given to a male child born on "Friday" (Atta indicates that he is a twin).

There are variants of each of the seven names as well, each of which have a meaning other than the day of the week one was born. For example, Yaw also means "earth," which might indicate a person who is down to earth, stable, etc. Kofi stands for "fertility," which could mean a person who is productive or creative. Female names also correspond with the days of the week, as well as with male names. For instance, a female Yaw would be Yaa, with the same basic meaning. A female Kofi would be Afua. And so forth.[24]

I had originally planned to name the first oil prospect in WCTP "Abenaa Píèsíe." Abenaa is female for "Tuesday", for the day the prospect had been identified. Tuesday represents ocean. Píèsíe means "first born." However, Ghana tended to be a country that often enjoyed controversy and division. So I thought if I suggested a female name or an Akan name, dissatisfied people would express outrage that we didn't use a male name, or that we used an Akan name. Because, in Ghana, controversy was as much a sport as was politics.

So it was back to the drawing board.

I then came up with names that should eliminate all debate:

---

[24] In addition to names that indicate what day of the week a person of Akan origin is born or whether they are a twin, there are also names that indicate what order in which a person is born, the circumstances of their delivery, etc. My friend Yaw Mensah, for instance, was born on a Thursday ("Yaw") and was his parents' third male child ("Mensah").

indigenous trees of Ghana. Mahogany, teak, odum, wawa, sapele and ebony. I gave these names to Kosmos. They picked mahogany and that was approved by GNPC. Thus, the first prospect in Ghana came to be named Mahogany.[25]

---

[25] Later in 2007, we made another discovery in the WCTP block and named the well Teak. In February of 2008, we made yet another discovery in the block, which we named Odum.

CHAPTER

10

TIME TO DRILL

In 2006, Joseph Kofi Addah took over as Minister of Energy from Professor Mike Oquaye, who had replaced Dr. Nduom. The position had become a revolving door of one or two-year duration, making it nearly impossible to establish a meaningful working relationship with anyone in that important Cabinet position.

While we performed the seismic acquisition and analysis endeavors, I searched for a shipping agent and set up crew change information and operations in preparation for when the drill ships would arrive. The ship crew change would involve people rotating off and onboard the ships every three weeks. The crew would be coming from all over the world. It was up to me to coordinate travel from Accra to Takoradi and back, locate housing and ground transportation, and deal with other crew and staff needs. I was still doing everything on my own, with no support staff.

In mid-2006, Kosmos completed the seismic work and we were ready to drill. But we found ourselves faced with three major problems. First, the price of oil had increased to the point where it was nearly impossible to locate an available drilling rig, as most of them were engaged.

Second, not only did we need a rig, but we could also have used a partner to help shoulder some of the associated costs, because Kosmos was tapped out at Blackstone. When a company explores for oil, due to the amount of money and risk involved, it's a wise strategy to have partners, to help spread the cost and risk. To drill one well could easily cost $50 million or more. If a company took on all of that expense and came up empty after just one, two or three exploration ventures, the entire company could collapse. On the other hand, if the partnership effort was successful, each company would reap a smaller percentage of the rewards, but at least they'd be alive to drill another day.

Our third problem was that our agreement with the GNPC called for us to begin drilling by 2007. It was 2006, and we didn't even have a drilling rig. We could apply to the GNPC for an extension, but the penalty would be excessive.

Our backs were against three walls. And they were pressing in—particularly for Kosmos. Their plan was to be drilling a well by the time we reached the first required milestone of the agreement, and both time and money were tight. They were already looking at a block in Nigeria and could only hope that might pay off or, at the very least, result in a soft commercial discovery.

But first, Ghana. For that, Kosmos needed a partner, because they had only $190 million on hand, and the funds were draining fast. Their business model was to farm out a certain portion of the Ghana project to a partner who would then pay for their ongoing costs, up to a certain point. They still had 86.5% of WCTP (to EO Group's 3.5% and the GNPC's 10%), so they had some room to play with—if they could entice a partner who was willing to acquire a share in exchange for working on the project.

Kosmos had a preexisting partnership arrangement with a Dallas firm called Pioneer Resources. In that deal, whenever Pioneer would fund some of Kosmos' overhead on a particular project, Pioneer would receive half ownership of the project. After the Government of Ghana had finalized our WCTP application process, granted us the license to explore the block, and we had completed the geological and seismic analyses and matured the project to the point where we were satisfied with its progress and potential, Kosmos then presented the package to Pioneer for their investment consideration.

Pioneer turned it down.

Kosmos then went to the oil industry to seek a partner. They sent out several dozen letters, soliciting interest from companies around the world. Many of them produced no response to the offer, not even to thank Kosmos for the opportunity and wish them good luck. There were a few responses from oil firms that thanked Kosmos for thinking of them, but they weren't interested, due to the high-risk factor. I could relate. I had gone through the same thing when I had approached the industry, trying to solicit partnership interest in getting the WCTP block set up years earlier.

Only a handful of companies replied that they would like to come to the Kosmos data room to look over the information: Exxon, Kerr-McGee, ARCO and Anadarko Petroleum. Of those four companies, Anadarko and Kerr-McGee (which was then in the process of being acquired by Anadarko) were interested.

Kosmos decided on Anadarko because Jim Musselman once had a relationship with the company.

Anadarko, based in The Woodlands, Texas, was one of the largest oil and gas exploration and production companies in the world. The firm had more than 4,000 employees, and had oil and natural gas operations in Algeria and China, and exploration blocks in Mozambique, Brazil, Liberia, Sierra Leone, Kenya, Côte d'Ivoire, New Zealand, Indonesia, and other countries. Anadarko had recently finished drilling several unsuccessful wells in India. They were bringing their rigs home through the Indian Ocean, headed for the Cape of Good Hope, and then on to the United States.

While discussing a possible partnership with Anadarko to drill in the WCTP block, Kosmos shared their seismic and related information with the firm. Anadarko's geologists studied the location of the WCTP acreage and analyzed the data. Their experts estimated that it probably contained less than fifty million barrels of oil—a completely different assessment than our geologists had arrived at. Yet, oddly, Anadarko seemed pleased. Why were they so convinced that it was only fifty million barrels? Why would such a huge oil firm even get involved in such a tiny resource in the first place?

Kosmos was convinced that Anadarko's estimate of the size of the field was low—by a long shot. But they needed an experienced oil exploration partner with drill ships, so Anadarko agreed to farm into the project. With one strange stipulation: they insisted on the right to become the Operator in Charge of the project if the field turned out to contain fifty million barrels of oil or less. If the find proved to be bigger than fifty million barrels, Kosmos would be in charge. It was a head scratcher. Not understanding the mysterious ways of the vastly experienced behemoth oil firm Anadarko Petroleum, Kosmos agreed that Anadarko could be the operator if the WCTP discovery turned out to be tiny.

Unknown to Kosmos was that Anadarko had been looking for an opportunity to test a new proprietary technology they had developed called MEPS (Modular Exploration Production System[26]), a system

---

[26] See: https://www.google.com/patents/US7458425

that was designed to develop small discoveries of oil in very deep water. They had been developing the technology for use in the deep waters of the Gulf of Mexico, a rough area with particularly strong currents. At the time, I am of the opinion that Anadarko wasn't necessarily looking for an oil project. They had just finished an unfruitful run in India and were going home to recharge and refit. But they were open to a small, deep-water opportunity in calm enough waters to be able to field test MEPS. And along came Kosmos.

In the meantime, halfway through our negotiation process with Anadarko, we heard that the GNPC was soliciting oil firms to license a block adjacent to ours that had become available. The block, called Deepwater Tano, had been licensed by Dana Petroleum in 1997 and contained a shallow water portion and a deep-water portion. Dana had drilled two wells, come up empty-handed, and abandoned the lease. Kosmos wanted this acreage, because when we had done our seismic study, our calculations concluded that our prospect extended into the abandoned Deepwater Tano block. It was a great opportunity for Kosmos to pick up protection acreage and hedge their bet.

Kosmos immediately filed an application with the GNPC for the Deepwater Tano block.

The GNPC sat on the application for nearly a year without acting on it.

Kosmos kept inquiring into the delay.

The GNPC adopted a wait-and-see attitude.

In the meantime, a company called Sabre Energy—led by Kofi Esson, another Ghanaian—had brought a company named Tullow Oil to Ghana, similar to how EO Group had brought Kosmos to Ghana. Tullow Oil, a multinational oil and gas exploration company headquartered in London, was founded in 1985 in Tullow, Ireland, a small town 35 miles south of Dublin. The company's first oil discovery was in Senegal in 1986. That was quickly followed by the acquisition of acreage in Spain, Italy, South Yemen, Pakistan, Bangladesh, India, Côte d'Ivoire, Egypt,

Romania, and the UK.[27] They were fast moving, highly efficient players.

Tullow put in an application for the Deepwater Tano block.

Kosmos complained to the GNPC that they had submitted their application for the block nearly a year before Tullow and had never received a response. They insisted they should be awarded the block instead of Tullow.

The GNPC responded that Kosmos already had the WCTP block and hadn't even begun drilling that yet.

The competing applications sat at the GNPC. A standoff ensued.

But the government of Ghana was desperate to bring more foreign investors into the country, particularly oil explorers. A century had passed; previous Ghanaian government administrations had not produced oil in commercial amounts, while neighboring countries had been pumping massive amounts of oil out of the Gulf of Guinea for decades. President Kufuor's marching orders to the GNPC and Minister of Energy were to drill wells in as many places as possible as soon as possible, with everyone who had been granted a license or was about to be granted one. He was adamant about developing the energy infrastructure and oil extraction capabilities of Ghana as quickly as possible. The country needed the resources.

Thomas Manu, the GNPC Director of Operations (who had vouched for me in my September 2003 meeting in Dallas with Kosmos geologist Brian Maxted), was working overtime to get as many oil companies as possible exploring and drilling in the gulf, off the coast of Ghana. The more wells Ghana got going, the higher the prospects of finding oil, and the better it would be for the country.

Finally, the GNPC announced their decision concerning the Deepwater Tano block: the block was to be divided into two parts, deep

---

[27] Today, Tullow's main production comes from six countries in Africa as well as the Southern North Sea and Asia. As part of the oil exploration consortium whose activities had originated with my efforts to license the WCTP block in Ghana in 2002, the Jubilee oil field would become Tullow's largest discovery ever (as it would for Kosmos Energy, as well).

and shallow, and they awarded the block to both Kosmos and Tullow, with each company owning half, and Kosmos being the operator.

However, Kosmos told the GNPC that they weren't interested in developing the shallow water portion of the block, because it contained gas. Tullow, on the other hand, responded that they had no problem with development of both the deep and shallow water portions of the block.

Then Kosmos made a costly business blunder. They had their lawyer send a letter to the GNPC stating that Kosmos geoscientists had determined that the oil in the Deepwater Tano block pooled over into their WCTP block, and since it was the same pool as WCTP, Kosmos could kill two birds with one stone by counting the Tano well as part of WCTP obligations.

After having made the decision to award Deepwater Tano to both parties, the GNPC didn't take kindly to Kosmos trying to force their hand with these developments. So, the GNPC reversed their decision and awarded all of Deepwater Tano to Tullow.

The GNPC wanted Kosmos to drill two separate wells, one on each block. But Kosmos was adamant they would rather drill only one well and argued that if they drilled two wells, they would both be in the same pool.[28]

As seismic data had shown that the prospect pooled into both blocks, it could be argued technically that it was right for Kosmos to have claimed that they had discovered the oil in both blocks (and certainly they wanted to save money by having to drill only one well). But their legal letter only infuriated the government, because the GNPC wanted the company to drill in each block, no matter whether oil pooled into both blocks. Had Kosmos never sent the letter, but simply maintained that since they had applied for the Deepwater Tano block first (a long time before Tullow had even shown up and expressed interest), they may have had a chance at being awarded Deepwater Tano block. Now,

---

[28] It was only in retrospect that it was discovered that Kosmos had been correct in their assertion.

they had missed the opportunity to get the extra block. It would prove to be a costly misstep. And it wouldn't be the last one Kosmos would make over the next couple of years.

Fortunately for Kosmos, however, they were able to undo some of the damage. Tullow didn't know what Kosmos knew about what was in the WCTP block that pooled over into the Deepwater Tano block. So Kosmos offered to farm into Deepwater Tano, and Tullow agreed to allow them to acquire a 40% interest in the block. However, GNPC Chairman Sekyere-Abankwa advised Tullow that might not be the wisest move. So Tullow revised their offer, agreeing to give Kosmos 40% of Deepwater Tano in exchange for 25% of WCTP. Kosmos accepted.[29] (It was brilliant free advice from the Chairman and would greatly benefit Tullow.)

Kosmos was not happy with getting a lower equity than they wanted, yet they didn't exactly get the shaft, because they now had a partnership with Tullow Oil and could share the risks of the investment.

Meanwhile, Kosmos was under pressure to get a drill rig into WCTP. They had chosen Anadarko Petroleum, who had the type of rig Kosmos needed. But Kosmos had entered the talks with Anadarko from a weakened position: with deep-water drilling rigs scarce, no rock solid guarantee there was a lot of oil in our block, and being in danger of losing our WCTP license if we didn't get busy drilling soon, Kosmos now had to deal with Anadarko, the big gorilla on the block.

Anadarko knew Kosmos needed them for deep-water drilling rigs.

---

[29] The enhanced GNPC additional participation interest of 5% in Tullow's Tano Deep Water block was due to the fact that Tullow had inherited a block that already had 2D and 3D seismic data, the value of which was to be credited to GNPC (through the enhanced additional participation interest of 5%, which was higher than the Kosmos 2.5%). Kosmos was to acquire their own 3D seismic data which was non-existent on the WCTP block, while Tullow took over the existing 2D and 3D seismic data (acquired by Dana Petroleum in August of 1997; thus the difference in the two additional participating interests. SOURCE: Steven Sekyere-Abankwa, former Chairman of the GNPC, in a statement he made to the Ghana Police, CID Station, on March 29, 2010, concerning the details of the negotiations between the government of Ghana, the GNPC, and EO Group/Kosmos Energy, which resulted in the granting of an oil exploration license and the signing of the parties' Petroleum Agreement in May of 2004.

So, in exchange for drilling services, Anadarko wanted half of Kosmos' share of the now combined WCTP and Deepwater Tano blocks. Kosmos accepted the deal and gave half of their stake in the combined blocks to Anadarko Petroleum.[30] It was an excellent business proposition for Anadarko.

Our partnership included EO Group/Kosmos Energy, Tullow Oil/Sabre Oil, the Government of Ghana, and Anadarko Petroleum. After calculating the new split, as well as the government's share, Kosmos had been squeezed down quite a bit from where they had started.

* * *

The infusion of funds in the 2006 expansion of the EO/Kosmos partnership into a six-member oil consortium allowed me to rent an office and hire some more personnel. I also managed to negotiate a raise from Kosmos to $8,000 per month (and would still only be earning around one-third of what my peers at the other oil firms were making). Still, I appreciated the few extra thousand dollars per month. Times were tough for working Africans. I felt very privileged.

A few weeks later, in August of 2006, my EO Group partner, Bawuah-Edusei, was appointed as Ghana's Ambassador to the United States. Since my efforts had collapsed in trying to set up a partnership

---

[30] As a result of the 2006 negotiation, Tullow Oil/Sabre Energy and Anadarko Petroleum farmed into the WCTP block, which had been acquired by EO Group and Kosmos in 2004, with Kosmos as the Operator. The percentages of ownership of the partners in this WCTP portion of the consortium were: Kosmos, 30.875%; Anadarko, 30.875%; Tullow, 22.896%; GNPC, 10%; EO Group, 3.5%; Sabre, 1.854%. Kosmos Energy and Anadarko Petroleum farmed into the Deepwater Tano block, which was adjacent to the WCTP block (subsequently discovered to be part of the same WCTP pool) and which had been acquired by Tullow Oil and Sabre Energy in 2006. Deepwater Tano was operated by Tullow Oil. The percentages of ownership of the partners in the Deepwater Tano portion of the consortium were: Tullow, 49.95%; Kosmos, 18%; Anadarko, 18%; GNPC, 10%; Sabre, 4.05%. In 2007, the combined WCTP and Deepwater Tano blocks were collectively renamed Jubilee Field. The percentages of ownership of the partners transposed to Jubilee were: Tullow (Operator), 34.705%; Kosmos (Technical Operator), 23.491%; Anadarko, 23.491%, GNPC, 13.75 (comprising 10% carried interest and 3.75% working interest); Sabre, 2.813%; and EO Group, 1.75%.

with Ennex Energy four years ago, I had been pretty much managing all operations on my own for EO Group, anyway. I was used to the work.

The operation was growing by leaps and bounds as drilling time approached. I was finally given a budget for an office. I found a former bank building and renovated it into an acceptable office environment, with amenities for our incoming staff. I had also located a shore base for all the tools, equipment, and drill pipes that were arriving. With the help of Air Force Captain Sam Oje,[31] I found a large tract of land at the Air Force Base in Takoradi, and negotiated a lease rate of a quarter of a million dollars per year. Captain Oje gave me a permit to go on and off of the base as needed, and guided me in navigating the business landscape (he was proving to be incredibly helpful in making my efforts a success in Takoradi). My efforts at initiating the introduction of an entire new industry to Takoradi—indeed, to all of Ghana—were intensifying.

The ground turned out to be waterlogged in many areas. I located some huge boulders to help hold the soil, and hired cranes, bulldozers, bucket loaders, and other equipment to build the base. I was doing things I'd never done before in my life, learning on the job, and asking a lot of questions.

There were other people who encouraged and helped me as I toiled away in Takoradi and Accra. At the GNPC, I met Emmanuel Tamakloe, a former employee of the GNPC and a highly experienced man who had been involved in much of the oil exploration activities that had taken place in Ghana before we had arrived. He understood how the GNPC operated internally and at all levels of the corporate hierarchy. He knew how to get things done in the oil business in Ghana in the most efficient ways possible. Emmanuel became a valued ally. Without

---

[31] Captain Oje was in charge of the Takoradi base at the time. His cooperation with me was the basis for building the logistics support for the oil industry in Ghana. He was later promoted to the position of Air Vice Marshall, in charge of the entire Ghana Air Force, and now serves as the Chief of Defense Staff.

his wisdom and experience, I would have struggled even more to get everything ready for drilling.

By now, Joseph Owusu had become one of my closest confidants and advisers. If there was any work I needed done from the U.S., he would ensure that it was done quickly and get it to me. He was always there for me and never asked for any money for helping me. A soft-spoken man, with a sharp mind and funny sense of humor, Joseph had become a highly valued and much-appreciated asset. And it didn't hurt that he could put on a face that looked like he could chew the top off of a Coke can with his bare teeth.

I would soon find out the hard way that when I came across trustworthy men like Joseph Owusu and Emmanuel Tamakloe, men of intelligence, deep loyalty, and a perfect blend of encouragement and steel nerves, I was halfway to winning any war that might be laid at my feet.

And several of those wars were on their way.

At last, in the spring of 2006, the Anadarko exploration drill ship Belford Dolphin, flagged out of Singapore, arrived from India.

It was time to drill.

CHAPTER

11

GUSHER

I had been asleep for nearly an hour on Tuesday, June 19, 2007, when the jangling of my bedside phone abruptly woke me. I glanced at the clock. The red numerals displayed 2:00 AM. I picked up on the second ring.

"This is George," I answered sleepily.

"George, we hit something."

It was Thomas Manu, from the GNPC. I snapped awake instantly.

"What did we hit?"

"There's a strong indication we made a discovery."

"Do we know what it is?"

"We're not certain. Smells like oil. Could be gas."

The smell of some fluids could mimic the odor of petroleum.

"How big is it?" I asked him.

"We don't know yet. But it could be big, George. We need to keep this quiet for now."

I got out of bed. My breathing quickened. I could feel my heart rate increase.

We hung up.

I realized I was shaking. I put on a pair of jeans, black loafers and a shirt, and took a walk around the hotel. It was dead quiet, hot, and muggy. I could barely contain myself. My mind was racing. I paced for hours, until daybreak. The Anadarko staff had worked through the night.

I would be awake almost nonstop for the next two weeks.

Most of the Anadarko staff was skeptical about what we had found. They thought it was only gas. We waited for a few days until the confirmation arrived. I could finally breathe. It was oil. Discovered in the WCTP block, it was located just off the continental shelf, approximately 36 miles off the southwest coast of Ghana. The field was on a downward slope in a central canal flanked by shallower western and eastern channels. It was massive. Something I had toiled on for years was coming to reality.

We needed to keep the discovery quiet, to prepare our announcement, to give time for GNPC Chairman Sekyere-Abankwa to inform the President and for the consortium partners to get ready for what we knew was coming. For the next couple of days I went about my business, knowing something big that the rest of the nation didn't know: history had been made.

* * *

The Belford Dolphin, which had drilled around 20 wells in India with no luck, was on its way back to the Gulf of Mexico to be refitted. With the agreement between Kosmos and Anadarko finalized, the ship had been diverted to Ghana to drill the WCTP well.

By Friday, June 22, we had verified all we needed to know about our find. It was time to tell President Kufuor.

"Don't joke," Kufuor replied when he heard the news of our discovery. "This is too expensive to joke about."

The following day I was to be on my way to Nigeria. I went through the airport, the whole time thinking about what this news meant, not only to Ghana, but to the world that had been almost convinced that there was no oil to be found in that part of the Gulf of Guinea. For anyone in the oil and gas business, traveling to Nigeria on business trips wasn't unusual. I had never been to Nigeria before. When we landed, I was both surprised and nervous to see the fanfare that was beginning to build up. There was also an armed security convoy waiting. It turned out that it was Kosmos' CEO Jim Musselman and his team who had come to meet me. They had been traveling with an armed escort because security was still a big issue in Nigeria at the time, and corporate executives never traveled without an armed escort.

It was the first time I had seen Musselman since our discovery. Our mood was jubilant as we exchanged high-fives.

On our arrival back in Accra airport, nearly two dozen black SUVs with government ministers and VIPs were waiting for us. I hadn't realized that the word had leaked out. We were treated like conquering heroes returning from battle.

We stopped at the Golden Tulip Hotel and planned our strategy. At four o'clock that afternoon, the convoy took us to President Kufuor's house, where an assembly of officials was waiting for us.

As was Ghanaian custom, even though he knew why we were there, we were formally asked the purpose of our visit to see the President. GNPC Chairman Sekyere-Abankwa announced why the Kosmos team was there.

"Ghana has finally discovered oil," the Chairman announced to President Kufuor.

The room erupted. A party atmosphere broke out. A former defense minister began dancing like a kid.

After thanking us, President Kufuor told us, "I am not going to tell the nation what you found. I want your engineers to tell the country that Ghana has struck oil commercially."

He then instructed us to go and get some of the oil and bring it back so we could show it to the world.

The following Sunday, at 11 o'clock, the Kosmos team, a GNPC Board member named Adu Gyamfi and I left Accra to Takoradi. We went to the rig to retrieve some samples of the actual crude oil from the WCTP well. On the oil rig, we filled a small bottle with crude oil, wrapped it up and I held it next to my chest like a little boy with a treasure. We brought it back to Accra. This time, there was another group of people waiting for us. I poured out some of the oil onto a white dinner plate and showed it to a very grateful and happy President Kufuor. He asked us to meet him at Osu Castle the next day to make the official announcement.

That night, I washed and dried a couple of shampoo bottles from the Golden Tulip Hotel and filled them with our oil.

The next day, a press conference was held in President Kufuor's office at Osu Castle. It seemed like every official in Ghana was present. The entire government and cabinet ministers were there, as well as the GNPC executives, Chairman Sekyere-Abankwa and the Kosmos staff. The office was overflowing with joy.

After pleasantries and greetings, Jim Musselman stood up to speak, asking me to stand beside him. Musselman held up a shampoo bottle of crude oil and announced, "Mr. President, Ghana has oil. We have made a significant discovery of high grade, commercial quality crude oil."

I took the bottle, uncapped it, and poured it onto a plate while the news media snapped photos and shot video, recording the event for posterity. I presented the oil to the President. The President was delighted.

George Owusu, the Country Manager of Kosmos Energy, pours a sample of the crude oil from the Cape Three Points for the benefit of President Kufuor. With them are CEO James Musselman, and Vice President Brian Maxted, both of Kosmos Energy.

"I can't believe my eyes," he said, flashing his big smile.

The plate of oil was passed around the room for all to see. For most of them, it was the first time they had ever seen crude oil extracted from the ground.

Within hours, the headline blared from newspapers, radio, and television outlets around the world.

As always in Ghana, no sooner than our announcement had been made, the nabobs of negativity reared their wagging heads. The political bandwagon went bonkers, with the NDC party and members of the news media claiming that the announcement was a hoax, a political gimmick to gain attention for the President and the NPP party, and claiming that the oil was not from our well but was merely a popular brand of dark cooking oil called "Adwengo."[32] The country hadn't found any oil in a century of trying, the naysayers were pointing out, so why would oil suddenly appear? They had gotten it spectacularly wrong, as they would many other facts related to our discovery over the next several years. But this was Ghana.

Regardless, everything changed in an instant. Our hunt had paid off. After nearly five years of believing, pursuing, pushing and pulling to prove my hunch about the West Cape Three Points block, my dream had become reality. Ghana was about to become an oil nation.

And I was about to be treated like a rock star.

---

[32] The discovery should have been celebrated by the entire nation without regard to political party affiliation but, Ghana being Ghana, it was turned into a political football instead of a great achievement. And ironically, these doubters were the very same people who would soon be jumping all over themselves to claim credit for the find.

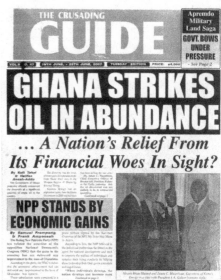

Newspaper headlines in Ghana in 2007/2008

CHAPTER

12

ROCK STAR

The discovery, comprising the WCTP block and the Deepwater Tano block,[33] was made just ninety days after the 50th anniversary of Ghana's independence from Great Britain. Later that year, Mr. Moses Oduro Boateng, Managing Director of the GNPC, named the combined ("unitized") blocks *Jubilee Field* to commensurate the 50th anniversary of Ghana's independence from Great Britain. The name became official.[34]

---

[33] As the discovery was just a few meters from the boundary between the EO/Kosmos WCTP field and the Tullow/Sabre Deepwater Tano field, Tullow had named their part of the well "Hyedua." However, by industry standards, this was not an actual discovery, but an appraisal well of our WCTP well, as Tullow had drilled in the same pool of oil after we had discovered the first pool.

[34] Jubilee Field, located in the Gulf of Guinea, 60 kilometers off the coast, was located at a depth

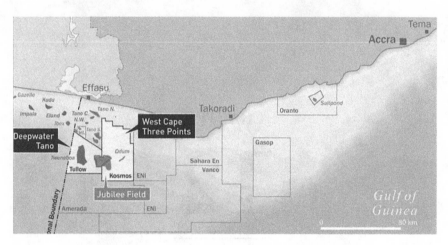

(Source: GNPC) Tullow and EO/Kosmos: West Cape Three Points and Deepwater Tano Fields

Jubilee Field was one of the largest in the world at the time, and the biggest in West Africa in a decade. Tests would reveal that the oil was among the very highest quality.[35] Initial estimates of the potential of Jubilee Field put its first production phase at more than 300 million barrels of premium grade crude oil,[36] for a capacity of 120,000 barrels per day. In January of 2007, oil prices had been $46 per barrel. By the time we discovered Mahogany in mid-June, the price had risen to $60, and was still climbing. At that rate, Ghana could reap a couple of billion dollars in revenue on their share alone, making the country a bigger oil producer than France and Spain.

However, in less than 48 months those estimates would prove to be way off-base, as the field would reveal itself to be astounding in

---

between 1,100 and 1,300 meters, a total depth between 3,400 and 4,200 meters, and covered 110 square kilometers. In geological terms, Jubilee Field is a continuous stratigraphic trap with combined hydrocarbon columns in excess of 600 meters.

[35] *Daily Graphic*, in an April 16, 2009, article by Mabel Aku Baneseh, titled "Kosmos to Assist in Electricity Production" (p.40).

[36] The WCTP crude oil was light and sweet. For oil refiners, that indicated a high quality oil that was ideal for worldwide refineries.

size, potentially containing as much as two billion barrels, and possibly more.[37] By then, the price of oil would rise to $80 per barrel, making the potential value of the field a staggering $160 billion, putting Ghana in a league with Africa's top oil producers.

We had done well.

After the find, development ratcheted up tremendously. As busy as I already was, my workload increased even more. We started bringing in outside contractors, logistics experts and other staff and crew essential to the operation. Annual personnel movements alone would soon reach nearly a thousand. There would be 75,000 tons of deck cargo to deal with. The Takoradi port was on its way to doubling activities in a few years. I was constantly being sought after by news reporters, for quotes, to discuss our find, production plans, and to be photographed with various dignitaries.

One night after a particularly long day, I was telling some of the employees how overworked I often felt. My $8,000 monthly pay was still not quite enough to comfortably take care of all my needs and obligations and send some money to my family in Houston, and put some aside for a rainy day and retirement. I was far behind in comparison to the salary I had given up when I had left Houston three years earlier to Ghana, and to the income my counterparts at Kosmos, Anadarko, and Tullow were making.

"George," one of the men said, rolling his eyes, "you are lucky! You're a Country Manager. Look at all the money you're making!"

"No," I responded, shaking my head knowingly, "I'm not making

---

[37] Estimates of the amount of crude in Jubilee Field ranged between 1 and 2 billion barrels. In their status report in 2008, the GNPC stated 800 million barrels as the total amount, ranging upwards of a possible 3 billion barrels (GNPC, 2008). In their base cases of 2008/2009, the International Monetary Fund (IMF) and the World Bank assumed a recoverable amount of approximately 500 million barrels (World Bank, 2009). The field also contained an estimated 1.2 trillion cubic feet of natural gas, the equivalent of approximately 162 million barrels of oil.

big money as a Country Manager, my friend."

"Don't lie, George," he quipped. "You know you're making a ton."

When I insisted that I was not, he looked at me for a moment, then said, "Are you kidding me? I'm making $45,000 a month."

At first, I thought he was joking. But his face said it all—he was not joking. This man was earning half a million dollars per year in the oil business and wasn't overseeing nearly as much activity as I was.

He added, "I'm also getting free accommodations, free transportation, a driver, a free mobile phone, my clothes laundered, free food."

I was speechless.

I said, "You're telling me you don't even have to spend a penny of your salary?"

"Not a cedi, if I don't want to," he replied.

There I was, Country Manager in charge of all of the shore and business operations, and I was being paid one-fifth of what my peers were earning.

I boarded the next plane to Dallas and went straight to the Kosmos headquarters. My pitch was simple: we just made a historic oil discovery and I was working the equivalent of two weeks every week to hold everything together on the ground in Ghana.

"There are guys over there doing half the amount of work I'm doing and they're being paid five times as much," I explained.

They agreed. My salary was raised substantially. And the raise would soon become a source of many problems in my life.

13

ON THE PROWL

The first battle we had to face after making the discovery was when to start production. Wrangling flared up between the partners after Tullow announced that, in order to better understand the block and do a proper job of developing it, they wanted to delay production for five years so they could do a further study of the field. They also had made a recent discovery in Uganda and were getting ready to invest money and resources in developing that field. At that time, Tullow wasn't a big company and would be financially stretched to try to move both their Ghana and Uganda projects to production simultaneously.

Anadarko was also content to put off production for a few years, because they had productions in the Middle East and elsewhere, and had recently bought a large company called Kerr-McGee, which was still in the process of being integrated into Anadarko.

But Kosmos, which was borrowing money at high interest rates, had no other productions underway, and in order to start paying off their loans, they had to get started on production of WCTP.

The Government of Ghana was also in need of money. And politically, the NPP government wanted to be able to show the world that they had found oil and were now in production. GNPC Chairman Sekyere-Abankwa sided with Kosmos, explaining to the partners that there were no good reasons to delay. He announced that production should start as early as possible.

It wasn't a happy conversation, but Tullow and Anadarko grudgingly agreed.

By now, Anadarko had begun to suspect that I, as the Ghanaian partner, was trying to shift everything in favor of Kosmos, my main counter-party partner, and that whatever Kosmos wanted, I was able to get for them. It seemed to me that Anadarko started nursing a grudge against me for their misperception.

The next problem to solve was the question of who would be the Operator in Charge of this monstrous project.

Anadarko, with their huge size, vast resources, and technical know-how, had found themselves on the outside, due to their having made a tactical error. In the beginning, when Chairman Sekyere-Abankwa had asked them if they would be the operator, Anadarko replied no, they would not. This was because they had assessed the field as containing less than 50 million barrels of oil and had insisted on putting into their agreement with Kosmos the stipulation that Anadarko would be the Operator in Charge only if the discovery was less than 50 million barrels.

But now that the discovery had been made and was found to be several times larger than Anadarko's experts had calculated, I imagine they now wanted to be the operator. They went to Tullow and asked them to side with them against Kosmos in pushing for Anadarko to be the operator of WCTP. Tullow agreed and allegedly stated that in their opinion, Kosmos was not technically sound, claiming that Musselman's Triton Energy discovery in Equatorial Guinea had made some errors in the development phase, which caused the integrity of some of the wells to be affected during the production from the field.

This became a big issue. We held a meeting in London to try to re-solve the trouble that was brewing. Chairman Sekyere-Abankwa, in his schoolmaster style, took the reins. He reminded Anadarko that when he had asked them if they wanted to be the operator, they had told him no. And now that they had made a big discovery, he was not about to allow them to change their position and push Kosmos aside.

Then Chairman Sekyere-Abankwa announced that the combined discoveries from both the WCTP and Deepwater Tano blocks (collec-tively known as Jubilee Field) would be unitized under the operatorship of one partner, and that partner would be Tullow.

"You are claiming that Kosmos is not qualified," Sekyere-Abankwa stated. "But if, for example, a doctor is going to perform surgery and he needs water, you bring water for him. If he needs oxygen, you bring him oxygen. So he can do his job properly. So, if you think Kosmos cannot do this, then we are going to form an integrated project team—an IPT—and all of you bring your engineers together to offer advice during development stage, but Kosmos is going to be the head of this IPT."

Anadarko and Tullow were to bring their engineers to Kosmos' office. Anadarko seemed appalled at the suggestion, humiliated and angry at being the biggest player and having to go to the offices of a tiny upstart partner who would be in charge of this huge and historic proj-ect. The confrontation that erupted over the idea nearly became physi-cal. But Kosmos stood their ground, because they knew that Anadarko had wanted to delay production in the first place, and if Anadarko was made operator of the project, they would come up with reasons to do exactly that.

In the end, Sekyere-Abankwa's word was law: Kosmos would be in charge of the technical operation of Jubilee Field until the production stage, when it would all be turned over to Tullow. And Anadarko, was left on the outside looking in. It felt as if Anadarko's antagonism toward me increased even more. They felt that, once again, I had been instrumental in moving the ball in Kosmos' favor.

This time, Anadarko shifted their strategy. Instead of siding with Tullow, they went to Kosmos and asked them to support Anadarko's bid to be the operator in charge of production of the unified field. Kosmos emphatically rejected Anadarko's request. And the infighting blew up all over again.

Chairman Abankwa, an astute and brilliant tactician and leader, once again stepped in and rode herd over the combatants, firmly stating what was best for the operation and for the partners in production of Jubilee Field and insisting that these acrimonious issues be resolved and that the partners move forward. Had it not been for Abankwa's prescient business acumen and firm leadership approach, production of Jubilee Field might very well have been delayed by several years.[38]

By early 2008, the world press was gushing about Kosmos Energy and our Ghana discoveries. On Wednesday morning, January 16, 2008, a deep-water floating drilling rig named Songa Saturn arrived in Ghana from Equatorial Guinea to drill a second well in the WCTP. It would be on location to drill the Odum well until April or May before departing for Libya. Four additional appraisal wells would be drilled beginning in mid-2008 (paving the way for production to begin in 2010).

That same month, Kosmos was named Explorer of the Year by the Britain-based World Junior Oil and Gas Congress. Kosmos Senior V.P. Paul Daily received the award in London on behalf of the firm. We were all basking in the glow of international fame. On January 11, 2008, the

---

[38] Tullow had made a small discovery in Uganda a few months earlier and wanted to take a few years to study the Jubilee Field discovery before starting production in Ghana. That, along with Anadarko's desire to also delay production on Jubilee Field, would have delayed production by years. Sekyere-Abankwa's disallowing Tullow or Anadarko to delay was as wise for Ghana as it was crucial to the future of Kosmos.

Daily Graphic newspaper quoted me in an interview about our activities and production plans: "Ghana will be the West Africa hub for Kosmos Energy. We are building for the long term and we are here to stay."[39]

Yet, just one year from then, everyone would be singing a different tune.

In 2008, I was surprised when the government of Ghana bestowed on me the Order of the Volta, an honor awarded for outstanding service performed for the country. I was given the award for the part I had played in initiating a new era that would bring the country into the top echelons of African oil-producing nations and bringing to a close one hundred years of efforts to discover oil in Ghana. My patient and untiring efforts of the past several years were at last being officially acknowledged.

President John Kufuor with George Owusu after bestowing him with The Order of the Volta, 2008

---

[39] *Daily Graphic,* in a January 11, 2008, article titled "Ghana to Become Oil Hub in Africa"; see: http://business.everythingghana.com/index.php?option=com_content&task=view&id=151 &Itemid=36

The first year after our oil discovery was a whirlwind of activity for me. I was given awards, invited to address panels, chair talks, and attend public appearances. I was the talk of the town, treated like a national hero wherever I went. Everyone wanted to know who this George Owusu was who had brought this opportunity, this company, this huge oil machine to Ghana. People were approaching me constantly with offers to buy my shares in Jubilee Field. I was featured in all of the newspapers, almost daily, often in front page stories, usually including a photograph of me with the President or some other Ghanaian dignitary. I was on television and radio constantly, my name mentioned everywhere. I had become an "instant" celebrity (despite my struggles in obscurity during years of dejection and heartbreak).

The happiest day of my life had been when we went to Osu Castle and announced to the whole world that Ghana had discovered oil. I thanked God that I was a part of that historic event, not only in Ghana but in Africa. Nothing beat finding oil in the place oil companies had referred to as "the graveyard." A place where scores of wells had been drilled and all had failed. A place where I came along, brought in a company and drilled in the right place. A place where we found hundreds of millions of barrels of oil. A place where everybody was convinced there was no oil. Playing a role in bringing about something like that? *Hallelujah!* A fantastic culmination of a long career in the petroleum industry.

I had left Ghana long ago as a young schoolteacher. I returned as a man twice as old to a country where nobody knew me and no one was aware of what I was doing as I worked under the radar. Then, suddenly, I was the toast of the nation. It was a wonderful feeling to have a half-decade of hard work in Ghana recognized at all levels of society. In a developing nation desperately in need of some way to economically lift up her citizens, I had become a national superstar.

My life would never be the same.

But the euphoria wouldn't last long, because my success had begun to fester ill will in the dark hearts of some people who were determined to bring me down.

The devil was on the prowl.

CHAPTER

14

FULL CONTACT

*"Pride, envy, and avarice are the three sparks that
have set these hearts on fire."*
—Dante Alighieri, The Divine Comedy: (Inferno, VI, l. 74)

Jubilee Field was expected to raise hundreds of millions of dollars a year in revenue for this impoverished country. It had the potential to improve the lives of Ghanaians by investing in education, health care, industry, and infrastructure. Yet, Ghana faced overwhelming challenges, due to her weak history of managing revenues in an open manner.

According to a story in the *National Geographic News*, doubts were openly creeping into the national discussion about the nation's new status as an oil behemoth. Some began to express fear that greed was going to turn Ghana into another Nigeria, an oil-rich neighbor that was plagued by corruption and experienced frequent oil spills that were often tied to vandalism. Oil had long played a role in civil strife in several other African countries too, including Angola, the Republic of Congo, and Sudan, countries that assigned income from natural resources as money to spend, rather than invest.[40]

Organizations such as the Africa Regional Coordinator for Revenue Watch Institute (a nonprofit that promotes transparency of government expenditures) and the Campaigns Coordinator for the Ghana-based Integrated Social Development Centre (an organization that promotes social and economic justice), jumped on the bandwagon of doubt, adding to growing concerns. Yet, we hadn't even produced one barrel of oil. Our discovery would continue to ignite emotions in Ghana for years to come. Some in good ways, some not.

None of the controversy stopped the world's oil industry giants from flooding into Ghana, however. In all of 2006, only four firms had applied for licenses to search for oil in Ghana. By mid-2008, GNPC Managing Director Moses Boateng reported that 20 companies had applied for oil and gas exploration licenses after our 2007 discovery, and 21 others had applied so far in 2008.[41]

The new pragmatic exploration and production policy of the NPP government had worked. We had started a classic oil rush. By the end of 2008,[42] we would drill six wells. During that time, Minister of Energy Joseph Adda would be replaced by Felix Owusu-Adjapong.

---

[40] A paraphrase of reporter Jeff Smith's December 15, 2010, *National Geographic News* article titled "New Oil—and a Huge Challenge—for Ghana." See: http://news.nationalgeographic. com/news/energy/2010/12/1012115-oil-ghana-environment-jubilee/

[41] Of those 41 oil companies, only six had been assessed to have the proven financial and technical expertise and were granted licenses. These included Yep-Dawant, Afren-Celtique, Sahara Energy Field Ltd., Tap Oil, South Atlantic Natural Resources, and Addax Petroleum. See: *Daily Graphic*, in a June 10, 2008, article by Mabel Aku Baneseh, titled "41 Firms Apply for Exploration" (front page).

[42] In addition to the Belford Dolphin and the Songa Saturn, the other drill ships would include the Eirik Raude, the Atwood Hunter, which arrived in March of 2009, and the Aban Abraham, which arrived at the end of 2009.

Still, the news of our big oil discovery wasn't a happy event for everyone connected to the oil industry in Ghana. The pundits shifted into overdrive, and the nation followed. Politics, Ghana's favorite sport next to football, was about to hit the airwaves. The game wouldn't let up for three long years. And I was the ball.

Tsatsu Tsikata had overseen the GNPC for nearly a decade and a half during a time when dozens of attempts to discover oil in Ghana had failed. Tsikata was supposedly a man with a power and reach that stretched back to the days of President Jerry Rawlings and still ran deep throughout Ghana. As an entrepreneur, I had always genuinely given anyone I met the benefit of the doubt, especially when I had not had any direct dealings with them. I certainly did not know Tsikata personally, and like all Ghanaians had given him respect for the work he had done for his country. Whatever the administration's supposed shortcomings had been were of no particular concern to me. I had no reason to denigrate him or any of his colleagues.

Even if the GNPC had struggled in previous years to attract investors, or their efforts had not resulted in the discovery of commercial quantities of premium grade crude, they may have very well done their best with the opportunity they had. But unfortunately I had been thrust into the crosshairs of a political fistfight, and I was bearing the brunt of legal backlash.

Two decades earlier, when Tsikata was a law professor, he had taught many of Ghana's future lawyers, government officials, and criminal justice professionals, several of whom could have remained loyal to him. I had no reason to suspect he might possibly have something to do with unsettling tremors that were about to ripple across my world.

By 2008, as America's banking, stock market, and home mortgage industry collapse continued to spread, many nations around the world began experiencing their own economic meltdowns. Consumers were losing their jobs at a frightening pace. Businesses closed down. Money was draining from the consumer market. Credit and finance sources were drying up. Economies were in freefall, with governments and municipalities struggling to maintain basic services.

In Ghana, where most citizens relied on the government to help house them, feed them, and provide economic assistance, people paid attention to who was representing their interests. The private sector was not well-developed in Ghana to begin with, and getting and keeping a job was the primary concern for the majority of the people.

The two things voters wanted to know about every candidate running for political office were, *What will you do to help me?* And, *How will you identify and eliminate what's not working for the best interests of the people?* This meant a political candidate couldn't just spout off their strong points or their advantages over their opponent. They had to convince the electorate beyond all doubt that the opponent was utterly corrupt and not worthy of representing the people.

Ghanaian politics was do-or-die politics. No middle ground. This approach created a winner-take-all, scorched-earth political atmosphere in Ghana, where the winning party (which had won office by convincing sufficient numbers of voters that the previous administration was a bunch of thieves, liars and con-men) must now do the "right thing" by cleaning house. Therefore, one of the first things the winner often did after taking office was to investigate everything the previous administration did, with the goal of proving to the people that what the winning politician had been saying all along (that the previous government was corrupt) was correct and that the saviors had now arrived and would put things right by meting out justice and jailing perpetrators.

This mindset had been in Ghana's "political DNA" for decades and was the same tactic used by her dictators in wresting power from their own predecessors. The only difference was that now, operating under a democratic system, it was done as part of a political voting process by forceful candidates and a willing press corps, rather than by a uniformed tyrant with guns and tanks.

As election rhetoric heated up during the 2008 Presidential campaign, it became evident that the NPP was in a tough battle to retain the Castle. Not because the NDC was making great strides in convincing the people they had a solid plan to lift Ghana up and improve the economy, fix the dilapidated infrastructure, and create equal business opportunities for all Ghanaians, but because the NDC was simply hammering an emotion-laden message of negativity against the NPP, with no proof, no specifics, and no coherency. Just endless pessimism. Harbingers of doom. The citizens deserved better. My only hope was that the NPP would not be tempted to sink into the same pit, in the name of trying to defend itself against the charges being thrown at it.

I took potential government regime change seriously, because in Ghana, politics is a full-contact sport. There is no objectivity. While the nation had enjoyed only a tiny history with a participatory democratic voting system, it seemed that the NDC party was more focused on proving their point and threatening that if they won office, they would put people in jail, rather than promise to work with the other parties in fixing the problems of our poverty-stricken nation.

The nascent oil industry's biggest champion in Ghana, President John Kufuor, was coming to the end of his second term and was constitutionally barred from running again. As campaign rhetoric began to shift, from euphoria over our new status as a potential world energy powerhouse, to expounding dark theories on how it had happened, I began to sense that there was a slim margin of possibility that the NDC opposition party might win the election in December. Still, we didn't expect much to happen in a major way that would disrupt our progress. After all, the people were aware of the good we were doing for Ghana. If an opposition government came in, we could only hope they would let us go about our business developing a huge new income source for the nation while they went about their business of governing the nation.

My naiveté was based in my having approached everything in connection with our historic oil discovery in an honorable and honest way.

I obeyed all laws and worked diligently in the pursuit of my business affairs, the way most hardworking people probably do. After all, I was doing nothing wrong, nothing illegal, nothing even remotely questionable. I had come to Ghana with an open heart to do my best with something I knew was good for the citizens.

I was in for a harsh lesson in politics, Ghana style.

> *"George always believed that since he did the right thing, since he had found something which is good for the country, nobody is going to question it.*
> *. . . being Americanized, he had somehow become naïve, thinking people would see the bright light and see the good that he'd done."*
> —Joseph Owusu, former Managing Director, EO Group

The first distant rumbles of trouble on the national horizon came when Vice President Alhaji Aliu Mahama was beat out at the NPP's convention by Nana Akufo-Addo as the candidate to run in December in the general election against NDC candidate John Atta Mills. It wasn't necessarily an indication of a rift in the party. Akufo-Addo was a popular economist and lawyer whose family roots went back to some of the founding fathers of Ghana. What was troubling was that V.P. Mahama had served President Kufuor and the nation faithfully for eight years, only to be badly beaten in the primaries. It almost felt like the party was out to fix something that wasn't broken.

I was far too busy to bother with it. It was interesting politics, but it didn't rise to the level of a red flag as to what was going on internally with the NPP. Besides, I wasn't exactly a government insider. Just a working man, holding down a job, trying to do something good for my country, and hoping the NPP wouldn't cause any unwarranted delays on the project, which could easily cost millions of dollars with each day of inactivity.

As the December Presidential election neared, political fervor was whipping up across the land. Candidate John Atta Mills' NDC party, which had been turned out of office nearly eight years earlier, desperately wanted to retake the Castle. They needed their negative campaign strategy to work in their favor, but the polls were still leaning toward the NPP. So Mills turned up the negative rhetoric.

And suddenly my name was tossed into the furnace of political demagoguery. I was being increasingly mentioned in nefarious terms by some newspapers and reporters, as if I were a scourge on my homeland. As the 2008 elections loomed, the ridiculous rumors not only increased, they took on a dangerous tint of bigotry. Stories began circulating that a former ambassador to Ivory Coast who was a friend of a former GNPC official had been told that everyone involved in the Jubilee Field discovery was an Asante—my ethnic group—and that we refused to work with, hire or deal with people who were not Asantes. This was an unfortunate assertion and sparked a string of erroneous inferences.

The truth, however, was that the company was very diverse. I was proud of having created a workforce from the drivers and personal secretary to the management team, all having come from different parts of the country. The farthest thing from my thought was to hire employees based on their tribal affiliations.

Presidential opposition candidate John Atta Mills, who was not an Asante, began stirring the pot even more, asking voters, *"Is all of this sudden oil really just coincidence?"* The insinuation was that there had to have been collusion in our securing the oil exploration license, and that EO Group must be surrogates for President Kufuor, whom some members of the media theorized was secretly set to receive millions of dollars from the oil deal as soon as he was out of office.

Theory turned to unfounded suspicion. Suspicion prompted Mills supporters to push for an investigation. Any politician knew that the words "being investigated for fraud" splashed across the front page of the newspapers in connection to the Kufuor administration was enough to make Ghanaians sit up and take notice—and maybe move Mills into the Castle in January and reveal President Kufuor and his cronies as having appropriated Ghanaian resources to themselves. If you repeat a lie loud enough and often enough, people begin to suspect there might be some truth behind it.

My star began to fall as suddenly as it had risen.

The rumor mill cranked into overdrive, pounding at the speculation that there had to have been favoritism at play in my securing the oil exploration contract. After all, how had Mr. George Owusu and EO Group so easily traipsed in from Texas and conveniently found oil where international experts had been claiming for a century there was none?

That September, I learned that other oil firms had applied for different exploration blocks in Ghana after we had received ours, and they had been denied. Apparently, these companies had been looking into how EO Group and Kosmos Energy had acquired our block. Then came a rumor that a couple of former cabinet ministers who were angry at having been dismissed from the Kufuor administration and had gone to Mills or the NDC and suggested that President Kufuor secretly owned the oil block and that his friend Bawuah-Edusei and his business partner George Owusu had been covertly put in place as Kufuor's front men, through whom oil proceeds would be quietly funneled to Kufuor.

Great fiction. But putting aside the fuzzy logic about how lawyer and businessman John Kufuor might have known there was oil in the WCTP block after renowned international oil industry experts had been asserting for decades there was none, and ignoring the conundrum that if Kufuor knew about the oil before he was elected, then Tsikata (the first and longest-serving Chairman of the GNPC) must also have known the oil was there. The theory suddenly becomes political comedy at its silliest. Yet, that was Ghana Politics 101. And the opposition party ran with it, shouting their theory from the rooftops and hoping the people would buy it.

It wasn't a tough sell. Politics was all about perception. Particularly in election years. Ghanaians loved politics, loved controversy, loved speculating on rumors. The political drumbeat of conspiracy soon became loud enough that I became concerned. I was still being treated as a respected businessman and hero for helping discover such an important resource for the country, but now the narrative was being tainted by a ridiculous and potentially dangerous tale.

And if Ghanaians loved anything more than politics, it was bringing big men down.

CHAPTER

15

A DARK SHADOW

In September of 2008, EO Group was informed that our joint venture partner, Anadarko Petroleum, was finally initiating their right to perform a comprehensive due diligence inquiry on EO Group as part of the joint partnership agreement with us, Kosmos Energy, and Tullow Oil.

The oil business was conducted in many places around the world where perceived corruption ran rampant. Thus, most companies performed their due diligence examination in advance of entering into agreements or partnerships where foreign governments were involved, to make sure that oil exploration blocks had not been fraudulently obtained, that there had been no underhand dealings involved in the acquisition of the blocks, and to verify that the partners had a history of operating in good faith and honesty. The reasoning behind these timely investigations was simple common sense: to make sure each partner had nothing in his history or on record that could potentially embarrass or harm the other partners or the proposed business dealings between them.

Anadarko, a huge and highly experienced international oil firm, had not yet signed the partnership's Plan of Development (POD). In my opinion they didn't perform their due diligence inquiry on EO Group before finalizing the agreement with EO Group/Kosmos Energy and Tullow Oil/Sabre Energy. They didn't do it after negotiations concluded. They didn't do it after they joined the partnership in 2006. They didn't do it in 2007. In fact, they had waited until late October of 2008, nearly three years after joining our joint venture partnership. The other partners had performed their due diligence with no delays. Why was Anadarko delaying?

Jim Musselman, head of Kosmos, was losing his patience. He wanted things buttoned up, the Anadarko due diligence inquiry of EO Group out of the way, the POD signed, and production started. Kosmos' investors had poured a ton of money into this venture and they were anxious to start producing oil and begin seeing a return on their investment.

Anadarko's delays were interesting timing, to say the least. Just sixty days before a Presidential election that could result in a party change in Ghana's government. Right in the middle of the most heated period of campaigning. Right when media stories of alleged illegal bribery on the part of President Kufuor, myself and my partner, Ambassador Bawuah-Edusei, in connection with our involvement in obtaining the license to explore for oil in Ghana were reaching a crescendo. Right at the time when opposition candidate John Atta Mills was telling Ghana that if he won the presidency, he was going to investigate our oil agreement. Curiously, Anadarko had timed their diligence investigation right as an excrement storm was descending on me. Why?

While it was nice to be publicly acknowledged as the person at the epicenter of having made Jubilee Field possible, the sensational charges being thrown about were frightening. Anadarko's timing of dragging me into their long-overdue due diligence was not helping my treatment by the news media in Ghana. Nor was it making Anadarko look like the sharp, professional, highly experienced oil firm it once was seen as. Unless something else was going on that neither I nor the Government nor Tullow nor Kosmos nor the media were aware of.

What was Anadarko up to? Were they still stewing over the fact that they had been refused the position of Operator of the integrated project team and had also lost their bid to delay production? I had heard that Anadarko was one of the oil firms that had applied to explore an oil block in Ghana and had been turned down, while other entities had received licenses. If that was true, were they disgruntled about that, and decided to join the pile-on against their consortium partner, EO Group? I was puzzled as to how Anadarko could possibly benefit from the appearance of deserting one of their own partners at such a crucial time. I sensed that a power play might be taking place in some way. I was somehow the pawn. The due diligence examination had to be a pretext for something else. If so, what was motivating them?

"Those who suffer from a power complex find the mechanization of man a simple way to realize their ambitions."
—Norbert Wiener, Ph.D., Author, Mathematician

Anadarko's due diligence exercise was scheduled to take place in Washington, D.C., where their law firm, Willkie Farr and Gallagher, and my business partner, Ambassador Bawuah-Edusei, were based.

Rather than be interviewed in the Willkie Farr offices, to avoid the appearance of having been summoned, Bawuah-Edusei offered to have the meeting held in his D.C. residence. As an ambassador, his residence and offices were considered legal territory of Ghana. If the lawyers balked at having the interview in his residence, Bawuah-Edusei offered to drop his ambassadorial privileges for as long as it would take for the questioning to be completed. That's how confident we were about the probable outcome of the questioning.

Although Bawuah-Edusei was rarely in Ghana during all that was going on in connection with Jubilee Field, he was as eager as I was to get the matter quickly resolved and put behind us. Not only was he an equal partner in EO Group, he brought a different level of perception to the situation: he was a personal friend of John Kufuor before Kufuor became president. And he was appointed by Kufuor to be Ghana's Ambassador to the U.S. after the license. The problem that created for me was one of *appearance*. Those facts had the effect of painting me with a brush of potentially negative perception in the eyes of the public.

Perception is the same everywhere. When people hear that someone close to the President is getting a big contract or becomes a millionaire overnight, they immediately think it's due to an unfair advantage afforded by proximity to the President. That's just where people's thoughts go.

The parties agreed to meet in October of 2008 in Bawuah-Edusei's ambassadorial residence in Washington, D.C. Willkie Farr lawyer Martin Weinstein would be the lead lawyer representing Anadarko. Jim Barnes, of Barnes and Cascio, represented EO Group. Kosmos Energy would be represented by the law firm Fulbright and Jaworski.

After introductions and initial pleasantries that October day in Washington, D.C., Anadarko lawyer Martin Weinstein got right down to business. He wanted to discuss alleged irregularities reported by unnamed Ghanaian officials that had been repeated by members of the news media concerning the EO Group/Kosmos Energy acquisition of the WCTP deepwater oil block offshore in Ghana in 2004.

I responded that I had grown weary of rumors and false accusations by politicians and news reporters. I told them that there had not been one single irregularity in the granting of that license to explore oil in Ghana.

Weinstein asked Bawuah-Edusei and me separately what we had done with the $250,000 fee paid to us by Kosmos in 2004.

It wouldn't be much of a problem to show what I had used some of the money for in the U.S. However, reconstructing how I had spent my money over the past couple of years in a cash economy like Ghana would pose a big problem. I could show cash withdrawals from my bank, but not necessarily how every penny of it was spent. Certainly there wouldn't be any large withdrawals, no cashier's checks, and definitely no payments to someone in the government.

Asking what I had done with that money wouldn't have been the lead-off question had Anadarko done their preparatory due diligence inquiry in the beginning, when most companies want to know who they're about to enter into business with. It was the kind of question, however, that you would ask if you had doubts about your business partner.

Due diligence inquiries were advance exercises to determine whether or not a company wanted to do business with a potential partner. If the investigating entity came across questionable information in the discovery process, then they would either decline entering into a relationship or they would ask the potential partner to deal with the matter before the parties moved forward. It was a safeguard, both to eliminate problems in advance and to provide an opportunity for full disclosure about how each partner had historically conducted themselves in business. It also helped the partners deal together with problems that might come up in the future, because if they had performed their due diligence inquiry on one another, then presumably they had vetted histories and accomplishments, checked references and so forth, and had reached a place of sufficient comfort with each other that they had felt assured that they were on solid footing and could handle the challenges of business together as a team.

It was the usual approach, the wise approach, the smart business approach. After all, we were consortium partners. Not competitors. Not enemies. *Partners*. It should have felt at least a little collegial in that room that day in Washington, given the immensity of our discovery together. There should have been at least a hint of camaraderie there that day. So why did it feel so icy in the room? Why did I feel I was being treated like a suspect in a crime?

What was Anadarko up to? Why were they initiating a years-late diligence inquiry right during a time when I was loudly being accused of wrongdoing? Why were they leading off with a question insinuating financial impropriety directed at the partner who was under increasing pressure related to recent unproven allegations? Curiously, Anadarko wasn't asking the Kosmos executives where they had spent their personal money over the past three years.

If their intention was to try to help me deal with those accusations, they never offered. Perhaps they were looking for a reason to get out of the partnership deal if the accusations against me proved true, because their reputation might be sullied by association if they continued with me. But it was highly unlikely that they wanted out of the deal. That would be like jumping off a train loaded with gold bars after it has left the station and is barreling down the track at full speed toward their own bank. And this particular train was a gravy train that was making news around the world and was estimated to be a long and lucrative one. No way would Anadarko leave that meal ticket after they had already been at the table for a couple of years. Truth was, they wouldn't sever their involvement in this consortium for any reason.

Bawuah-Edusei and I told the lawyers we didn't have a specific breakdown of exactly where we had spent every penny of our $125,000 each four years ago. We asked them why they needed those numbers.

When Kosmos had made that payment to Bawuah-Edusei and I back in 2004, I was broke. I used most of my share of the money to prepare to relocate from Houston back to Ghana. I bought a car. I used some of the money to continue construction on the house I was building in Kumasi. I bought a house in Accra and purchased all of its furnishings. The list was mundane and innocent.

Their next query drove home what the lawyers were getting at.

"Did any of it go to any government official?"

Did you pay a bribe to Kufuor?

It was a question freighted with criminal implications. Weinstein, a specialist in the Foreign Corrupt Practices Act (FCPA), was referring to a U.S. law that barred Americans doing business in foreign countries from giving gifts or making payments to foreign officials that might benefit the donor. It was a serious felony that could involve America's Department of Justice and the Federal Bureau of Investigation (FBI).

The question revealed Anadarko's suspicion that allegations about me funneling money to Kufuor in relation to the oil license could be true. Otherwise, they never would have asked—certainly not if they were aware of how politics play out in Ghana. But these were smart lawyers. Why would they ask such a question that was so poorly thought out that it bordered on dumb? What was Anadarko up to?

The question assumed that John Kufuor had ordered everyone at the GNPC—Director of Operations Thomas Manu, Managing Director Moses O. Boateng, Minister of Energy Albert Kan Dapaah and his replacement Minister Dr. Paa Kwesi Nduom, and Chairman of the Board Steven Sekyere-Abankwa—to sign off on my original MOU, the subsequent Production Agreement, and the granting of the license to explore.

For presumably smart lawyers to ask their client's own business partners such a question was odd, to say the least. Most insulting of all, the question had to assume that I, a longtime former manager at one of the world's largest oil firms, and Bawuah-Edusei, Ambassador to the United States for Ghana, had the hearts, the minds, and the intentions of criminals.

"Of course not," I answered. "Why would we give money to President Kufuor?"

"Can you prove you didn't?" they asked.

It was a typical prosecuting lawyer's question.

In my frustration, I blurted, "Could you prove you're *not* gay?"

He looked at me, surprised. After a moment it dawned on him what I was getting at.

You can't prove a negative.

It would be like me asking if they could prove they hadn't given cash to Mills. Besides, the burden of proof was on my accusers to prove their accusation. It was not up to me to prove it for them.

Nobody on the Kosmos team offered one word in our defense during the entire interrogation. Perhaps that was because Anadarko's attack on me put Kosmos in an interesting situation. They could side with the accused, but run the risk of facing tremendous business and legal implications. Or they could stay neutral and hope for the best. Or, if media pressure became too much and they felt too tainted by association to me, they could turn on me, too.

Time would reveal the character of each man in the room that day. All I could do was hope that the man at the top at Kosmos Energy, Jim Musselman, CEO and founder of the company, would back me. Although he too would soon be experiencing his own problems in Ghana.

Bawuah-Edusei and I had each originally given Anadarko forty-five minutes for the interrogation session and their lawyers had been grilling us for over two hours. It was clear where they were headed. They had focused almost solely on that $250,000 Kosmos Energy had paid us in April of 2004, and where the money had gone.

Round one was over. And it had shaken me. I figured the matter would be quickly resolved if I furnished the lawyers with bank records and expenditure receipts.

I figured wrong.

As their employee, Kosmos offered to provide me with legal counsel for the follow-up Anadarko meeting. EO Group's lawyer, Jim Barnes, was a good oil and gas lawyer and would be there with me, but he didn't have the area of expertise I was going to need to go up against the forces lining up against me. Kosmos would continue to be represented by Fulbright and Jaworski, but Bawuah-Edusei and I would need counsel well-versed in international law, criminal law, and business law. We needed a heavyweight, preferably located in Willkie Farr's own back yard, Washington, D.C.

Fulbright and Jaworski contacted the D.C. law firm Crowell & Moring, who assigned Adrian Mebane, a former U.S. DOJ Fraud Section lawyer, to represent me.

By the time I returned to Ghana, the national sport had reached fever pitch. The news media had turned vicious. Most of the reporting wasn't even making the most basic professional effort at investigative journalism. Stories had switched from accusations of fraud against me, and were now focused on new rumors of a rift between Ghana's first big oil partners.

Someone was feeding false stories to the press. It would be a while before I would discover the surprising identity of at least one of those parties. And the dark theory they had reported about me to some very powerful people would be a kick in my gut.

CHAPTER

16

LIES AND RUMORS

On November 28, 2008, just one month after the Anadarko diligence inquiry, an unsettling "news" story edited by one named Raymond Archer appeared in a local tabloid called *The Enquirer*. It told about the "Eric Amoateng drug saga" and the arrest of a man named "George Owusu," who had been charged by the Narcotics Control Board with drug trafficking. I was not the George Owusu who had been charged by the Narcotic Control Board, of course, and *The Enquirer* had known this for a fact, yet the paper had omitted that important distinction in their recounting of the incident. In fact, on the last page of the original police report referred to in *The Enquirer* story was a note that the drug dealer was "*not* oil businessman George Yaw Owusu of Kosmos Energy."

The misleading story was a temporary headache that a quick phone call should have cleared up. But this wasn't a casual and honest mistake by the newspaper. It was a deliberate smear campaign—and not just against me. I was well known as the George Owusu of the Jubilee Field oil discovery. My name had been in the news almost daily during the past year and a half in connection with my partnership's historic discovery. *Owusu* was a common surname in Ghana. *George*, even more so. Clearly, Archer and Focal Media had deliberately sought to give the public the impression that EO Group's George Owusu, the man who had spearheaded the biggest oil discovery in Ghana's history, and "friend" of President John Kufuor, was a drug trafficker. Meaning that the article was a crude attempt to smear President Kufuor's name by association to me, in an effort to affect the outcome of the upcoming Presidential election.

My lawyer filed a defamation lawsuit against *The Enquirer*, Focal Media, and Mr. Archer. It was assigned to the High Court, Fast Track Division, in Accra, and I put it out of my mind. Even in the Fast Track Division, the lawsuit would take a while to wind its way through the system. But the election was just one week away. The damage had been done.

The incident was only a foreshadowing of worse things to come. As rumors and attacks in the news media increased against me, my oil partners began to distance themselves from me, for fear of being tainted by accusations of back-room political favors and being dragged into negative news reports. Though I had done nothing wrong, committed no crimes or illegal acts, and no evidence of any wrongdoing had been presented against me by anyone at any time, I had become a pariah in my own country. There was even a persistent and troubling rumor that the U.S. DOJ was investigating me. There could only be one reason they would be involved: the FCPA. And why the DOJ would think that an American in Ghana had violated the FCPA could only be for one reason: somebody had gone to them with a tale. I could only wonder who was spreading rumors all the way to the United States about me.

There were a few legitimate news outlets that performed actual investigative journalism, rather than peddle rumors. Newspapers such as the *Daily Graphic* stuck strictly to the facts. Another paper, the *Crusading Guide*, published very serious, thoughtful, and well-researched political pieces.

I would watch the television news and read the papers each day and could quickly pinpoint which ones were telling the truth. Their reporters included documentation to support their claims. I began to notice a pattern: most of the fact-free attack stories had no reporter's name or byline associated with them. Whereas, those that examined the facts and evidence were attributed to specific writers. I started following only those news outlets and writers who were publishing facts and reality, and ignoring those that were fabricating tales according to what they wanted the public to believe.

A man can take only so much public berating. It was not a good feeling, especially after having been euphoric when our oil discovery had been made a year and a half earlier. Fortunately, my work as Country Manager for Kosmos Energy kept me busy and focused, so I didn't have time to get depressed. As the election drew near and the attacks increased, I tried to remain steadfast that truth would prevail, even in the face of so many serious charges against me. I had faith that God would protect me. After all, I had done nothing wrong. This was simply Ghana politics at work, I told myself. I faced the mounting attacks with as much of a positive attitude as I could muster.

But my attitude was about to take a turn for the worse.

After a bitterly contested election on December 7, 2008, the NPP's Nana Akufo-Addo lost his bid for the Presidency. After the elections, people seemed more convinced than ever that I belonged to former President Kufuor. They were convinced that Kufuor had known where the oil had been all along, as if he was some sort of magical shaman. They assumed that because the oil had been found during the time this man had been President, he had been caught in the act, and it was up to the NDC to put things right for the nation.

Even as Mills was setting up his new government and appointing his cabinet in the weeks prior to his official inauguration on January 7, 2009, his administration received those who were claiming to have evidence of Kufuor's wrongdoing, people who were insisting that Bawuah-Edusei and I were surrogates for him, and that EO Group's share of the WCTP license actually belonged to Mr. Kufuor. Apparently their "smoking gun evidence" had come from those disgruntled former cabinet ministers from the Kufuor administration who'd gone to Mills claiming that Kufuor was guilty. Yet they had offered no proof of their accusations. But the Mills administration believed them, apparently reasoning that if people from Kufuor's own party were coming forward to inform on him, then it must be true.

Mills' government went after EO Group with all they had, determined to destroy us and invalidate what they assumed we had obtained illegally.

Madness had gripped the nation. The war against me went into overdrive.

> *"In 2008 when I finished my term and stepped down, the opponents got into office and made many allegations, going as far as the U.S. to talk of corruption."*
> —John Kufuor, President of Ghana, 2001-2009[43]

---

[43] John Kufuor, former President of Ghana, to author M. Rutledge McCall during an interview on June 7, 2013.

CHAPTER

17

DARK DAYS

Immediately upon taking over Osu Castle on January 7, 2009, the Mills administration began appointing new cabinet ministers and directors over various departments, including Energy, Justice, and the GNPC.

A few weeks after the election, Kosmos CEO Jim Musselman and other Kosmos executives and I made a visit to the Castle to pay our respects to incoming President Mills for having won the hard-fought election. Our visit was publicized in a newspaper article a week later . . .

"KOSMOS COMMITTED TO PRODUCTION SCHEDULE"

"Mr. Musselman congratulated President Mills on his election as the new President of Ghana, adding that the outcome of

the 2008 poll had demonstrated without any shred of doubt that
democracy had come of age in the country. Mr. Musselman said
Ghana was now a shining example of undiluted democratic governance on the continent and called on other African countries to
emulate such impeccable credentials. President Mills commend-
ed the giant oil concern for its operations in Ghana and said 'you
can always count on our support.' He reminded the company of
the need to conform to the legal requirements of the company's
investment in the country . . ."

—*Daily Graphic*, January 16, 2009[44]

If Mills wore a Presidential ring, the story would have had
Musselman on one knee, kissing it. In the photo accompanying the
story, I was standing front and center, shaking hands with Musselman
while President Mills and V.P. John Mahama loomed over my left shoulder, grinning at the back of my head as if they were sizing my neck for
a rope.

The story added that Kosmos was "close to signing a development
plan on the oil project and for that reason called for greater cooperation between the government and his outfit for the smooth and or-
derly development of the oil fields." That wasn't true at all. In fact, we
were nowhere near close to signing the POD, because both Anadarko
Petroleum and the Government were dragging their feet on signing it.[45]

The article went on to claim that Musselman had "explained that a
letter of intent between his outfit and the Government of Ghana had
already been signed to move the project forward, stressing that his company has committed to doing business in the country." On the surface,
Musselman's line about Kosmos being "committed to doing business in
Ghana" sounded like a friendly promise from the company to hang in

---

[44] *Daily Graphic*, in a Jan. 16, 2009, article by Kweku Tsen, titled "Kosmos Committed to Production Schedule"; (p. 24).
[45] Anadarko had served notice on the partners that they would not sign the POD until the alleged violations were fully resolved.

there with the nation and help improve the economy.

During the election campaign, Mills had been bitterly airing his displeasure about the structure of the WCTP agreement signed by the previous administration under John Kufuor. Mills was convinced that at 10% of Jubilee Field, Ghana had gotten the shaft, and that the terms we had negotiated in the WCTP deal had been based on a secret arrangement between me and former President Kufuor. Mills was a politician. And right now, the politicians were the experts when it came to shaping public opinion and whipping up public anger against the big foreign oil firms gearing up to take the resource and its income out of Ghana. Their newest battle cry had become, "Why did EO Group get such a huge cut for bringing nothing to the table? Why did two guys get 3.5% when the entire country of Ghana got 10%?"

But there were several problems with that complaint:

1. Nobody was whining about the 4.05% belonging to Sabre Oil in the Deepwater Tano agreement, which was also led by a Ghanaian, Kofi Esson.

2. EO Group's 3.5% was all coming out of Kosmos' share of the WCTP block, not from Ghana's.

3. Ghana's overall income generated by the deal, including tax income, was between 50–55%.

4. What EO Group had brought to the table was the *entire table*: despite all the efforts of the GNPC, there had been no meaningful oil industry in Ghana before we single-handedly initiated and spearheaded the effort that had resulted in creating the nation's oil industry in the first place. In fact, I had gone to incredible lengths to help get things to where they were, to help get Kosmos set up and operating in Ghana after leaving all I had in America, walking away from a secure career and a great job,

sacrificing everything to make it possible for Ghana
to one day enjoy the fruits of my labor.

How quickly people forget—which is exactly what politicians hope
for. Still, rumor mills continued working overtime, hinting that the
government was mounting an investigation of me and would soon be
handing down charges. Investigators from the CID supposedly had me
in their sights and would be pulling me in for an interrogation any day.

I had no choice but to deal with the brewing storm like any apo-
litical businessman would. I smiled in public and acted like everything
was fine.

It's only politics.

Business as usual in Ghana.

I have more important business to deal with.

But inside, I was reeling from the public attacks I was being subjected to. I did my best to keep my already high blood pressure from
putting me in a hospital from worry about how far the government was
willing to go to take me down.

* * *

As if it wasn't bad enough that the new government was now breathing down my neck, in early January of 2009, a plane full of Anadarko
Petroleum lawyers arrived from Texas and prepared to grill me for the
second time in ninety days. My lawyer, Adrian Mebane, had arrived
in Accra the first week of January to help get me prepared for the
interrogation.

We met on January 17, just ten days after Mills was sworn in.
Present at the session were Mebane and EO Group's lawyer Jim Barnes,
the Anadarko lawyers from Willkie Farr and Gallagher, and the Kosmos
lawyers from Fulbright and Jaworski. This time, I was the only one
being grilled. The questioning wasn't a quick two hours like the session

we'd had in Washington, D.C. This one lasted eight solid hours. Martin Weinstein, lead lawyer representing Anadarko in the previous interrogation, was not present. Perhaps he had already accomplished in D.C. what Anadarko had set out to do. Private financial forensic investigators had poured through my accounts and documents with a fine-tooth comb. They'd found nothing improper, no dark money trail, no wrongdoing whatsoever.

It was evident during the interrogation that Anadarko's lawyers were focused on finding a connection to support their theory that I, a man who had met President Kufuor before he had been elected President, and my partner, who'd had a prior friendship with Kufuor and had been appointed by him as Ambassador to the U.S., Switzerland and Austria, had used influence to gain a special advantage in the WCTP block license acquisition. Their questions indicated that they were going using information and circumstances they had received from people they had talked to who were on the periphery, who had at one time assisted EO Group, or who were connected in some way to the Ministry of Energy. The lawyers were responding to innuendo, rumors, and whatever innocent information I was confirming for them during the interview, about people that we knew or had some dealings with.

I gave them my bank records. I showed them receipts for what I had spent of my share of the 2004 fee Kosmos had paid to us. I answered their questions about Newbridge Hospitality Services, the car rental company Kosmos had approved of and signed off on. Nothing was out of order. Taxes had been paid. Licenses were up to date. Everything was in the open. Nothing hidden or shady. I hadn't bribed anyone, or broken any laws. I was a regular citizen, a family man, a hardworking oil industry manager with decades of legitimate energy experience under my belt. I was not a rich man. Not a political firebrand. Not powerful or "connected." I didn't speak out against the government.

I was just another business man, once raised in poverty, educated as a teacher, who had moved to America, got a job in the oil business, and became inspired by a fellow Ghanaian who challenged us to go find oil in Ghana. That man happened to go on to become President of Ghana. I happened to find oil in Ghana. In fact, each of the government's key ministers, executives, directors, and managers who had been involved in vetting, approving, verifying, and negotiating with me, had signed off on the MOU. Several of them had remained in their positions when the Mills administration came in.

So, I wasn't overly concerned.

But I should have been. Because the Mills machine was going after no one but me. Why? Why was little EO Group, one of only two Ghanaians involved in the entire Jubilee Field oil consortium, being singled out—me in particular? The answer was clear: we were the easiest target. The smallest partner, the least wealthy. And in Bawuah-Edusei, we had a direct connection to Mills' archenemy, former Ghanaian President John Kufuor, who had appointed Edusei to different ambassadorial posts during his two-term administration.

Right now, none of that mattered. What mattered that muggy day in January of 2009 was that in the space of two years I had fallen from national hero for putting Ghana on the map, to national pariah for ripping the country off in the process.

I was afraid. Any normal man would be, in my circumstances. Truth may be a powerful weapon, even against detractors who refuse to let it get in the way of their agenda, but how do you fight a political machine run by the man who was once the vice president and second-in-command to the country's most recent leader—a man who was now in charge? John Atta Mills had an entire army, police agencies and secret investigators at his disposal. Even his new Attorney General, Betty Mould-Iddrisu had started uttering threats against me—and I'd never even met the woman. It was almost as if Ghana was determined to make the anonymous adage a national motto. *No good deed goes unpunished.*

When I had done my original work with John Craven in 2003, we had the data, the science and the analysis, and we negotiated a MOU and obtained a license to explore oil. It was the ultimate dream for a man like me who had worked professionally in the petroleum industry for decades in the United States. Anyone could have done exactly the same thing. It was a matter of obtaining a license from the Ghana government and then just going and giving it a try. There was no guarantee, no attachment of intellectual property rights to assert. It was a shot in the dark. All we had was a reasonable hope that our analysis of this particular deep-water section would prove fruitful.

Even when Ennex and John Craven had backed out and declined to sign the MOU, I still had hope. Even when Kosmos had first backed out due to lack of funds, I still had hope. Hope is all any company has when they enter into virgin territory. I was simply dogged and determined enough to find a drilling partner with the resources, the experience, and the equipment to drill. I could easily have failed. After all of the previous failures to find oil—in and near our very same block—I knew how extremely lucky I was to have been the one to help make the discovery.

It was a miracle. Not a crime.

All I knew was that I loved Ghana. I was born there, raised there, educated there. I had family there. I owned land there. Ghana was in my soul. She was my roots. My family's blood was deep in her soil.

Yet, if history taught me anything as a former schoolteacher, it was that history was often rewritten by the victors. If Paul Rusesabagina, author of the book *An Ordinary Man*, was right when he wrote, "a false view of history is a toxin in the bloodstream of [a] country,"[46] then it seemed as if Ghana had a lot of poison to exorcise in deciding how to portray her newly evolving history to future generations of Ghanaians.

For now, I could only hope her poison wouldn't harm me permanently.

---

[46] Paul Rusesabagina, *An Ordinary Man* (the book that inspired the hit movie "Hotel Rwanda"); Penguin Books, 2006 (p.54).

As an employee, I had to subject myself to the Anadarko interrogations or I could be fired. If I was fired, I would have a more difficult time protecting my contractual interest in the field. All they needed to do was to find a clause they could claim I had breached. In fact, any partner in the consortium could try that tactic against me. Conditions were perfect for it.

I had certain protections as an employee, of course, but I had obligations, too. Such as having no choice but to subject myself, at Kosmos' direction, to their partner Anadarko's diligence inquiry. And I could face liability if it was proven that I had been involved in illegal activities that could harmfully impact any member of the partnership. Particularly if such activities were serious crimes in Ghana, such as bribery or fraud. Or, as a U.S. citizen, federal crimes such as violation of America's FCPA.

I was in a tight spot. If Anadarko could prove any sort of illegal activity on my part, they could potentially force EO Group's share of ownership in the WCTP into default and, ultimately, a possible relinquishment of our shares over to the other partners.

For a large international corporation like Anadarko, that task would be far easier than taking on Kosmos, who was backed by private equity giants Warburg Pincus and Blackstone Group. Or Tullow, the largest single shareholder in the Jubilee Field. Or even my business partner, Bawuah-Edusei, a former ambassador for Ghana and a respected physician living in America. That left me, the only partner being accused by the government and the news media of having committed serious crimes. Weakest buffalo in the herd. And if I was proven guilty, Kosmos could file a lawsuit against me and effectively side with Anadarko in finishing me off. Appropriation of my shares, perpetrated under color of a diligence inquiry. Even the mere threat of all those big men going after me might have been enough to make me give up the fight and run back to Houston—especially with the government of Ghana sharpening their knives to go after me, as well.

Is that what Anadarko was up to, attempting to find cause to appropriate EO Group's interest in the joint venture partnership, or was I just being paranoid? It was an interesting theory, and I sure hoped it stayed theoretical. But if it wasn't just theory, who could I turn to for help? Kosmos had valued me a great deal, in the early days. But that was waning as Anadarko was pushing against me, and the new government was going on the offense, and the news media was ramping up their attack.

I was on my own in figuring it all out. Even my lawyer, Adrian Mebane, was abandoning me. He'd accepted a position with another firm and would be departing soon, handing my case off to another Crowell & Moring lawyer. I began to feel very alone, strung out there with so many forces arrayed against me. I was just a guy who believed in loyalty and hard work and decency and honor (tenets not generally held in high esteem among the combatants vying for control over Africa's resources). Yet, I was also the guy who had brought his efforts, contacts, and opportunities to both Ghana and Kosmos, and had developed legitimate business relationships with those executives. I could only hope and pray they would suddenly see the light, trust what they had seen and experienced with me during the past half decade, and not abandon me or betray me or attack me in my hour of greatest need.

I was innocent.

And here was the irony in the entire situation: from the beginning, Anadarko had never expected us to find so much oil in WCTP. Anadarko had been so certain of their expert analysis that WCTP was a small find that they had bet on it, insisting on being the Operator in Charge of production only if the field contained fifty million barrels or less. When the field had been shown to contain up to fifty times more than the Anadarko experts had calculated, Anadarko found themselves playing second fiddle to their partners. In my opinion, now, instead of being thrilled that they were part of a historic and massive discovery, Anadarko became disgruntled that they, the big gorilla on the block, would be subordinate to little Kosmos Energy on the project. And for nearly three years they dragged their feet on performing their diligence inquiry and balked at signing the POD when it could have been in 2008.

Then came the change of government, and it was a whole new ballgame. Not only was I now in the government's crosshairs, but Anadarko started going after me.

Fate seemed to be having a lot of fun at my expense.

On January 14, 2009, a few days after I had slogged my way through the Anadarko interrogation, I was notified that the defamation lawsuit I had filed against *The Enquirer* gossip tabloid for insinuating that I was a drug lord had been delayed. The paper's publisher, Focal Media Limited, and its editor, Raymond Archer, had evaded service of the writ by a bailiff of the court. Both had refused to file a responsive declaration and had failed to enter an appearance at the preliminary hearing.

On January 16, 2009, the *Daily Graphic* newspaper announced EO Group/Kosmos Energy's third major oil discovery (dubbed "Mahogany-3") in the six wells Kosmos had drilled in the WCTP block. It was nice that some of the reporting in some of the news outlets was sticking to the facts. But news of our success was not improving the spirit of cooperation and mutual solidarity between me and my oil consortium partners. No doubt feeling tainted by association with me, they soon began to distance themselves from me—in spite of our joint ownership of what was shaping up to be a colossal golden goose in the form of the Jubilee oilfield, now estimated to contain at least one billion barrels of oil. At the current price of $60 per barrel, that kind of money was worth going to all-out war over. The combatants were lining up.

Kosmos Energy, in particular, began pulling back from me. They were mentioning me and EO Group less often to the news media, whereas before, they had trotted me out like their golden boy. They were increasingly taking full credit in the news media for the WCTP discovery and were no longer mentioning my name, whereas before, they were proud of what I had done in putting their little firm on the map. During the next few months, Kosmos grilled me five more times. In Dallas, in Houston, in Accra, in Washington D.C.

Coming just months after Anadarko had alerted the government that they were suddenly doing a due diligence examination of me, an investigation of me by Kosmos Energy—the first partner I had brought into the deal—was a hard blow to take. Even Tullow Oil, which had remained neutral throughout the Anadarko attacks, now requested that I go in for questioning.

My partners were piling on. I was tired, weary, hurt, disappointed. My heart ached.

I began to wonder if there was anybody out there *not* trying to destroy me.

CHAPTER

18

VIEW FROM UNDER THE BUS

In late March of 2009, a small window of light appeared on the dark horizon: Anadarko suddenly agreed to sign the joint venture partnership POD for Jubilee Field. Though they didn't explain why they had finally decided to sign, I could only assume that each of their two recent diligence inquiries of me may have produced encouraging results. Yet, even that good news was about to hit a wall.

After Anadarko had agreed to sign the POD, the Minister of Energy refused to sign off on it. The consortium partners, particularly Kosmos, had a fit. If the POD wasn't approved by the Minister of Energy, production couldn't move forward.

It had taken some time for Dr. Joe Oteng-Adjei, the new administration's Minister of Energy, to be appointed and vetted and get up to speed. It was understandable that, since there had never been a significant oil discovery in Ghana, the minister didn't want to make a mistake, so he had taken the time to solicit input from experts both inside and outside of Ghana who had sufficient experience and knowledge to offer input into a petroleum POD that would protect the interests of the government.

But Anadarko's and the minister's delays had been stacking up, and Jim Musselman was getting impatient for things to move forward. Without a POD, Kosmos' ownership share in Jubilee Field would be far more difficult to monetize, because they couldn't take their investment to the world market to either sell or get a loan against. Kosmos had been dead in the water and bleeding cash, with no money coming in. And Blackstone was breathing down their necks to *sell, sell, sell*. That kind of pressure can cause people to do things they might later regret.

A meeting was convened in March to try to work out the issue. All of the players were present; EO Group, Kosmos, Tullow (which had just discovered Tweneboa,[47] a major deepwater oilfield that rivaled the size of Jubilee), Sabre, Anadarko, the Minister of Energy, the GNPC Chairman, the Managing Director. Nearly two dozen people were in the room, anticipating that the POD was going to be signed that day. When we were informed that it would not be signed, Jim Musselman started to become very agitated.

One of the men from the GNPC sidled over to me and quietly told me to tell Musselman to calm down.

I leaned to Brian Maxted, who had recently been elevated to Chief Operating Officer of Kosmos, and urgently asked him to ask Musselman

---

[47] Located east of Jubilee, Tweneboa Field was similar in size to Jubilee Field and was estimated to contain up to 1.4 billion barrels of oil. In addition to these two major discoveries, several smaller wells were found nearby. In all, the oil firms operating off the coast of Ghana would discover 15 wells by 2011. Large parts of the Ghanaian waters have yet to be explored.

to step outside with me. The three of us excused ourselves and went out onto the corridor.

I told Musselman that he needed to calm down, that the Ghanaians would not respond well to an angry diatribe against them. This was not Houston, Texas. In Ghana, things were handled differently. Musselman needed to get a grip. But his emotions had escalated too high for him to calmly accept the incessant delays any longer.

We went back into the room. Tension mounted as Minister Adjei continued to balk at approving the POD. The GNPC was looking for any excuse not to sign, because they were convinced Kosmos was in the pocket of the NPP and were Kufuor supporters. To the new management of the GNPC and the Ministry, it seemed as if Kosmos had always been getting their way.

Then Musselman, normally a friendly and unflappable executive, suddenly blew his stack and told Minister Oteng-Adjei where to go. That nailed the coffin for Musselman. The room went cold. I hung my head, mentally willing Musselman to back off and calm down. He could kill the entire deal right then and there. Our oil consortium was in Ghana at the pleasure of the government. The men across that table were decision-makers who had our economic futures in their hands. If we kicked and complained and shouted too much, we would be invited to pack up and get out. It wasn't good business to bite the hand that feeds you.

I felt like I was watching more than half a decade of hard, gritty, thankless work going down in flames.

Musselman's days were numbered.

I was hanging on by a thread.

And the government's war against me ratcheted up another notch. For them, it boiled down to simple numbers: if they could prove that I had criminally bribed my way into this deal, then they could confiscate EO Group's 3.5% share. The same cunning motive I was beginning to suspect may have been behind Anadarko's attack on me earlier. Prove

criminal charges, point to stipulations in our agreement against partners engaging in illegal activities, force a turnover of EO Group's shares.
Even if charges were not sustained, maybe they could wear me down
with police interrogations, endless government inquiries, whatever it
would take. If that had been Anadarko's surreptitious plan too, if they
had indeed fanned the flames of suspicion against me by feeding false
information to the media and to the government, possibly through a
former GNPC executive, then it seemed to be working. Because the
government of Ghana was bearing down on me full bore.

In the meantime, Kosmos kept their head down, pushed carefully
toward production, and hoped they wouldn't come under the scrutiny of
the government themselves. Which meant they would have to deal with
Musselman, who had become a liability for openly rebuking the Minister
and ticking off a roomful of his associates. So, to get Musselman out of
the way, Kosmos kicked him upstairs to the position of Chairman, and
moved Chief Operating Officer Brian Maxted into the CEO slot.

The whole situation had put Anadarko and Tullow on edge, because
the entire project could go down the tubes at the whim of an angry new
government. As for me, a founding partner in the consortium, with a
contract tying my shares directly to Kosmos and being an employee of
Kosmos, I was now a liability to Kosmos. If Kosmos wanted to mend
the fence with the GNPC and get their oil out of the ocean, several
matters would have to be delicately handled. Particularly EO Group,
who now had a bright red bull's-eye on our back.

The government's attack against me was now being led by newly
appointed Attorney General Betty Mould-Iddrisu. And she was preparing to come down on me like a hammer on an anvil. It would be
worth the fight for the new administration. Three point five percent of
a multibillion dollar oil discovery represented a significant increase in
Ghana's share—hundreds of millions of extra dollars if they could hang
a case on me and get me behind bars. If they could hang something on

me, they could prove to the world that the NPP and former President Kufuor were corrupt.

I was reminded of the old Chinese curse. *May you live in interesting times.*

Maybe it was time to move back to America.

CHAPTER

19

INTERESTING TIMES

In July of 2009, Kosmos, tired of the increasing political and press scrutiny, and with former CEO Jim Musselman sidelined, had decided it had had enough. Kosmos opened a data room and put out feelers for interested buyers for their stake in Jubilee Field. Kosmos notified potential bidders, as well as their partners in the oil consortium, that they had until July 17 to submit bids. They failed to get the consent of GNPC.

When they found out, the GNPC expressed extreme displeasure that Kosmos hadn't informed them of their intentions before talking to other oil companies. They asserted that Kosmos had no right to solicit buyers for the field without approval by the government. They had a point. As the government represented the Ghanaian citizen-owners of the land in which the oil was located, and, in accordance with Article 16.4 of the July 22, 2004, Petroleum Agreement, Kosmos was required to officially notify the GNPC before opening the data room and soliciting bids for the stake.48

Kosmos CEO Brian Maxted countered that he did give an advance notification of their plans, to both Energy Minister Joe Oteng-Adjei and GNPC Chairman Ato Ahwoi.

GNPC said they deserved more than a mere notification.

Maxted notified GNPC Director of Operations Thomas Manu that Energy Minister Oteng-Adjei had earlier assured Kosmos that if the firm had involved the GNPC in the bidding process, the government wouldn't stand in the way of a sale.[49]

The GNPC informed Kosmos that the government of Ghana must be informed in advance and give permission before Kosmos' share in Jubilee could be sold.

Kosmos strenuously disagreed.

Minister Oteng-Adjei requested that Kosmos step down as Technical Operator of Jubilee Field, since they were now trying to sell their share.

Kosmos refused.

The GNPC warned Kosmos not to attempt to sell their share.

A battle was about to ensue between Kosmos and the GNPC.

In the meantime, I received good news and bad news, all in one: I found out why Anadarko had suddenly wanted to sign the POD back

---

[48] Article 16.4, under the Article 16 Confidentiality clause of the July 22, 2004, Petroleum Agreement signed by the parties, stipulates, on page 59, "All data, information and reports, including interpretation and analysis supplied by Contractor required or produced pursuant to this Agreement, including without limitation, that described in Articles 16.1, 16.2 and 16.3, shall be treated as confidential and shall not be disclosed by any Party to any other person without the express written consent of the other Parties."

[49] The *Washington Times*, in a March 26, 2010, online story by Chuck Neubauer, titled "Ghana Discovery Sparks Fight Over Oil." See: http://www.washingtontimes.com/news/2010/mar/26/ghana-discovery-sparks-fight-over-oil/

in March. The reason would both please me and tick me off all over again for how I was being treated. Sometime between January 16 and January 22, 2009, officials from Anadarko Petroleum had contacted the U.S. DOJ and informed them that their diligence investigation of me, Bawuah-Edusei, and Kosmos Energy had found "several red flags and lots of smoke" but no evidence of FCPA violations. No one had informed me of that good news. Then, a few weeks later, in mid-February, lawyers from Anadarko's law firm had met with officials from the DOJ, provided them with documents and more specific information, and reiterated that there had been "no smoking gun" evidence that would justify a probe by the DOJ into EO Group or Kosmos. No one had informed me of that meeting, either.

In fact, I was not informed until many months afterward that the results of the October 2008 and January 2009 Anadarko interrogations had cleared me and EO Group of involvement in all suspected illegal activities. In fact, only in June of 2009 did lawyers Martin Weinstein and Theodore Whitehouse have a meeting at the Willkie Farr offices in Washington, D.C., and made it official, by announcing that, after having conducted their 2008 and 2009 Anadarko due diligence investigations of EO Group, they "had not found any specific violations of the FCPA and were not able to find any link between a prohibited act and any Ghanaian governmental official and/or party official."

They added, "Without such a linkage, there had been no violations of the FCPA." They also noted that the oil block concession had been "awarded prior to Mr. Bawuah-Edusei's appointment as an ambassador"—not after the block was granted. In attendance at that June announcement were Ghana's new Attorney General Betty Mould-Iddrisu, Robert Reeves (General Counsel of Anadarko), Luis Derrota (Associate General Counsel of Anadarko), San Francisco lawyer Duke Amaniampong (a Ghanaian national) and Baffour Assasie-Gyimah (of

Ghana's Bureau of National Intelligence).[50]

Willkie Farr then contacted the U.S. DOJ to officially inform them of their findings, provide them with specifics and documents, and report that with regard to the activities of American citizens Mr. George Owusu and former Ambassador Kwame Bawuah-Edusei, the investigation had "not found a 'smoking gun' that would lead them to conclude that there had been an FCPA violation."

There had been no illegalities involving Ghanaian governmental or party officials, EO Group, or Kosmos Energy in the oil block concession. Anadarko's report had essentially absolved all parties, including the former President of Ghana, of any wrongdoing. Yet, for four months, nobody had informed me. For four nerve-wracking months I had been kept in the dark, left to sweat it out, thinking Anadarko's investigators and lawyers were still lurking out there. And all the while, they had already cleared me.

Perhaps Willkie Farr had assumed that the DOJ or Anadarko or the Ghanaian officials would inform me of the news. Perhaps the Ghanaian officials had assumed that the DOJ or one of the other Americans, such as my joint venture partner Anadarko or my main counter-party partner Kosmos would inform me. Maybe Kosmos was not even aware. But nobody had told me. It was a huge relief to be cleared. Still, Anadarko's timing in initiating their late diligence inquiry couldn't have been more destructive. The months between exoneration and disclosure had allowed more time for more damage to be done.

And it was getting worse.

Upon examining the investigators' reports revealing no wrongdoing, I imagined Ghana's new Attorney General would inform the CID to stand down. She would have told them that Owusu was innocent, that the results of the investigation had proved it. That didn't happen. Obviously, news that the U.S. DOJ had been informed that I'd been

---

[50] GhanaWeb online news website *General News of Saturday, 16 January, 2010*; see: http://www. ghanaweb.com/GhanaHomePage/NewsArchive/artikel.php?ID=175233

cleared and that the issue was closed as far as Anadarko was concerned did not sit well with Ghana's new Attorney General, Betty Mould-Iddrisu. Unless the Ghanaian government was playing a different game altogether.

After being informed by Anadarko's lawyers and investigators in January, in February, and in June that there had been no smoking gun, no wrongdoing had been committed, and that I had been exonerated, I expected the Attorney General would pack it up, close the file, notify EO Group that they were no longer under suspicion, and move on to the next case. Instead, the Mills government decided to investigate the entire matter themselves. Maybe because some of Anadarko's investigation had taken place mostly during the previous administration under John Kufuor. Maybe because the Mills administration thought the high-powered American lawyers got it wrong. Maybe because Mills wanted to embarrass Kufuor, or to vindicate the NDC as the choice of the people in electing him as President, or because he just wanted to find fault and point fingers.

All I knew was that it had started all over again. This time with Ghana Government investigators and police agencies. Being investigated by Anadarko and Kosmos had been mere minor league warm-ups compared with what was about to happen to me.

CHAPTER

20

THE CROSSHAIRS

Meanwhile, the battle between Kosmos and the GNPC over Kosmos' attempt to sell their stake in Jubilee had reached a fever pitch. GNPC Director Thomas Manu notified all potential bidders for the Kosmos stake whom the government suspected had been given data or other information pertaining to Jubilee Field, WCTP, or Deepwater Tano, that all such data was proprietary property of the Government of Ghana, and that it was just as unlawful for them to possess it as it had been for Kosmos to have allowed them to access it.

The Mills government was ticked off that Kosmos was trying to sell, and they were determined to make that impossible. A simmering of anger set in between the GNPC and Kosmos. Now, Kosmos and I both were in the Government's crosshairs.

The news media got wind of the rift and began looking into things, taking sides, offering opinions, facts, fantasy. Of primary concern was that the GNPC was claiming that, according to section 23(2) and 23(5) of the Petroleum Exploration and Production Law (PNDC Law 84), all data relating to oil and gas activities in Ghana was the property of the GNPC.[51]

"KOSMOS-EXXONMOBIL TRANSACTION— NO DEAL!"

"The authority for the Government is provided in the Petroleum Exploration and Production Law, whilst that for GNPC is captured under Article 25 of the Petroleum Agreement it signed with Kosmos Energy, a company which has now metamorphosized into off-shore company in Cayman Island. Under the law, the Government Ghana, represented by the Minister of Energy, has an unconditional right approval before any direct for indirect assignment of a petroleum agreement or part of it. This is captured under article 8 of Ghana's PETROLEUM EXPLORATION AND PRODUCTION LAW, 1984 P.N.D.C.L. 84, subtitled, Non Assignment of Petroleum Agreements, which reads: 'A petroleum agreement entered into under this Law shall not directly or indirectly be assigned, in whole or in part, by the holder of such agreement to another person without the prior consent in writing of the Secretary.' Secretary in the agreement means the Minister of Energy."

—*The Enquirer*, October 26, 2009[52]

Considering all that was being thrown at them by a new government desperate to own a larger cut of Jubilee Field, it was understandable that Kosmos wanted out. They were also primarily an oil exploration

---

[51] *The Enquirer*, in a Nov. 2, 2009, story titled "GNPC To Buy Out KOSMOS"; front page banner (story p.12).

[52] *The Enquirer*, in an Oct. 26, 2009, story titled "Kosmos-ExxonMobil Transaction – NO DEAL!"; front page banner (story p.4); and an Oct. 28 follow-up story in the same newspaper by the same title (p.14).

company, not a production firm. They saw what was on the horizon even before an intractable opposition government had taken over Ghana: the super-major oil companies were ramping up their march across the African continent. And their sights were on the big new player in the game. Ghana.

In their plan to offload their share of Jubilee, Kosmos entertained an offer from oil giant ExxonMobil for the prize. The GNPC warned Kosmos that failure to comply with provisions of PNDC Law 84 was illegal, and hinted that the government might want to take over the firm's share in Jubilee (which was starting to look like a probable motive for why the Mills government wasn't making it easy for Kosmos to try to sell). Kosmos' troubles with the government were mounting by the day.

My troubles were about to become even worse. Months earlier, when Ghana's new Attorney General, Betty Mould-Iddrisu, had been informed that I had been cleared by Willkie Farr investigators and that the U.S. DOJ had been pulled into the case, rather than standing down, she had put in a call to the CID, and a case file was started. Mould-Iddrisu then began openly pursuing her agenda, through CID interrogations. They looked into my financial records to see for themselves if I had made any politician, any government official, any former president, an improper payment. Then they began calling me in for questioning.

After the CID interrogation of me began, the media cranked up the accusations, and were now insinuating that I had managed to fool the lawyers and investigators hired by Anadarko. What was once smoke was fanned into flaming controversy. Corporate investors tended to shy away from anyone who brought controversy or even a hint of scandal to their investment. As a result, Kosmos began to pull away from me even more. A business partnership with me was not a relationship that would please their investors.

The pressure was on me from all fronts. Far from winding down after being cleared by Anadarko, my battle was just heating up. If it continued much longer, or became any worse, it could separate me from my share of the very oil field I had initiated the discovery of. And the only thing that could make it worse was one word from a jury: *Guilty*. I had originally thought Anadarko was the only party that was out to do me harm. However, while Anadarko's timing and attitude had done much damage to me, they had cleared me and were no longer a threat.

Yet, it was obvious that someone—whoever was stoking the government and the news media with misinformation—had it out for me. They were still out there. In fact, I was beginning to think there was more than one, working behind the scenes to destroy me. And not necessarily out of anger (it's the knife you don't see coming that hurts the most).

Whatever the reason for the surreptitious attacks against me, the political winds had shifted one hundred and eighty degrees in one fast year. I didn't know how I would survive it. I thought about my grandfather the preacher, and all he had taught me about faith, about truth being the victor, about praying to God in times of trouble. Throughout my life, whenever I had experienced emotionally trying situations, I would repeat Bible verses that fit what I was going through, to try to calm my fears. Psalm 35—*Fight against those who fight against me, O Lord. Arise and come to my aid. May those who plot my ruin be turned back in dismay.* Psalm 46—*God is our refuge and our strength. An ever-present help in trouble. Therefore, we will not fear.* With so many powerful people determined to take all I had, to smear my reputation, to put me behind bars, it wasn't always easy to remember that God was with me. I was only human.

I wondered if it was all worth it. I missed Houston. The whole situation, the CID interrogations (three in as many weeks), false stories in the media, my consortium partners' increasingly cold shoulders toward me, and everything else I was dealing with, was pushing me to the edge of a heart attack. My doctor increased my blood pressure medication dosage and warned me to cut back my work hours and try to relax. That was like telling a man running down a train track in a dark tunnel to try to ignore the heavy rumbling and the bright light barreling at him from behind.

The train hit me later that month when I was forced into a cash-only existence and had to begin living as if I was a fugitive who hadn't even been charged with any crime. At least not formally.

But it looked like that was coming.

I was informed by a letter mysteriously left on my desk at my office.

The letter began, "You are required to report to the CID . . ."

Having no choice, I went to the CID offices in Accra with my lawyer Addo Atuah, where I was interrogated by investigators in a tedious repetition of the nearly-identical questions I had been asked by the Anadarko lawyers from Willkie Farr last October and earlier this January.

Only this session was scarier, because these guys had badges and guns. So I answered their questions.

They asked over and again if I gave money to any government official.

"I told you, I didn't pay anyone anything. Why would I pay anyone money?" I tried to explain.

They pushed further to insinuate that they had been told that I had received confidential data from the GNPC and that I had used that information for my own personal gain.

"I did not. There's nothing to confess. I've done nothing wrong."

It went on like that, over and over and over, for hours. They were trying to break me, scare me, force a confession from me.

The next CID interrogation focused on why I was being paid so much money as Country Manager for Kosmos Energy. CID investigators became convinced that I was using my income to pay bribes to people. What they didn't seem to consider, however, was that I had a home and family to maintain in the United States, I had car loans, a mortgage on my house in Houston, and living and housing expenses in Ghana. Nor did they seem to realize that I was being paid one-third of the going rate for an oil industry Country Manager in Africa. I was even supervising staffers such as Logistics Managers who were being paid more than I was.

The CID was soon forced to drop that approach. After all, there was no law in Ghana against being paid for your work.

Then the CID fixated on how large of an interest EO Group had in the WCTP partnership.

"Who decided to give you guys three and a half percent?" the interrogator asked. "That's a huge amount."

"What is three and a half percent of zero?" I asked back.

"Zero?—it's worth much more than zero, Mr. Owusu."

"When we made the deal, there was no oil. It was all speculation."

"So *you* say."

"We did not have a fortune teller on the technical and engineering team to tell us oil was down there. Besides, our three and a half percent was coming out of Kosmos' share, not the government's share, not from the people of Ghana. And the government approved the license."

"Oh, we're looking at Mr. Kufuor, too. You can be sure of that. Tell us about the two hundred and fifty thousand dollars you received. What was it for?"

"We already discussed that. I told you, it was because we had nothing. I had been investing my time and effort exploring for oil and wanted at least to get the benefit of our sweat equity if we didn't discover anything. If all we ended up with was a block that didn't pan out, then I wanted to make sure I was paid for my time and effort."

"That's a lot of money."

"I only got half. Plus, I had quit my job and moved here to Ghana. If Kosmos hadn't gone forward with it, I would have been left a pauper. Besides, the money was part of their investment, just like any other part, whether it was hiring staff or putting physical infrastructure into place."

"So why didn't you ask for millions?"

"Because Kosmos was a start-up and didn't have that kind of money. Besides, I was doing it for Ghana, not for me."

"That's not what our sources say."

Who were these "unnamed inside sources" cited in news reports? Who were the "government insiders" the media kept referring to as they fanned the flames of suspicion against me? Had disgruntled former GNPC employees been feeding disinformation to the government, the media, and acquaintances at Anadarko during the 2008 campaign, and then to the police?

Things had gone far beyond merely frightening. I was facing what was looking like guaranteed prosecution and possible prison time.

CHAPTER

21

LAWYER UP

I flew to Houston. It was time to talk to Phil Inglima, the new lawyer Crowell & Moring, Kosmos Energy's law firm (Fulbright and Jaworski), had assigned to replace Adrian Mebane.

While Mebane had been a fine man and very skilled lawyer during our brief association, the relationship between Kosmos and me was deteriorating. I could only hope this new guy was not more beholden to his employer than to me.

When Mebane had handed off the case file to Inglima in March of 2009, he told Inglima that he had become convinced there was nothing to any of the charges against me and that he assumed the Ghanaian government would see the light and drop their pursuit.

"If you could take care of this client when I leave," Mebane had told

Inglima, "I'd appreciate it. I think it's all over. There was nothing to it."

Talk about famous last words.

I met Phil Inglima and his associate, Femi Dekalu Thomas, a Nigerian, at the Houston home of my EO Group lawyer, Jim Barnes.

Inglima had the appearance of a young tech entrepreneur. He was in his early 40s, his hair was slightly graying at the sides, and he had an energetic demeanor. He was a 1988 graduate of Georgetown Law Center and had clerked for a federal judge before being offered a position as a prosecutor in the D.C. District Attorney's office. He turned down the offer and went to work for one of the leading lawyers in D.C., working on public corruption for a major U.S. petroleum company as well as for individuals in some notable scandals, including a huge case in Nigeria. He became a partner in the firm and spent two years as Special Prosecutor and as Senior Associate Independent Counsel, investigating domestic bribery through campaign contributions, on cases involving the White House, the Department of the Interior, and the Democratic National Convention. He then went to Crowell and Moring, in 2005, where he became a partner and Co-Chair of the firm's white-collar practice.

Inglima was not only off-the-charts smart, but he seemed to be a genuinely nice human being. However, with what I had been going through lately, I trusted no one. Nice meant nothing. Only time and experience revealed a man's true heart and intentions.

I was fortunate that Jim Barnes was protective of me. He had coordinated with Mebane earlier and had been aware of every aspect of my activities in the oil partnership. With Inglima coming into the picture, there was a certain amount of suspicion—on both sides. For me, the question was whose side was Inglima on. After all, his paycheck came from Kosmos, who was busy making my life miserable, along with the other players aligned against me.

When I first met Inglima that day in Houston, there were moments when Barnes and I would step out of the room for quick sidebars.

Inglima and Thomas must have thought this was going to be a challenging situation because, frankly, I didn't trust anyone at that point. Mebane had suddenly left after only a handful of months, and I was very apprehensive. Scared, actually. I had enemies of the most powerful kind, and they were out to get me. I felt very alone. Even my EO Group business partner Bawuah-Edusei wasn't much involved in the oil consortium (other than my giving him various updates as necessary), and never in its daily activities. He wasn't even in Ghana. In the beginning, he had his medical practice in the U.S., then his ambassadorial duties for several years in different countries, and then he'd gone back to his medical practice.

I was facing a huge government investigation and had no idea what was going to happen. I needed a legal team to stick with it; not come and go. I had no time to ascertain motives, personalities, abilities. On top of all that was the fact that Inglima had been assigned by Kosmos' law firm. And Kosmos wanted to interview me yet again, because they had become distrustful of me—and here I was, being represented by their employee, essentially. It felt like the definition of conflict of interest. It was natural for me to wonder if this was really my lawyer or just another Kosmos lawyer. How was I to know he wasn't a spy in my midst? I didn't know the man. To say I was apprehensive would be a gross understatement.

Inglima tried to assure me.

"We have one duty," he explained at our meeting at Barnes' house. "And that is to represent you. Doesn't matter whether we won a raffle that appointed us as your counsel, or somebody connected to it brought us in. Everything you say to us stays here. Everything you want and that we perceive as our objective, is aligned from you to us. We keep on the same page going forward. There is no Kosmos in the room. There's no Anadarko in the room. So don't fear that that is going to be the case."

It would take awhile to build trust. It was to my advantage that Crowell & Moring had a friendly relationship with Fulbright and

Jaworski, who had appointed Crowell to represent me on behalf of Kosmos. All I could do was hope that Inglima wasn't too much of a skeptical audience himself. It wouldn't help my case at all if he was looking at me with suspicion like it seemed everyone else was. I reminded myself that relationships took time to build.

Inglima knew little about Ghana, and virtually nothing about me. But he did know Nigeria. In the two cases he'd had involving Nigeria, he had learned that you couldn't get much business done there without greasing the skids. That was true in many countries. Our challenge was that it was illegal for an American citizen to do so—and that was at the heart of all of the suspicion being leveled at me.

Fortunately, the Kosmos lawyers had shared a fair amount of what they had constructed from the Kosmos investigation of me and my bank records, so he knew there had been no payments going in questionable directions. He also knew from Adrian Mebane the diligence and effort Mebane had put into preparing me for the Anadarko interview in January. Those things comforted me, somewhat.

Inglima had brought Femi Dekalu Thomas with him for two reasons. First, as Thomas was black and from Nigeria, he would be a sort of cultural ambassador who could help Inglima understand Africa more broadly. And second, Inglima was concerned because he was a white guy replacing Mebane, who was black. I didn't particularly care what shade my lawyer came in, as long as he was good. Although, with all of my oil consortium partners being white, it couldn't hurt to have a white guy fighting on my side. I appreciated Inglima's sensitivity. The temptation for many Americans was to think of most African countries as primitive, backwater cultures built on corruption and easily exploited by the powerful and the wealthy. There tended to be a high amount of skepticism about Africa and Africans that was fueled in part by cultural ignorance and in part by racism. That was not to say these lawyers were racist, but everyone has biases.

I had hired a lawyer in Ghana named Addo Atuah, who'd been

representing me as my personal lawyer in Ghana. Atuah, a former police officer and investigator, had the necessary background and relationships that would help me in Inglima's absence in Ghana, as well as aid Inglima in understanding the methodology and psychology of Ghanaian police and prosecutors.

That first meeting with Inglima and Thomas went as well as could be expected under the circumstances. Yet, I flew back to Accra unsure. Unsure who I could really trust. Unsure who would abandon me next. Unsure of my entire life.

In the meantime, Inglima went to work trying to understand the political dynamics of the different players and to devise a strategy for pushing back against the players opposing me. It would be frustrating and difficult for him to be on the other side of the ocean and not be able to appear in a court or at a CID or Bureau of National Investigations (BNI) interview with me in Ghana, but those days would come soon enough. For now, he coordinated his efforts through my lawyer, Addo Atuah.

Inglima's first challenge was to reassure Kosmos Energy's law firm, Fulbright and Jaworski, that he was on the job and had a plan of response to the increasing attacks against me—which were tainting Kosmos by association. Negative information was coming almost daily. Leaks from the Attorney General's office and the CID. Harmful stories in the media. Rumors on the street. All Kosmos wanted was to be able to operate peacefully with the Mills administration, weather the storm, and get out unscathed.

Kosmos didn't know Ghana.

My next CID interrogation went off and on for two or three days. These investigators were drilling deep. Their first few interviews had focused almost entirely on money they were convinced I had somehow funneled to former President John Kufuor. When they repeatedly struck out on that theory, they switched to less glamorous accusations.

Newbridge Hospitality, Kosmos Energy's in-house car rental company, became the CID's new pet issue.

"Tell us again about your car rental company, Mr. Owusu. Tell us how you funneled money through it."

And on and on. I was tempted to look outside to see if Siberian snow was falling.

The CID knew that was a non-issue. They were Ghanaians. They knew the local car rental approach wasn't bringing in big cash. It was uncles and aunties and cousins and making a couple of extra *cedis* on the side. The CID grudgingly let it go.

But I sensed they weren't done with that issue.

Next, they checked with the Ghanaian IRS, to see if I had earned any money for which I had not paid taxes. That effort was quickly shot down when the IRS instead owed *me* ¢356 Ghanaian *cedis*, the equivalent of about $110 at the time.

After the Newbridge automobile rental agency inquiry produced nothing to hang a case on, and I hadn't cheated on my taxes, the CID moved on to their next charge against me and called me back in, even more determined to hang something on me. They wanted me locked up, *period*. Every little thing connected with me and my work in Ghana became shocking, overblown, serious issues to them.

Through the last half of 2009, I would be interrogated a total of thirteen times by the CID. Rumors were running amok. Ghana's Bureau of National Investigation investigated me. The Attorney General was breathing down my neck. My business partners were giving me the cold shoulder. My wife was missing Houston. Daily TV and newspaper reports depicted me as a criminal. Rumors said I was going to be arrested and imprisoned any day.

It was the 21st century. Ghana was flush with oil. Ghana should have been magnificent. But for me, it was becoming hell.

With all of their different approaches fizzling out, the CID searched for their next big break in the case they were trying to build against me.

And they found one.

"Mr. Owusu, who signed your EO Group partnership business registration form in 2002?" I was asked during the next interrogation.

"I did."

"Who else signed it?"

Our eyes locked. I knew instantly what he was probably referring to. And I was in trouble. At least in his mind, I was. Because in that police officer's mind, he was seeing a felony.

I responded carefully, feeling my heartbeat tick up a notch.

"My business partner is Dr. Kwame Bawuah-Edusei."

"I didn't ask you what his name is," the interrogator said. "I asked you who signed the document."

I pictured the document in my mind. The name below the signature line read *Dr. Kwame Bawuah-Edusei*. The handwriting above the line was mine.

I knew what the officer's next question would be. *Did you forge your partner's signature on an official document, Mr. Owusu?*

As I sat there in the CID interrogation room, the investigator hounding me over and over with the same questions I had already answered again and again, and my Ghanaian lawyer content to let the session play out rather than take control of it, I recalled the first conversation I'd had with Phil Inglima in Houston.

"My main objective, George," Inglima had told me, "is to keep you out of jail. Now I need you to identify your objectives to me."

"That's my main objective, too," I had responded. "But I don't see how it could end that way. These people are trying to take my ownership rights from me in this oil development project. I worked hard for this. Why should I be stripped of it? I have as much of a right to it as any of the other partners."

"Absolutely," Inglima had responded. "But that's our second objective. Our first is your life and liberty."

As I read my handwriting under Bawuah-Edusei's signature line on
that form, it suddenly struck me: Inglima had been right. This situation
was not just about trying to void my agreement so my share of the oil
discovery could be taken. For the CID, the Attorney General, and the
government of Ghana, it was all about putting me in prison. It was
about my liberty.

This signature situation was going to be a problem. If the signature was false, then there was no legitimate business, no EO Group. If
there was no EO Group, the original MOU the government had signed
back in 2003 was null and void. If the MOU was invalid, it could be
argued that everything that had flowed from it ("fruit of the poison
tree") could be negated. EO Group's partnership with Kosmos Energy,
signed in 2004, would be gone. The license to explore the WCTP block
for oil, which the Ghanaian Parliament had approved in 2004, gone.
The agreement Kosmos had entered into with Anadarko and Kosmos'
counter-party partner EO Group, gone. EO Group's stake in the Jubilee
Field oil discovery, gone. Anadarko, Kosmos, the government of Ghana,
everybody and their Ghanaian uncle would sue me. I'd be defending
lawsuits until my hair turned gray. Probably from my jail cell in Nsawam
Prison.

I told the officer that I alone had signed the EO Group business
registration form. For both Bawuah-Edusei and myself.

That was all he needed to hear.

CHAPTER

22

FULL CIRCLE

Tuesday, June 16, 2009, was a seasonably humid day in Accra. I had come from an appointment with my doctor and stopped at Addo Atuah's law office. I had just stepped inside when his phone rang.

As Atuah answered the phone and listened, a look came over his face that I'd seen enough times to know who it was.

I mouthed the words, *the CID?*

He nodded to me and said into the phone, "No, inspector. Mr. Owusu cannot come in again. Not today."

I felt my blood pressure begin to rise. I had just been to the doctor's office and here they were again, requesting yet another interrogation. These officers weren't giving up.

"Mr. Owusu is on medication for high blood pressure and is under doctor's orders to rest," Atuah said to the investigator on the line.

He listened a moment, then covered the mouthpiece of the phone and whispered to me, "It's about a form you forgot to sign after they questioned you yesterday. A minor matter. He says it will only take a minute to drop by and sign it."

I shook my head and muttered something under my breath. In Ghana, a country where the police were often seen as corrupt, nothing was ever a *minor matter* with the CID. The officer on the phone was one of the same ones who had interrogated me several times during the past few days—sessions that had driven my blood pressure to deadly levels lately.

My lawyer suggested that I go and sign the form.

I relented and agreed to go to the CID headquarters. The way things had been going lately, I was in no position to butt heads with the police.

A half-hour later, Atuah and I were on our way across town with my lanky nephew, Ransford Mensah-Boateng, at the wheel of my Toyota 4-Runner.

Ransford had recently earned his degree in economics at the University of Cape Coast and was working as my executive aide, driver, and confidant while he decided whether he wanted to go into business or go back to school to earn a Master's degree. But if the past few months were any indication of what lay ahead, the next three years with me would give Ransford a Master's degree worth of experience in how *not* to do business in Ghana.

Ransford dropped me and Atuah off at the entrance of the CID building and pulled into the parking lot to wait for us to finish our business.

Atuah and I went inside and treaded down the sterile, sparse hallway I had become so depressingly familiar with over the past several weeks.

The nervous gloom of hopeless governmental oppression that settled over me must have been similar to the feeling my father had experienced under Kwame Nkrumah's rule exactly fifty years ago that month.

After waiting for nearly two hours in a bare room, a group of uniformed and plainclothes police officials entered and escorted me and Atuah to another room, where several dozen more policemen were waiting. One of the investigators informed me and my lawyer that, as part of their inquiry into various activities involving EO Group's acquisition of oil exploration rights in the WCTP block five years earlier, the court had issued search warrants for my home and my office. They were to be served at once.

Numb and disbelieving, I was escorted across town to my office in a wailing convoy of police cars and a bus full of armed, uniformed and plain-clothed officers, with blue lights flashing and sirens wailing all the way.

As we sped through the streets, Accra's perpetual crowds of street beggars peered in through the windows, trying to get a glimpse of the criminal in the back seat.

When we arrived at my office, I was ordered to wait outside while investigators descended en masse to the confused looks of my staff members. Addo's objections were ignored as officers confiscated files, computer hard drives and countless documents.

When they had taken what they wanted from my office, the speeding police convoy took me all the way down the Tema Motorway to my house, where my wife and our young grandson watched, frightened and helpless, as a phalanx of armed, uniformed officers and plainclothes detectives stormed in. Every room was searched, personal items pawed through, more computer drives taken, other documents seized, and every item photographed.

It was embarrassing and degrading. I protested, of course, as any innocent man would who was being victimized by his own government. But it was no use.

How does a man, who has faithfully gone to work every day, performed his duties flawlessly and honestly, provided for his family and paid his taxes, deal with suddenly finding himself in a situation he has only seen on the nightly news and in television dramas? How do you explain to your wife that you have done nothing wrong, when the mere presence of police with guns and badges searching her home seems to contradict your pleas of innocence?

After Ransford posted a surety bond on my behalf, travel restrictions were placed on me and I was warned that if I moved or wanted to leave the country for any reason, I would have to inform the police and the Attorney General in advance. Which, in this political atmosphere, meant get permission first.

Early the next morning it was on the front page of the newspapers, on the radio, on television. One news story even told a lurid tall tale about how I had been "stripped naked" by the police in front of my wife and child. Of course, I had neither been arrested nor stripped naked, but the news media would have their mischief, whipping up sentiment against me and doing all they could to join the government in humiliating and embarrassing me.

I had been in the national spotlight for 24 long months. The first three-fourths, basking in the euphoric glow of being fêted like a national hero in Ghana. And the last fourth as a villain.

How I missed my idyllic days as a fresh-faced twenty-something school teacher, long before America had called, and set me on this twisting path.

CHAPTER

23

LET THE GAMES BEGIN

In July of 2009, the Minister of Energy grudgingly agreed to sign off on the Jubilee Field POD. Oil revenue was cash income the country badly needed, and the government didn't want to be seen as delaying things.

That same month, Kosmos released a statement that they had voluntarily and fully cooperated with an inquiry by the Ghana Attorney General's office. They added that their legal team had performed an exhaustive investigation of me and EO Group and had found no violations of America's FCPA—by Kosmos or anyone associated with the company's endeavors in Ghana. It was a true statement and I was glad they made it, but their timing, in light of what they were about to do to me, was surprising—to say the least.

EO Group issued our own public statement, as well, stating that we had given our full cooperation to the government's investigation of me, and asserting that we had neither paid nor promised anything to anyone in the Ghanaian government to secure our MOU to explore for oil in Ghana in 2003, nor had we done anything illegal involving our partnership with Kosmos in 2004, nor with the WCTP exploration license we had been granted by the government that same year.

The dispute between Kosmos and the GNPC grew worse when the GNPC discovered that Kosmos had not only continued to solicit bids from oil companies to buy its stake in Jubilee Field after they'd been told not to, but were now working on an agreement with ExxonMobil to buy them out.[53]

The GNPC was outraged. The GNPC's Thomas Manu stated that the government of Ghana had "an exclusive pre-emptive right" to buy the oil field, adding that the GNPC "takes a serious view of the illegal manner in which data belonging to GNPC has been made available."[54]

Kosmos shot back that the GNPC had no right to buy their stake in Jubilee Field, asserting that they had complied with all confidentiality requirements and had gone as far as to suspend the bidding twice

[53] According to a report titled "Basic Overview of Ghana's Emerging Oil Industry," by Thomas Kastning (for FES Ghana, 2011; Friedrich Ebert Stiftung), "The most detailed public base case has been published by the World Bank staff in December 2009. Interpreting the World Bank data, the bank's staff calculated total companies' (excluding GNPC) revenues of US$8.29 billion. Assuming the World Bank was right, the Exxon bid for 23.5% of the field was far too high--if they do not expect production in other fields. The German development agency GIZ estimates the annual Government revenue between US$200 million and US$1 billion, while the World Bank predicts the highest Government revenue (in year 2016) to be US$1.8 billion. These variation shows, how different institutions interpret different data." The same report stated that, according to the World Bank, the effective share for the government of Ghana could create revenues totaling between US$15 billion and $20 billion over a 19-year period. Any way it was estimated, the field was a monster.

[54] The *Washington Times*, in a March 26, 2010, online story by Chuck Neubauer, titled "Ghana Discovery Sparks Fight Over Oil." See: http://www.washingtontimes.com/news/2010/mar/26/ghana-discovery-sparks-fight-over-oil/. However, this information was incorrect, as the government had no such right. The government did, however, have the exclusive right to give consent for a sale.

in efforts to resolve the issue and give the GNPC an opportunity to prepare a bid themselves for Jubilee Field, but that the GNPC never entered a bid.[55]

As the year dragged on, the battle of words and wills between Kosmos and the GNPC intensified. News outlets reported every blow. Even American news outlets jumped in on the battle. The *Washington Times* reported that, "while its petroleum agreements with Ghana say Kosmos cannot assign its interests without the written consent of the energy minister and the GNPC, the agreements also note that such consent 'shall not be unreasonably denied, withheld or delayed.'"[56]

If Kosmos wanted out of Ghana unscathed, they would have to figure out a way to placate the government or hunker down for a long cold spell.

Before July was over, even President Obama weighed in . . .

"GHANA DISCOVERY SPARKS FIGHT OVER OIL"

"'The people of Ghana have worked hard to put democracy on a firmer footing, with peaceful transfers of power even in the wake of closely contested elections,' President Obama told the Ghanaian Parliament in July. He noted that Ghana had shown that 'development depends upon good governance,' which he said had been missing in too many places in Africa. Even as Mr. Obama told the members of Parliament that 'oil brings great opportunities,' the newly elected Ghanaian government was quietly beginning to challenge Kosmos for control of the offshore oil sites—which promise to bring billions of dollars in revenue to the country."

—*Washington Times*, March 26, 2010[57]

---

[55] The *Washington Times*, in a March 26, 2010, online story by Chuck Neubauer, titled "Ghana Discovery Sparks Fight Over Oil." See: http://www.washingtontimes.com/news/2010/mar/26/ghana-discovery-sparks-fight-over-oil/
[56] Ibid.
[57] Ibid.

As if it were even possible to squeeze one more drop of ink out of the situation, the news media shifted into overdrive. The headlines ratcheted up their reporting on anything having to do with me, EO Group, Kosmos Energy, the CID, Ghana's Attorney General, Jubilee Field, and oil in Africa. It was about to become a 36-month feeding frenzy that would involve America's FBI and DOJ, some of the largest oil companies on the planet, and the untimely death of a President.

CHAPTER

24

YOU'RE FIRED

On Thursday, July 9, 2009, my lawyer, Phil Inglima, received a call from Bill Jacobson, lead lawyer at Fulbright and Jaworski, the firm representing Kosmos Energy. By the time Inglima phoned me, I had already received the news—possibly the hardest blow yet of all that was being thrown at me.

That afternoon I was working in my office when Kosmos CEO Brian Maxted stepped into the room and handed me a note. He told me that I had been relieved of my duties, and that the company was parting ways with me.

I looked at him uncomprehendingly.

"What? Why?" I asked.

"Attorney General Betty Mould-Iddrisu says you are being

investigated for fraud, forgery, bribery, money laundering, and several other crimes."

I started to try to explain that being investigated for those offenses didn't mean I was guilty of perpetrating them.

He cut me off and said stonily, "Your own country's Attorney General told us you are being investigated, George."

I knew the NDC had it out for me because of my perceived connection to former President Kufuor, and I understood that lately the government seemed to want me behind bars, but I was so surprised by the tone in Maxted's voice that I felt my heart rate instantly tick up.

"We're sorry, George," he added, "but we can't work with you anymore." And I was fired.

The odd thing about the firing was that Kosmos had recently concluded in their own diligence investigation of me that I had done nothing illegal or improper. So why let me go? Obviously, it had nothing to do with the performance of my duties as Country Manager of Kosmos Energy.

It was just as Phil Inglima had said. Kosmos was in the crossfire of animosity between the NDC and the NPP political parties, and was feeling intense pressure from Kosmos' financial backer Blackstone Group—which had invested hundreds of millions of dollars in Kosmos. With everything happening all at once, it was understandable why Kosmos was feeling that all the hostility was preventing them from conducting business in the best interests of the firm. The only solution they could see, in order to be perceived as a neutral party, was to disassociate themselves from me. They wanted out. They wanted out of Jubilee Field. They wanted out of Ghana. And they wanted out of their relationship with me.

Maxted refused to discuss the matter with me any further. After having helped make it possible for the Jubilee Field consortium to make a historic oil discovery that in one decade would grow Kosmos from a firm with only six employees to more than two hundred, it brought me great sorrow and pain to be told to leave.

I was allowed just a few minutes to vacate my office. I was evicted from my corporate apartment. I was ordered to surrender my company car, computer, and mobile phone. I was paid no compensation, given no severance package, and offered no "golden parachute." I was left with nothing. I still had my share of EO Group's 3.5% of the WCTP block, but it was not monetized—and the production phase wasn't even set to start until 2010. After that, EO Group's share of the cost would be tens of millions of dollars—money we were nowhere near having and the default on which would completely wipe out the value of our 3.5% share.

Thank God a friend of mine named Alex Bruks was gracious enough to offer me a house in Accra where I could stay for free for a few months. It was a life-saver. I had a brief sanctuary where I could try to figure out what to do next. Those types of very kind gestures would make me forever grateful for the rare people who were brave enough to stand by me in my darkest days.

By getting rid of me, Kosmos may have thought they could get rid of a few problems. They had been receiving so much heat during their clash with the GNPC about selling their stake to ExxonMobil that they may have thought that if they dumped me, it might somehow soften the anger from the government and help resolve that issue.

Or perhaps Kosmos was trying to absolve themselves from any involvement in crimes the CID and the Attorney General were stating that I had committed. The constant news stories announcing that I was under investigation often connected my name to Kosmos Energy. If Kosmos investors perceived my deteriorating public image to be dragging down their monetary value, then it would be a simple business decision to let me go.

Also, Blackstone had invested more than $400 million in Kosmos and they wanted to collect their share of the sale. To give Maxted the benefit of a doubt, if Blackstone had been putting intense pressure on Kosmos to sell, and if his meeting with Attorney General Mould-Iddrisu had been the final straw for him, then Blackstone may have seen the CID's relentless investigation of me as the issue standing in the way of the GNPC approving the POD. I was a multibillion-dollar thorn in the side for everyone—Mills, Blackstone, Kosmos, the GNPC. My mere presence as a partner in the consortium could potentially unravel any deal. I had to be dealt with.

Whatever the real reason Kosmos fired me, the episode brought up a sad reality for me about doing business in Ghana: a certain "anti-business" attitude seemed to be permeating much of the government's approach to business and law. An undercurrent of selective enforcement of the nation's laws and constitution was creating a fear in businesspeople of being wrongly accused by the government or law enforcement, and possibly suffering reprisals—which caused business partners to bicker with one another, rather than to stand in solidarity in dealing with a government that came across as arbitrary and often unreasonable in some of their dealings with business matters.

Fortunately, when they fired me, Kosmos assured Phil Inglima that they weren't going to terminate the contract between EO Group and Kosmos Energy, and that they would continue paying my lawyer fees. This was a kind gesture, because I was still up against the formidable power of the CID and their ongoing investigations of me. If the Attorney General could prove that I had forged my partner's signature on that Ghanaian business registration form, then both Kosmos and I could lose, because the government would then claim that the partnership between Kosmos and EO Group had been invalid all along, and our ownership shares in Jubilee Field could be contested. Likewise, if I were to be proven to have committed any serious crimes in Ghana, then Kosmos and I could lose. And if I were to be proven to have committed a violation of America's FCPA, Kosmos and I could also lose. We were joined at the hip in every way. The only way for Kosmos to have avoided what lay ahead for them, would have been to have chosen unity with me instead of division, to have worked with me instead of firing me.

Instead, Kosmos seemed to have been outmaneuvered by the government. And there was probably only one way to try to undo that blunder: was it possible that they were considering offering testimony against me if the Attorney General decided to arrest me? Would Kosmos even think of doing something so sinister to me?

I was a man who believed in loyalty, hard work, honesty, and fairness. I had brought all of those efforts and attributes to my dealings with Kosmos, and had once enjoyed very close relationships with most of their executives. Yet, I had been betrayed, and was now being treated with contempt. The only partner at the time who didn't overtly join the attack on me was Tullow Oil. But even they interrogated me.

Still, many players were working against me. The ability of my new lawyer, Phil Inglima, was about to be severely tested. I was relieved when he arrived in Ghana in late July. We got busy preparing for what was shaping up to be an epic battle.

Inglima's immediate worry was that the government's endless interrogations were wearing me out. In America, we are accustomed to invoking the Fifth Amendment privilege against self-incrimination, in order to know what government witnesses are saying against us, so we could respond and gauge their reaction to those facts. That doesn't happen in Ghana. In Ghana, they ask the questions and you answer the questions. Period. No matter how long it took for them to be satisfied with your answers. Because, in Ghana, the authorities don't necessarily bring an indictment on day one. They bring an accusation. And it could be a long time before they issued formal charges. That would be followed by another long period of waiting before the start of trial.

There was no swift "due process" in Ghana. It could be a *very long* process. Years, even—just to get to trial.

CHAPTER

25

So-Called "News"

By late 2009, the news media feeding frenzy was out of control. Even so-called "legitimate" news reporters didn't seem to understand that since not a drop of oil had been pumped yet, and wouldn't be for another year, I didn't have "millions" of dollars (in fact, closer to hundreds). I'd been fired from my job and was living on savings that were fast dwindling.

It was times like those that once again revealed to me the importance of family members who stuck by me. Among others, my nephew Ransford was one of those people. After he had earned his college degree a couple years earlier, I had taken him under my wing while Country Manager of Kosmos Energy. He had wanted to get a job at Kosmos, but because of the partisan charges against me, I didn't want him to be tainted by association. So he became my unofficial personal executive aide.

When I moved into my friend's house, Ransford became even more valuable as my assistant and confidant. I respected his intelligence and appreciated his calm, peaceful demeanor and upbeat outlook on life. He was somebody I could talk to during these times when I was out there alone, feeling the whole world crashing in on me. He was there for me to lean on. He would also explain to me how Ghanaians thought about whatever I was being subjected to, or what was being said about me publicly. Even though I was Ghanaian, I had been out of the country for a long time and was not up to date on rules, customs, and cultural etiquette. Ransford was a great asset, and a comfort in the increasing storm of my life.

Meanwhile, the news media's disinformation campaign had a field day with my firing. In a front page national news story titled "WAR AT KOSMOS ENERGY—MD FIRED!"[58] a "business" writer misstated my title, made up numbers about my ownership share in WCTP, and wrote a fiction that my shares had "been slashed." I could only wonder why he hadn't contacted me to verify what he intended to print.

September of 2009 closed with an eye-popping story titled "KOSMOS BOSS IN US CELLS - GEORGE OWUSU ARRESTED BY FOREIGN INTELLIGENCE."[59] The story announced that I was in jail in America, that my "shadowy" company had registered Kosmos as our "subsidiary" and that I was involved in a "fraudulent sale of Kosmos to shadowy figures."

While I occasionally appreciated the break from reality these rather comedic pieces brought me, I realized there might be a few people in Ghana who would mistake them for actual journalism or truth.

These bawdy attempts at journalism were embarrassing—to me,

[58] The *Business Guide*, in a Sept. 28, 2009, front page article by Felix Dela Klutze titled "WAR AT KOSMOS ENERGY – MD Fired!"
[59] *The Ghanaian Eye*, in a Sept. 28, 2009, article titled "KOSMOS BOSS IN US CELLS– George Owusu Arrested by Foreign Intelligence"; front page banner (story p.3).

certainly, but definitely to their writers and publishers. Yet, every country that allowed freedom of the press had been following the trend of "news" outlets that didn't really report news so much as tell wild, speculative, self-congratulatory styled "infotainment." The pieces were blatant attempts to stoke fear and play on the emotions of their readers, and stroke the ego of the people who wrote and published them. Rather than simply inform people, these "shock tabloids" wanted to shape and control the direction of thoughts in the minds of the populace in an effort to elicit specific responses from them. Even worse, they were cavalierly harming the victims of their lies.

It was sad that adults didn't seem to have anything better to do with their time than trash others with lies. I suspected that if the tables were turned, and these publishers and writers found themselves as victims of a relentless smear campaign based on deliberate deception, they would cry the loudest.

If news reports were any indicator, October was shaping up to be a month bordering on hysteria and schizophrenia, with headlines all over the map, accusations flying and, as usual, with me front and center. The news banner headline I awoke to on Tuesday, October 6, 2009, made an effort at correcting the record: "EX-KOSMOS COUNTRY DIRECTOR NOT ARRESTED, STILL A FREE MAN IN GHANA!"[60] Yet, just 48 hours later, headlines blared in a "confirmed" story titled "US SECURITY QUESTION GEORGE OWUSU"[61] that had me back in America and "cooperating with the CIA." I could only wish I were in the U.S. Thankfully, by the end of October, the media decided that I had not been arrested after all and that the CIA was not involved, and that angle subsided.

One of the beauties (and the burdens) of Ghana was that it had

[60] *The New Crusading Guide*, in an Oct. 6, 2009, story titled "EX-KOSMOS COUNTRY DIRECTOR NOT ARRESTED, STILL A FREE MAN IN GHANA!"; front page banner (story p.3).
[61] *The Ghanaian Eye*, in an Oct. 9, 2009, article titled "US Security Question George Owusu"; front page banner (story p.7).

freedom of the press to the point of being oppressive. Newspaper businesses were being run out of every little print shop and ink store and everybody had an opinion to publish. The truth was, there wasn't much well-researched news in Ghana. It was mostly opinion, conjecture, rumor, and the peddling of particular viewpoints, mixed in with just enough fact to render these stories somewhat plausible at first glance. Yet, "news" like that could upset powerful people.

In late fall of 2009, Phil Inglima was contacted by Nathan Dimock, a DOJ prosecutor. Inglima hadn't dealt with Dimock before. We could only hope he would be impartial and fair.

During the early phone calls, the DOJ was extremely suspicious of me and EO Group. Obviously, Anadarko and Ghana's Attorney General had convinced them something was amiss.

"There had to have been a payment," Dimock told Inglima. "There must have been."

The DOJ had opened a file on me, but they weren't pressing me to go and talk to them personally. Not yet. They were biding their time.

I was past overload. I was being watched constantly and followed everywhere I went, by undercover operatives of the BNI, the CID, and who knows what other government agencies. I was besieged by news reporters. I was approached by people who wanted money because they thought I was rich. I was hounded by people who were convinced I had somehow ripped off Ghana, and were threatening me.

And soon, I would be fighting battles on two different continents, thousands of miles apart, with the governments of both countries in which I held citizenship.

CHAPTER

26

SEIZURE

In October, Kosmos informed the government that it had reached a "contractually binding agreement" to sell its stake in Jubilee Field to ExxonMobil for an undisclosed price. The news quickly became public. Media coverage went viral . . .

"LURKING FOR THE BIG KILL:
KOSMOS TANGOS WITH GHANA"

"On October 6, 2009, a wired news report attributed to an unnamed source and authored by James Herron of Dow Jones Newswires [it is] alleged that a U.S. oil giant ExxonMobil Corp. has bought Kosmos Energy's stake in oil blocks offshore Ghana. The share price of Kosmos' partners in the blocks – Tullow Oil PLC and Anadarko Petroleum Corp. were reported to have soared on the basis of the take-over speculations. But this, *Public Agenda* has learned, could be yet another ploy in the company's bid to make a 'kill' out of its stake in the jubilee field.

". . . analysts at Morgan Stanley [reportedly put] a value of $3.3 billion $5 billion on Kosmos' stake in the blocks. . . .It is be-lieve [sic] that the actions of Kosmos are intended to hype their share-holding and to discourage the Government of Ghana from acquiring the stake. This is not the first time Kosmos has been linked to such a story. Sometime in May this year, news went around that Kosmos was looking for a buyer for its 30% stake in the Jubilee Field, valued at some US$3.1 billion. Kosmos was quick at the time to deny the story, even though it was apparent that backed by venture capital fund they couldn't stay around for long.

"Industry experts say it is usual practice for small companies like Kosmos to make the discoveries, sell off and move on for the 'big boys' like the ExxonMobils to move in."

—*Public Agenda*, October 12, 2009[62]

The government went ballistic. The next day, competing newspapers followed up with their take on the news . . .

"CNOOC, EXXON VIE FOR STAKE IN JUBILEE FIELD"

"Last week, Dallas-based Kosmos told bidders by letter it had 'entered into an exclusive binding agreement' with Exxon to sell its 23.5% stake in Jubilee. Kosmos is partly [owned] by private equity firm Blackstone Group LP and Warburg Pincus. A rival bid could

---

[62] *Public Agenda*, in an Oct. 12, 2009, front page story by Steve Manteaw titled "Lurking for the Big Kill: KOSMOS TANGOS WITH GHANA."

set up months of legal and political wrangling, said one person
familiar with the matter, because Kosmos feels it can sell the stake
to whomever it wants, so long as the Ghanaian government gives
its consent. News of the Exxon agreement infuriated the Ghanaian
government and GNPC, which had been trying to negotiate to increase its 13.8% stake in the field."

—*The Chronicle*, October 14, 2009[63]

On October 15, GNPC Director of Operations Thomas Manu
wrote a letter to the *Financial Times of London*, stating that the GNPC
had actually been "negotiating with Kosmos prior to the announcement
of the ExxonMobil agreement."[64] Manu told the media, "I don't see the
Exxon-Kosmos deal as done," adding that Ghana had the right to block
the offer.[65]

The GNPC then rejected negotiations between Kosmos Energy
and ExxonMobil,[66] denied permission for the sale, and hired investment bank Morgan Stanley to advise them in their efforts to acquire the
Kosmos assets at a "fair-market value."

Kosmos insisted that Ghana had no right to stop the ExxonMobil
sale, and stated that the GNPC had never even submitted a bid.

The GNPC went to ExxonMobil and, according to a story in *The
Washington Times*, instructed them to "confirm that the agreement with

---

[63] *The Chronicle*, in an Oct. 14, 2009, story by Daniel Nonor titled "Cnooc, Exxon Vie for Stake in Jubilee Field" (p.7).

[64] *The Enquirer*, in an Oct. 22, 2009, story titled "VODAFONE, KOSMOS-EXXONMOBIL-COMMON ORIGINS, COMMON AGENT! – Kosmos – Exxon-Mobil Deal; Kosmos In Breach" (p.4).

[65] *The Chronicle*, in an Oct. 14, 2009, story by Daniel Nonor titled "Cnooc, Exxon Vie for Stake in Jubilee Field" (p.7).

[66] *The Chronicle*, in an Oct. 26, 2009, story by Emmanuel Akli titled "GOV'T SNUBS $4B KOSMOS EXXONMOBIL DEAL...As Mills Fails to Grant Audience to CEO"; front page banner (story p.15).

Kosmos is no longer in effect," admonishing the juggernaut oil company of "the importance we attach to companies wishing to invest in Ghana respecting our laws and the sovereignty of Ghana."[67]

Kosmos fired back that just because the GNPC had the contractual right to approve an assignment of a petroleum license, didn't mean they had the right to buy Kosmos' stake in Jubilee.

The GNPC asserted that their agreement with Kosmos did not allow the oil company to assign its interests without obtaining the written consent of the Minister of Energy and the GNPC.

Kosmos countered that such consent, according to *The Washington Times* story, "shall not be unreasonably denied, withheld or delayed."[68]

The ExxonMobil sale was put on hold while Kosmos and the GNPC slugged it out.

Meanwhile, the *Public Agenda* newspaper speculated in a front page story as to what the GNPC was up to: "The plan according to Government sources is to acquire Kosmos' shares, trade them for a profit, and use the profit margin to finance additional interest for GNPC."[69] That suggestion only made things worse between Kosmos and the GNPC.

An October 9 news story tried to succinctly explain the dispute:

"JUBILEE PARTNERS ENDORSE KOSMOS-EXXONMOBIL TRANSACTION"

"...the government's right to approve an assignment is sometimes misconstrued as a right to buy the Kosmos stake. These approval rights are designed to ensure the optimum development

---

[67] The *Washington Times*, in a March 26, 2010, online story by Chuck Neubauer, titled "Ghana Discovery Sparks Fight Over Oil." See: http://www.washingtontimes.com/news/2010/mar/26/ghana-discovery-sparks-fight-over-oil/

[68] ibid.

[69] *Public Agenda*, in an Oct. 26, 2009, front page story by Steve Manteaw titled "CHINA, U.S. CLASH OVER GHANA'S OIL – BP to Neutralize the Americans."

of the reserves requiring license holders to be financially capable
and technically efficient. As the world's biggest and most profitable
oil company, it would be hard to find a more qualified partner for
Ghana [than ExxonMobil]."

—*Daily Graphic*, October 9, 2009[70]

Though I had my own battles to fight during the brawl, and was
doing my best to keep my head down and stay out of the news, even I
was dragged into the fray. An *Enquirer* article, true to their style, butch-
ered the details and set tongues flapping with their slant on the facts:

"VODAFONE, KOSMOS-EXXONMOBIL—COMMON ORIGINS, COMMON AGENT!—HOB's New Clout"

". . . ExxonMobil is also seeking to acquire the interest of the
EO Group – nominally held by Ambassador to Switzerland and
the US Barwuah [sic] Edusei and George Owusu, former Country
Manager of Kosmos in Ghana. The latter was recently sacked by
the company after he was said to have made certain damaging
admissions in certain police investigations in Ghana in July this
year, about the over US$300 million Kosmos interest, according
to intelligence gathered by the Enquirer.

"The EO Group's 3.5% interest in the Kosmos Agreement has
been entirely paid for by Kosmos. This free 'earned interest', as it is
known in the industry, was granted as a result of the direct access
that the EO Group gave to Kosmos to former President Kufuor,
access which the former President himself has acknowledged.
...Various attempts by Kosmos to maintain this kind of access to
the new Presidency in Ghana are in full gear as Kosmos media

---

[70] *Daily Graphic*, in an Oct. 9, 2009, article titled "Jubilee Partners Endorse Kosmos-ExxonMobil Transaction" (p.25).

blitz give credence to the ExxonMobil transaction."

—*The Enquirer*, October 22, 2009[71]

Once the news was out that Jubilee was in play, the floodgates opened. Some news outlets hinted that Kosmos had made a calculated move solely to jack up the value of their share of Jubilee Field—a move that was unwittingly bolstered by the press and led to an international clash for control of the asset . . .

"KOSMOS/EXXONMOBIL TRANSACTION—NO DEAL!"

"The news of the purported deal, which could not name a source, was uncharacteristically carried by Dow Jones and Reuters Newswires, and was picked [up] by major international media outlets, including the Wall Street Journal and the Financial Times. The reports indicated also that news of the purported deal had led to gains in the shares of Kosmos' partners in the block, Tullow Oil and Anadarko Petroleum. Many companies, from Europe, Asia and America, have shown interest in buying the Kosmos interest in the West Cape Three Points (WCTP) and Deepwater Tano blocks."

—*The Enquirer*, October 26, 2009[72]

"CHINA, U.S. CLASH OVER GHANA'S OIL"

"The question of who buys Kosmos Energy's stake in Ghana's Jubilee Field won't be answered for a little while as the jostling for the shares, valued at anywhere between US$3.1 BN and US$3.7

---

[71] *The Enquirer*, in an Oct. 22, 2009, story titled "VODAPHONE, KOSMOS-EXXONMOBIL—COMMON ORIGINS, COMMON AGENT!—Kosmos—HOB's New Clout; Kosmos, George Owusu and Kufuor" (p.4).

[72] *The Enquirer*, in an Oct. 26, 2009, story titled "Kosmos-ExxonMobil Transaction – NO DEAL!"; front page banner; story p.4; and an Oct. 28 follow-up story by the same title (p.14).

BN assumes new twists and turns by the day. Industry watchers have describe [sic] the ever changing dynamics around Kosmos' attempt to offload its shares as largely influenced by Chinese and American interests in Ghana's black gold."

—*Public Agenda*, October 26, 2009[73]

It turned out that Kosmos hadn't been the only oil firm the Ghanaian government had been talking to about buying the little Dallas firm's stake in Jubilee. The GNPC had also gotten cozy with the Chinese, hosting CNOOC Chairman Fu Chengyu for a visit to Ghana . . .

"CNOOC, EXXON VIE FOR STAKE IN JUBILEE FIELD"

"Exxon and CNOOC would both be vying for Kosmos Energy's stake in Jubilee, a discovery estimated to hold 1.8 billion barrels of oil.

"Cnooc sent a senior delegation of officials to the Ghana capital of Accra a couple weeks back, including Chairman Fu Chengyu. They committed to an equity stake for GNPC in this deal and talked about wanting to help the Ghanaians develop their national oil company. Cnooc has been linked to several possible deals in recent months but Mr. Fu said he is more interested in buying specific assets such as oil or gas fields instead of buying companies. Cnooc told Ghana it 'could help them develop their national oil company' and that they 'are kindred spirits' in that process . . .

"The Kosmos bid was to be Exxon's first major purchase in a decade and give it a major foothold in the region. Jubilee is the type of expensive and complex deep-water project that Western oil companies have traditionally excelled at. Not only do they offer

[73] *Public Agenda*, in an Oct. 26, 2009, front page story by Steve Manteaw titled "CHINA, U.S. CLASH OVER GHANA'S OIL – BP to Neutralize the Americans."

technical expertise and experience, but also a deep balance sheet. Since many of the new, large oil discoveries—including Angola, the Gulf of Mexico and Brazil—have been under thousands of feet of water, western [expertise] have dominated this new arena.

"The Chinese, however, have long coveted this deep-water know-how and in 2005 tried to purchase it by bidding for U.S. oil company Unocal Corp. Chevron Corp. ultimately wrestled it away from the Chinese in a highly political struggle. Cnooc's efforts in Ghana appear more successful because they are willing to bring in GNPC as a partner."

—*The Chronicle*, October 14, 2009[74]

At the news that ExxonMobil had some serious, cash-heavy, potentially unsavory competition for attempts to buy them out, Kosmos raised the stakes. They began a furious local, regional, and international campaign to frame the discussion in stark "us against them" geopolitical terms, rather than the simple business matter that, at its core, it actually was. The Kosmos game plan, *The Enquirer* newspaper speculated, "involves giving very little information about the actual terms of the so-called 'binding exclusive agreement' between Kosmos and ExxonMobil . . . but projecting the whole issue in geo-political terms— Chinese interests against US interests, instead of focusing on Ghana's national perspectives, which GNPC has been articulating."[75]

In response, *Public Agenda* reported, "sources close to GNPC have describe [sic] Kosmos' behavior as recalcitrant and selfish," adding that the sources had described Kosmos execs as "misbehaving and now resorting to tricks to cover their misdeeds." The story went on to say that

---

[74] *The Chronicle*, in an Oct. 14, 2009, story by Daniel Nonor titled "Cnooc, Exxon Vie for Stake in Jubilee Field" (p.70). Also see: http://www.wsj.com/articles/SB10001424052748704429304574467861885329846

[75] *The Enquirer*, in an Oct. 22, 2009, story titled "VODAFONE, KOSMOS-EXXONMOBIL-COMMON ORIGINS, COMMON AGENT! – Kosmos – Exxon-Mobil Deal; Kosmos In Breach" (p.40).

Kosmos' share-trading deal with ExxonMobil was "having no effect," adding that the move by Kosmos "was clearly intended to hype the value of its stake and use that in its subsequent negotiation with the Ghanaian government."[76]

Kosmos' tactic in framing the controversy as an East versus West battle may have backfired on them, as it only seemed to drive the GNPC closer to the Chinese—who then stepped up their campaign to acquire the Jubilee asset. President Mills refused to meet with the CEO of ExxonMobil. Although ExxonMobil held out hope that they could convince the government to consider allowing them to be involved in Jubilee, President Mills had lost all interest in talking to them, shutting the door to talks and giving the cold shoulder to their CEO . . .

". . . MILLS FAILS TO GRANT AUDIENCE TO CEO"

"A source in the Energy Ministry confided in this reporter that if ExxonMobil had followed the right procedure in buying out the [Jubilee] fields, government would have considered it, but now the door has been shut. The Chief Executive Officer of ExxonMobil, Rex W. Tillerson is reportedly making frantic efforts to meet President Mills for his company to lend money to Ghana, to enable her [sic] buy the fields, but the request has been turned down. . . . all efforts by the ExxonMobil CEO to meet President Mills has proved futile."

—*The Chronicle*, October 26, 2009[77]

---

[76] *Public Agenda*, in an Oct. 26, 2009, front page story by Steve Manteaw titled "CHINA, U.S. CLASH OVER GHANA'S OIL – BP to Neutralize the Americans."

[77] *The Chronicle*, in an Oct. 26, 2009, story by Emmanuel Akli titled "GOV'T SNUBS $4B KOSMOS EXXONMOBIL DEAL...As Mills Fails to Grant Audience to CEO"; front page banner (story p.15).

Meanwhile, Blackstone was pressuring Kosmos to sell. But it was beginning to appear as if Kosmos might not have the ability to pull off a proper sale of their own reserves.

Throughout the rest of the year, the media was sunk deep in a frenzy of speculation and battling "news" stories. As many as half of them were actually right, too. However, unfortunately for Kosmos, it was becoming increasingly obvious that the deal with ExxonMobil was not going forward . . .

> **"KOSMOS/EXXONMOBIL TRANSACTION – NO DEAL!"**
>
> "Contrary to propaganda being wage through major international news networks, suggesting a sealed deal between Kosmos Energy and ExxonMobil over the former's interest in the Ghana Jubilee Field, The Enquirer can report that there is no deal. This is because the approval rights of the Government of Ghana and the Ghana National Petroleum Corporation (GNPC) over any such transaction are unconditional and absolute. . . . Sources close to GNPC state that 'GNPC is not just looking at companies with technical and financial muscles, which requirements are important, but also those strategic-fit for the petroleum field of Ghana.'"
>
> —*The Enquirer*, October 26, 2009[78]

Amid all the hubbub surrounding the controversy, it was easy to lose sight of the fact that it was Kosmos that owned the stake in Jubilee. Yet, even their suitor ExxonMobil soon seemed to abandon them, in spite of the January 2010 deadline the two had agreed upon as the date they would sign their official purchase agreement.

While sources stated that BP was "less overbearing and easier to deal with" than Exxon Mobil,"[79] ExxonMobil still had their supporters, some

[78] *The Enquirer*, in an Oct. 26, 2009, story titled "Kosmos-ExxonMobil Transaction – NO DEAL!"; front page banner (story p.4); and an Oct. 28 follow-up story by the same title (p.14).
[79] *Public Agenda*, in an Oct. 26, 2009, front page story by Steve Manteaw titled "CHINA, U.S.

of whom took to writing well-reasoned op-ed pieces—which probably didn't help Kosmos' deteriorating relationship with the GNPC . . .

"GNPC SHOULD BITE WHAT IT CAN CHEW"

[The GNPC is] "trying to scare off other possible suitors, including ExxonMobil, as well as undermine the value [of Jubilee Field]. . . . What is amazing is that the GNPC is said to be already struggling to meet its financial commitments on their small paying interest. How is GNPC going to pay for the massive current and future expenditures associated with the Kosmos interest? How is it going to pay for 8 times its current participation when it cannot meet its current financial obligations? Perhaps Ghana is missing the real point: if we break down our own laws when it suits us how will Ghana be viewed by current and future investors? Sources familiar with the current impasse say what is more baffling is the fact that the ExxonMobil Kosmos agreement when announced included additional participation for government - the very reason for which GNPC wants to go to other parties."

—*Daily Guide*, October 27, 2009[80]

The *Daily Guide* op-ed writer then hit it on the head with a closing suggestion about what might really be going on: "Perhaps there are more personal considerations at play than we realize and as usual, to the detriment of Ghana."[81] The "personal consideration" was that the GNPC simply didn't want any oil firm put forth by Kosmos.

These were complex times for Kosmos Energy as they fought to offload their stake in Jubilee while trying to keep the government of Ghana from interfering with what could be a colossal payday for the

CLASH OVER GHANA'S OIL – BP to Neutralize the Americans."
[80] *Daily Guide*, in an Oct. 27, 2009 op-ed titled "GNPC SHOULD BITE WHAT IT CAN CHEW" (p.18).
[81] Ibid.

little Texas firm. The battle Kosmos was waging had been the front page news story nonstop from back in June when Kosmos had opened their data room to ExxonMobil, and it would continue all the way through the following year. It was a battle that Kosmos probably should have more carefully thought through before embarking on. Now, Kosmos found themselves stuck between a rock and a hard place, and would soon become like a small animal struggling to extricate themselves from a tar pit they'd dashed into while chasing a shiny object. Not heavy enough to be dragged down, not strong enough to pull themselves out.

Ghana was becoming their purgatory.

CHAPTER

27

SERIOUS FRAUD

The third week of November of 2009 brought the blow I'd been hoping for weeks was only another rumor. On November 17, the Managing Director of my bank received an official request from the Head of the Banking Supervision Department at the Bank of Ghana. The request, dated October 20, 2009 (a full month before my bank received it), stated that the Executive Director of the Serious Fraud Office had ordered the Bank of Ghana to freeze, "with immediate effect," my bank accounts, financial assets and other assets. The other companies and individuals included in the asset freeze order were Dr. Kwame Bawuah-Edusei, EO Group, Kosmos Energy, Newbridge Hospitality Services, Ecquiva Services, and two other related individuals. Commercial banks across Ghana received the freeze order from the

Ghanaian Serious Fraud Office.

On November 16, the *Daily Guide* newspaper had written a story scooping the asset freeze. The story quoted Ghana's Deputy Minister of Information as denying that any bank freeze action was going to happen. But the *Daily Guide's* scoop forced Mould-Iddrisu to take action, or back off and appear weak.

On November 17 of 2009 (according to documents leaked two years later[82]), the same day the bank letters finally went out to freeze my accounts, Donald Teitelbaum, America's Ambassador to Ghana, happened to have had a conversation with A.G. Mould-Iddrisu about the Kosmos asset sale situation. During that talk, the Ambassador had urged Mould-Iddrisu that "any dispute with Kosmos be resolved transparently and within rule of law." Mould-Iddrisu had responded that "the investigation would be carried out in a fair and transparent manner," and noted that "the companies in the consortium would be asked to meet with the GOG [Government of Ghana] in the next week." Meanwhile, Kevin Black, my replacement as Country Manager for Kosmos, contacted the U.S. Embassy in Accra on November 17 and informed them of the asset freeze. It was then that Ambassador Teitelbaum realized that when he had spoken with Mould-Iddrisu earlier that day, she had never revealed to him that our financial accounts had been frozen, according to documents.[83]

It was Teitelbaum's first posting as Ambassador after having served at embassies all over Africa. He'd only been on the job in Ghana for sixteen months, serving from one year after Ghana's major oil discovery through the final six months of Kufuor's last term in office. And things were deteriorating. Teitelbaum requested guidance from the U.S. State Department on cleared language for use with the Ghanaian government

---

[82] Source: Wikileaks; for the original, unredacted version, leaked to Wikileaks on Sept. 1, 2011, (reference id 09ACCRA1226; aka Wikileaks ID #235396); see: http://wikileaks.org/cable/2009/11/09ACCRA1226.html
[83] Ibid.

★

BANK OF GHANA

TELEPHONE: 666902 - 8
666174 - 6
BSD FAX NO. 662038
OUR REF: BSD/65/2009
YOUR REF:

P. O. Box 2674
ACCRA-GHANA

DATE: 2nd November, 2009

The Managing Director
Ecobank Ghana Limited
19, Seventh Avenue
Ridge West
Accra

Ecobank Ghana Limited
Managing Director's Office
1 Z' NOV. 2009

Dear Sir,

FREEZING OF BANK ACCOUNTS, FINANCIAL ASSETS AND OTHER ASSETS PURSUANT TO S. 13 (9) OF THE SERIOUS FRAUD OFFICE ACT 1993, 466

The Executive Director of the Serious Fraud Office, in a letter Ref. No.SFO/ED/054/VOL.9/101 dated October 20, 2009 to the Bank of Ghana requested that the bank accounts, financial assets and other assets of the under listed individuals and companies at your bank be frozen with immediate effect.

Individuals
1. Dr. Kwame Bawuah Edusei
2. George Yaw Owusu
3.
4.

Companies
1. E.O. Group Ltd.
2. Kosmos Energy LLC
3. Kosmos Energy Ghana HC
4. Newbridge Hospitality Services Ltd.
5. Equiva Services Ltd.

Please take note and act accordingly.

Yours faithfully,

D.O.K. OWUSU
FOR: HEAD
BANKING SUPERVISION DEPARTMENT

Bank of Ghana Letter Re Serious Fraud Office Asset Freeze Order, 2009

in response to the asset freeze. It wasn't his first cable to State Department about the situation.[84] In fact, the Ambassador had already alerted the State Department about the Owusu, Mills, Kosmos, GNPC matters when they had flared up after the new administration took the Castle eleven months earlier.

Teitelbaum had reported to the State Department that Kosmos had told him, "so far, only the bank accounts have been frozen, and there was some confusion over whether Kosmos's banks would freeze both offshore and onshore accounts. The GOG [Government of Ghana] has not moved to seize computers or other company property but the CID is asking Kosmos and other oil company representatives to come in for questioning on November 26. Kosmos characterized the GOG move as an attempt to damage the company's reputation in Ghana and to force the company to sell its share of the Jubilee Field to the GOG at a sharply reduced price."[85]

Teitelbaum's communiqué to the State Department continued, "an NPP parliamentarian chastised the NDC for its unfair treatment of Ghanaians involved in bringing Kosmos Energy to Ghana—namely George Owusu of the EO Group—only to have Owusu publicly deny unfair treatment, which led to an NPP retraction of the statement." The ambassador's cable went on to say that I was, "currently under investigation by the CID, something that Kosmos Energy Country Manager Kevin Black feels has restricted Owusu's ability to speak freely about accusations that he is an NPP loyalist who served as a front for former President John Kufuor, something that has never been proven."[86]

Other cables between Ambassador Teitelbaum and the State Department about the issue as it played out in 2009 would make for interesting reading when they were leaked by Wikileaks in September of 2011 after the dispute had been set in motion by Kosmos soliciting

---

[84] Ibid.
[85] Ibid.
[86] Ibid.

the ExxonMobil offer and then making it public—ticking off the government of Ghana:

> "According to Maxted, the company feared that the GOG was trying to damage its reputation . . . [he] feared that although an asset freeze would not affect development of the Jubilee Field because it was not the operator, it could affect Kosmos's two drilling operations of exploratory appraisal wells, which he said cost the firm USD 1 million/day to operate. Maxted said that the GNPC had most recently asked Kosmos to come to Accra on November 30 to try to resolve a separate outstanding legal issue between the parties. Maxted characterized the GOG motivation for the rumored action as 'retribution' against Kosmos for the way in which it secured funding from the World Bank's IFC so that GOG approval was not necessary. The [Ghana] A.G. stressed that the GOG was not singling out U.S. companies and that all actions would be carried out in a transparent and legal fashion."
> —Wikileaks, September 1, 2011[87]

Over the next few years, I would be forced to continue to use cash only, as all banks in Ghana were on alert not to transact business with me. Having lost my job, and with no access to bank accounts, the new stress added to my already overloaded plate. I was not a wealthy man. How was I to support my family, pay my bills, provide for my children? It would also be a challenge to travel to business meetings, many of which were in connection with my position as a partner in the oil consortium and were held in London, Houston and Dallas. I did my best to maintain appearances as a functioning and effective businessman.

What Kosmos had done in firing me without cause had been hurtful and embarrassing enough. But what the government had done in

---

[87] Ibid.

freezing my bank accounts was worse. Kosmos had been happy to take the business opportunity I had handed them in Ghana, but they now wanted me gone. And Ghana was happy to have the income the oil discovery would bring the nation, but they now wanted to make it nearly impossible for me to stay.

Some said I should have fled Ghana. Just leave the country, return to America, rebuild my life, and regain my sense of peace and balance. But I don't run. Especially when I had committed no wrong. It was not easy staying in Ghana, low on money, constantly followed by shadowy figures, suspicious eyes cast at me by everyone who had seen me in the news, my every move scrutinized, everything I said in a CID interview leaked and splashed across tabloid headlines the next day.

There were occasional respites from the storm swirling around me, however. While the news media usually mangled several of the details, a fairly positive profile came out in the November 19 issue of one of the larger, more prominent Internet information sites in the country. Titled "History of Oil Discovery In Ghana-The EO Groups Role!!!" the piece told about EO Group and the key role it had played in the discovery of Jubilee Field. It was a relief to sense that some news sources were taking a stab at putting an upbeat face on Ghana's good fortune in the oil business, and giving credit where credit was due.[88]

Five days later, *The New Crusading Guide* newspaper ran a comprehensive historical analysis of the entire sequence of events, starting from July of 2004 when Parliament had approved the oil exploration agreement between EO Group/Kosmos Energy and the GNPC. Titled, "KOSMOS/EO GROUP & GHANA's OIL . . . No Smoking Gun . . . No Kufuor Or NPP Connection!" the two-page story was refreshingly accurate in nearly every facet of their examination of the facts. The story concluded, "The EO Group, from all indications both at home and

---

[88] The online news website GhanaWeb.com, in a story titled, "General News of Thursday, 19 November 2009." See: http://www.ghanaweb.com/GhanaHomePage/NewsArchive/printnews. php?ID=172153

abroad, has been transparent and cooperative. Sources close to it (EO Group) have intimated to *The New Crusading Guide* that the Group will assert its right at all times to safeguard its integrity."[89]

Still, the press bashing in general made me feel like I was in the middle of a boxing match that featured me being batted around by the heavyweights—the CID, the GNPC, the Attorney General, Kosmos Energy, and whoever else wanted to take a swing at me. I did my best to stay on my feet and roll with the punches. I stubbornly refused to go down.

My pattern became working late into the night on preparing my case, sleeping until early afternoon, and scrambling to scrape together enough money for basic necessities as my funds dwindled away. There were still a few friends and associates I could borrow money from, but times were becoming lean. I had a feeling it would be a long spell before the pressure began to ease. 2009 had been a wild year for me. And 2010 would be just as wild.

---

[89] *The New Crusading Guide*, in a Nov. 24, 2009, story titled "KOSMOS/EO GROUP & GHANA's OIL...No Smoking Gun...No Kufuor Or NPP Connection!"; front page banner (story p.2).

28

THE TAMING OF THE PRESS

The new year launched with another *Financial Times of London* story on January 7, 2010, that set off a firestorm of reaction from Kosmos, from me, and from former President John Kufuor . . .

"CORRUPTION PROBE INTO SALE OF
GHANA OIL BLOCK"

"The ongoing Ghana investigation risks complicating efforts by Kosmos to cash in its share of the country's biggest field. U.S. and Ghanaian authorities are investigating corruption allegations involving a Texas oil company and the local partner that helped it secure control of the Ghanaian oil block that yielded one of

Africa's biggest recent discoveries. . . . Kosmos, which denies any wrongdoing, is owned by US private equity groups Blackstone and Warburg Pincus.

"According to people close to the investigation, Ghana is preparing to file criminal charges against EO, a company set up by two political allies of John Kufuor, former president, whose party lost tense elections a year ago. The US justice department is also understood to be probing the relationship between EO and Kosmos . . .

"Duke Amaniampong, a California-based lawyer working for the Ghanaian investigation, told the Financial Times that Ghana's attorney-general had accumulated 'enough evidence of criminal culpability to bring charges against the EO Group and its directors'. The charges would include 'causing a financial loss to the state, money laundering and making false declarations to public agencies' . . .

"Ghana, Kosmos said, now wants to secure a share of the profits by forcing Kosmos to sell itself at a knock-down price to GNPC, the state oil group, which could then sell it to the highest bidder. 'Some factions in the country are clearly seeking to spread rumours and untruths in an attempt to undermine the company so that its assets can be [pushed] below fair market value,' Kosmos said.

"According to a senior Ghanaian official, Kosmos's financing of EO's costs was 'widely regarded in the industry as unusual' especially as the terms of Kosmos's deal with the government and state oil group were 'more favourable [to Kosmos] than from any other agreement'."

—*Financial Times of London*, January 7, 2010[90]

---

[90] *Financial Times of London,* in a Jan. 7, 2010, story by William Wallis, Martin Arnold, and Brooke Masters titled "Corruption Probe Into Sale of Ghana Oil Block." See: http://panafricannews.blogspot.com/2010/01/corruption-probe-into-sale-of-ghana-oil.html

There was much more than that in the story, and it was vicious—and only partially correct. It was a textbook example of stating conjecture as if it were fact, statements that were not properly attributed, misquotes, and inaccuracies.

For an entire year, the government had been demonizing me in the public domain, in newspapers, on television, over the radio. Now the financial news media in London was going after me. And they hadn't done their homework. But I couldn't rebut it, because even though the *Financial Times* reporter had asked to interview me for the piece, I had been instructed by my lawyer to decline the request, given that the government of Ghana was threatening to file charges against me.

"George," Inglima advised me, "let them say whatever they want. The issues happen in the courtroom. Not in the press. So don't say anything."

It was good advice. But I was up against the reality that Ghana had what was referred to as a "Rent a Press," where many newspapers in Ghana were the mouthpiece of the government. Even my CID interrogators were leaking to the press. When I was being questioned by the police, everything I said in the interrogation room would appear the next day in the newspapers, but with their negative spin on it. So it wasn't easy to shut up and say nothing in my defense. Nonetheless, we took Inglima's advice and issued only a generic statement that read in part, "EO's directors played an important role in opening Ghana's oil industry, and had done so lawfully and without using 'improper influence.'"

Considering the increasing vitriol of the attacks on me, it wasn't always easy to keep in mind that to the average Ghanaian there was a more historical perspective on the issue, as explained by Diarmid O'Sullivan on the "Global Witness" online website in response to the *Financial Times* story . . .

"GHANA CONTROVERSY SHOWS NEED TO SHINE
A LIGHT ON OIL DEALS"

"...any hint of murkiness, or of secret connections between oil investors and government officials, automatically leads to suspicions of corruption. And looking at other countries in the region, suspicion is a reasonable response. In neighbouring Nigeria, for example, it is an open secret that the allocation of oil rights has been used by rulers in the past to reward their cronies. Ghanaians are acutely aware that far from growing out of poverty on its oil wealth, Nigeria has been nearly wrecked by corruption and misrule.

"And further down the Gulf of Guinea is Angola, a country with a reputation for severe corruption which Global Witness has been reporting on for the last decade. Sonangol, the state oil company, has pre-qualified a large number of private companies (most of them little-known) to bid for minority shares in Angolan exploitation licenses. Global Witness reported last August that one of these private companies had a shareholder with the same name as Sonangol's chairman (who declined to answer questions about it).

"President Obama pointedly chose Ghana over Nigeria for his first African visit as Head of State. . . . his speech to Ghana's parliament contained advice to the continent's other leaders (and perhaps an encoded message to the Ghanaians): 'No country is going to create wealth if its leaders exploit the economy to enrich themselves . . . No person wants to live in a society where the rule of law gives way to the rule of brutality and bribery.'"

　　　—Diarmid O'Sullivan, "Global Witness," January 10, 2010[91]

---

[91] Online news website "Global Witness" in a Jan. 10, 2010, story by Diarmid O'Sullivan, titled "Ghana Controversy Shows Need to Shine A Light On Oil Deals" See: http://www.globalwitness.org/library/ghana-controversy-shows-need-shine-light-oil-deals

I bit my tongue and didn't reply to the *Financial Times* attack. My time would come. I also didn't reply to the next salvo, fired at me four days after the *Financial Times*' story in an article that quoted Attorney General Mould-Iddrisu's plans to prosecute me and Kosmos . . .

"GOV'T SWOOPS ON KOSMOS ENERGY—AS BETTY MOULD-IDDRISU READIES FOR PROSECUTION"

"According to the Attorney General and Minister of Justice, Mrs. Betty Mould-Iddrisu . . . the government had gathered enough criminal evidence against the [Kosmos Energy] group, and would soon press charges against them. [The] charges could include, 'causing financial loss to the state, money laundering, and making false declarations to public agencies.' . . . [the] government began conducting intensive investigations into the activities of Kosmos and its partner, EO Group . . . 'This is a case of criminal activities which has extended beyond Ghana's country's criminal code,' she . . . confirmed reports of ongoing investigations by the state and United States authorities into corruption allegations . . . with the US said to be particularly interested in probing the relationship between EO and Kosmos."

—*The Chronicle*, January 11, 2010[92]

The next day, January 12, 2010, I got a small break from the press battering when *The New Crusading Guide* re-ran the comprehensive historical analysis of the events they had originally published on November 24. In this new edition, the paper also ran a story that mentioned a curious figure named "Duke Amaniampong" known to some of his friends from his childhood years as "Kwabena Dogo," who had also been mentioned in the January 7, 2010, *Financial Times of*

---

[92] *The Chronicle*, in a Jan. 11, 2010, front cover story by Daniel Nonor, titled "GOV'T SWOOPS ON KOSMOS ENERGY – As Betty Mould-Iddrisu Readies for Prosecution."

London story. Amaniampong, a San Francisco, California-based lawyer who the media had referred to as "protégé of Tsatsu Tsikata" and also a relative of the Attorney General Betty Mould-Iddrisu, was working for the Ghanaian investigation.

"YET ANOTHER WILD GOOSE CHASE—KOSMOS/EO PROBE FIASCO UNDERWAY"

"Yet another wild goose chase is underway as the Serious Fraud Office (SFO) and the Attorney-General embark on investigations into alleged criminal deals involving KOSMOS and the EO Group relative to their stake in West Cape Three Points block of Ghana's oil field. . . . our sources at the AG's Department have intimated that investigations have so far failed to establish any solid and factual basis (prima facie) for the allegations . . .

"Our sources also revealed that as far back as June 2009, a meeting attended by Attorney-General and Minister of Justice, Mrs. Betty Mould-Iddrisu, one Duke Amaniampong, widely believed to be a Tsatsu Tsikata protégé, Robert Reeves, General Counsel of Anadarko and others, in Washington D.C., USA, was briefed that no specific violation of the Foreign Corrupt Practices Act (FCPA) had been committed in the Kosmos/EO deal in Ghana or the US . . . The said meeting was also told that the Ghana government/ Anadarko-sponsored international investigators were not able to find any link between a prohibited act and any Ghanaian government official or party official . . .

"'In view of the abysmal failure of both Ghanaian and external investigators to find a 'smoking gun,' the Attorney-General is now inclined to pursue the third option of forgery or false declaration to public agencies against one of the partners of the EO Group. There is talk of the said partner allegedly forging signatures of his other partner and his wife for the purpose of registering the EO

Group and other related companies with the Registrar General's Department' . . .

"On-going investigations by The New Crusading Guide have revealed that the investigations by the SFO and the AG are driven by suspicions, wild-cat perceptions, unfounded allegations and sheer bitterness on the part of certain persons who once held sway over Ghana's oil industry and are scheming in the shadows to re-assert their influence, control and command. 'Those persons . . . are not accountable to anybody. They are virtually shadow Attorney Generals and Ministers of Energy. They are driven by unbridled bitterness and hatred which have no real foundation. But history will surely expose them and their evil plans,' reflected our sources who spoke to us on condition of strict anonymity."

—*The New Crusading Guide*, January 12, 2010[93]

Four days later, on January 16, 2010, GhanaWeb.com ran a lengthy story on their website, titled "EO—KOSMOS PROBE HEADING FOR AN ANTI-CLIMAX," which opened with the statement, "Protracted and in-depth investigations sponsored by Anadarko Petroleum and the Government of Ghana (GoG) into alleged criminal deals including possible violation of the Foreign Corrupt Practices Act (FCPA) of the USA . . . have hit a wall as no credible evidence of criminality and illegality was uncovered by the investigators."[94]

It was nice to know that I had more supporters in the media than I had assumed. But there was only one problem with this back and forth newspaper slugfest: they were all citing "unnamed, highly placed, inside sources." Somebody had to be wrong. No matter what I knew to be true, no matter what the newspapers were saying, no matter what I

---

[93] *The New Crusading Guide*, in a Jan. 12, 2010, story titled "Yet Another Wild Goose Chase – KOSMOS/EO PROBE FIASCO UNDERWAY" (p.3).

[94] The online news website GhanaWeb.com, quoting a story titled "EO – Kosmos Probe Heading For An Anti-climax!" on their "General News of Thursday, Thursday, 16 January 2010" page. See: http://www.ghanaweb.com/GhanaHomePage/NewsArchive/artikel.php?ID=175233

hoped would happen, the final decider would be Betty Mould-Iddrisu. And she didn't like me. In fact, her steadfast, public drumbeat that I was guilty of committing a crime and was going down felt downright personal. And powerful international players would soon be expressing the same sentiment about her.

Then, on January 18, 2010, came the game-changer, something I had feared more than all else during the most nerve-wracking year I had ever spent on earth. The title of the story in *The New Crusading Guide* headlined the news in such light-hearted, almost trivial terms, sounding like more of the same tit for tat, negative versus positive stories, that I nearly missed one number and three tiny words:

> **"MILLS' 'WITCH-HUNT' IN TOP GEAR! . . . AS AG**
> **PREPARES TO FILE A CHARGE OF '25 COUNTS'**
> **AGAINST EO MINUS KOSMOS"**
> "Alleging Causing Financial Losses of $1Bn, $300m, $250,000
> To A Public Body (GNPC), Illegal Transfer Of $175,000, False
> Declarations to Public Agencies (Forgery), Failure to Call Annual
> General Meetings Of The Company & Failure to Circulate Profit &
> Loss Account, Balance Sheet & Reports, etc, etc!"
> —*The New Crusading Guide*, January 18, 2010[95]

"25 Counts," the headline had stated. That was a lot of charges. Probably enough to make some of them stick with a jury. I was in trouble. And what about that *"Minus KOSMOS"* tag line? All along, the news reports—both pro and con—had, for the most part, lumped EO Group and Kosmos Energy together, with only every other story or so focusing exclusively on me and my alleged misdeeds. How had Kosmos

---

[95] *The New Crusading Guide*, in a Jan. 18, 2010, story titled "MILLS' 'WITCH-HUNT' In Top Gear! ...As AG Prepares To File A Charge of '25 Counts' Against EO Minus KOSMOS; front page banner (story p.2).

suddenly been removed from the A.G.'s steady, angry attack of the past year? Had they traded in their deal with ExxonMobil in order to save their own skin?

How had EO Group, all by our little old selves, caused a one-and-a-third billion-dollar loss to the State of Ghana? It was illogical to assume, as the news report had, that the omission of Kosmos from the charges was an indication that the July 22, 2004, Petroleum Agreement was above board and properly and lawfully executed, because if the A.G. considered the agreement to have been legitimate, then there would have been no reason to prosecute EO Group for causing a ten-figure loss to the State. What was their premise by which my actions had caused something like that? It didn't make sense. None of the other charges added up to the state losing over a billion dollars of their above board and lawful share of Jubilee Field, either.

The story continued . . .

> ". . . The 'Witch hunt' has began [sic]. . . . the 'stubborn cats' in the Mills Administration are bent on pursuing the course of malicious prosecution with reckless abandon. . . . the Attorney General and her collaborators including one Duke Amaniampong and a former GNPC top shot (identity withheld for now), have opted, against sound legal advice, to file charges against the owners/directors of the EO Group . . .
>
> "They know that investigations have proved that the charges have no basis and cannot stand a test of critical judicial scrutiny in a court of competent jurisdiction. They have been so advised by both their internal and external legal advisors and consultants (minus Duke Amaniampong) but they are not interested in listening to wise counsel.
>
> "Our sources noted the significance of the omission of Kosmos and any official of GNPC or Ministry of Energy or the Kufuor Administration on the charge sheet, and wondered how

the owners/directors of the EO Group could on their own and by themselves have conspired to willfully cause over one billion and three hundred million United State dollars financial loss to a public body (GNPC) and the Republic (State) of Ghana for that matter without collaboration from people in the GNPC and the Ministry of Energy/Government of Ghana. They also added that omission is also a loud declaration by the powers that be that the July 22, 2004 petroleum agreement among Kosmos, EO, GNPC, Ghana Government was above board and properly and lawfully executed.

"'The owners and directors of EO Group are mere scapegoats. After the futile search for evidence to link former President Kufuor and his men to the Kosmos/EO Group, something still had to be done, hence the targeting of George Owusu and Bawuah Edusei . . .' reflected a senior staff member of the AG Department."

—*The New Crusading Guide*, January 18, 2010[96]

It still did not explain how Kosmos had suddenly gotten themselves off the A.G.'s hook. Had they cut a secret deal? And what was the meaning of the parenthetical phrase "minus Duke Amaniampong" in reference to the fact that the A.G. and her internal and external legal advisors and consultants had been advised to drop their pursuit of the 25 charges against me? Who was Duke Amaniampong, this "protégé" of Tsikata? It was looking increasingly likely that someone was the puppet master stirring things up against me, and was now pushing this mysterious Duke Amaniampong to lean on the Attorney General. Why did this "San Francisco lawyer" disagree with all the other professional investigators and legal advisors who said that prosecuting me would be futile? Who was this guy, and what was his problem against me? Was it a proxy war against Kufuor and I was just a pawn?

Who knows? I had bigger things to worry about: the story revealed that the A.G. was getting ready to hand down 25 criminal charges

---

[96] Ibid.

against me. Mould-Iddrisu's next move would be to formally file charges against me, revoke my Police Inquiry Bail, and set a trial date. That would officially lock me inside Ghana indefinitely. The trial could last for *years*.

A story two days later appeared as a front page banner headline, "TSATSU TSIKATA 'FINGERED'". . .

"TSATSU TSIKATA 'FINGERED' . . . AS AG'S PROTRACTED 'FISHING' FOR FCPA VIOLATIONS ENDS WITHOUT 'A CATCH'"

". . . former Chief Executive of Ghana National Petroleum Corporation (GNPC), Mr. Tsatsu Tsikata has been playing an active role in investigations being conducted by Attorney General's office into the acquisition of exploration and production rights in Ghana's Jubilee Fields . . .

"Until this paper stumbled upon the evidence, Mr. Tsikata's role had been largely a matter of speculation and conjecture . . . However, last week, our research counterparts in San Francisco, California, United States of America, (USA), were able to 'intercept' enough material of great evidential value which conclusively es-tablished a linkage between Mr. Tsikata . . . and Ghana's Attorney General, Betty Mould-Iddrisu, Duke Amaniampong, a Ghanaian lawyer resident in USA and Mr. Kweku Mortey, the Executive Director of Ghana's Serious Fraud Office (SFO) . . . as far as the Kosmos/EO Group investigations are concerned.

"The 'evidential material' courtesy [of] sources close to Duke Amaniampong, clearly underscored Mr. Tsikata's directive to Attorney General Betty Mould-Iddrisu, Duke Amaniampong and Kweku Mortey, to study a 'press release' dated February 11, 2009 on what he (Tsikata) saw as, 'A LOT HAPPENING ON THE FOREIGN CORRUPT PRACTICES ACT (FCPA) FRONT'. . . . 'Apparently . . . Mr. Tsikata had a hunch that something similar [to the 2003 U.S. Department of Justice FCPA violation investigation and February 2009 conviction of KBR, a Halliburton subsidiary in Nigeria] might have transpired in the Kosmos/EO Group's dealings with the GNPC in July 2004, hence his decision to call the attention of Betty Mould-Iddrisu, Duke Amaniampong and Kweku Mortey to 'A lot happening on the FCPA front' . . . Duke Amaniampong, motivated by Mr. Tsikata's directive and or information, quickly communicated his 'confirmed itinerary' to both Mrs. Mould-Iddrisu and Mr. Tsikata on November 2, 2009, just a day after Mr. Tsikata's 'red alert' (directive information) . . .

"Both our AG Department and San Francisco sources expressed great surprise that in spite of the clear and solid evidence available to the Attorney General to the effect there had been no specific violation of the FCPA, she (AG) would still allow Mr. Amaniampong and Mr. Tsikata to propel the pursuit of a fruitless 'fishing expedition' in search of a non-existent crime at huge public expense.

"By June 2009, the Attorney General and her collaborators knew that chasing a violation of the FCPA was bound to be a mirage and yet 5 months down the line in November 2009, Mr. Tsikata was alerting the Attorney General on 'A lot happening on the FCPA front' relative to the Halliburton saga in Nigeria, while his protégé (Duke Amaniampong) was busily confirming his itinerary to Accra, Ghana, to help investigate Kosmos/EO Group's equity in the Jubilee oil fields which the Attorney General had in July 2009 declared legal and above board."

—*The New Crusading Guide*, January 20, 2010[97]

---

[97] *The New Crusading Guide*, in a Jan. 20, 2010, story titled "Fall-Outs From Kosmos/EO Probe - TSATSU TSIKATA 'FINGERED'...As AG's Protracted 'Fishing' For FCPA Violations ends Without 'A Catch'"; front page banner (story on p.3).

As the news media finally fit this last puzzling piece into place as to who had been stirring things up against me for so long, a revelation hit me: all I had been put through hadn't been initiated by politics and a crazy Attorney General. The vendetta against me seems to have been launched by a formerly connected Svengali who had been pushing Mould-Iddrisu, pushing Mills, pushing the CID, to do his bidding. Just as I had initiated my quest for oil as a way to lift up my fellow Ghanaians who were struggling in our country, this person may have initiated his quest for revenge as a way to lift himself up over a fellow Ghanaian who was innocent. The time for honoring himself was coming to an end.

It was a relief to have public confirmation of the identity of one of my most bitter detractors and his California sidekick. It was also nice to feel such support and to finally read some real investigative journalism from the media.

But the fight wasn't over. Not by a long shot.

CHAPTER

29

25 COUNTS

In mid-January, before A.G. Betty Mould-Iddrisu had had a chance to officially file the 25 criminal charges against me, someone on her staff leaked them to the press.

The document had been prepared by Gertrude Gladys Aikins, Director of Public Prosecutions, on the orders of Attorney General Betty Mould-Iddrisu. The list went on and on. Among them were four counts of Conspiracy to, or Causing, Financial Loss of $1.3 billion to the government of Ghana; two counts of Money Laundering, for transferring tens of thousands of dollars outside of the country; seven counts of Conspiracy to, or Forging of, Official Documents; six counts of Willfully Making a False Statement; one count of Deceit of Public Officer; and several others.

I felt like the blood had drained from my body after I read the 25 counts.

Around the same time the 25 charges were announced, Nathan Dimock, a trial lawyer with the U.S. DOJ, reached out to Phil Inglima. Inglima told Dimock he would make a proffer presentation to the DOJ of exactly what I would tell them under oath. Inglima requested two things in exchange for the proffer.

"First," Inglima told Dimock, "we want you to see through what's happening here with George. We believe Anadarko may have gone to you guys to manipulate this process for purely commercial gain, to use the U.S. DOJ and the Ghanaian Ministry of Justice to strip EO Group of their interest in the petroleum transaction."

Inglima explained to Dimock that it was obvious what Anadarko and Ghana's A.G. were trying to do. This was a huge oil discovery, for which more than $4 billion dollars had been offered just for Kosmos Energy's share alone. It was all about money, pure and simple.

"They're working you guys," Inglima told Dimock. "Please tell us that you are not going to take at face value anything you hear from them. Give us an opportunity to address the issues from our side. Give us a chance to show you the lay of the land in Ghana."

"The second thing we want," Inglima told Dimock, "is that if we persuade you, then we want a promise that you will clear our client. Because he's under the sword of Damocles in Ghana right now. We really think George is in peril. We are convinced that they want not just to strip him of his interests, they want him in jail. This is tantamount to a political prosecution."

Inglima was aware that the U.S. Justice Department didn't want to get involved in the internal politics of Ghana and how they went about their justice system. He knew the DOJ wasn't going to call Ghana and tell them to back off. But he was genuinely concerned that I was on the verge of being railroaded into what could be an indefinite incarceration.

Dimock assured Inglima that the DOJ would make an independent

decision and would not allow themselves to feel constrained by anything going on in Ghana. He also told Inglima that they had received
no transcripts from my many sessions with the CID in Ghana and were
interested in what I had to say about the accusations against me.

Inglima reiterated how hopeful he was that the DOJ's outcome
might have some influence on the Ghanaian process, which was clearly
politically motivated and seemed to be headed for a disaster for me. He
impressed on Dimock that the U.S. DOJ taking a stance on the situation would have an enormous political impact in Ghana, because the
people understood the resources, rigor, and integrity the United States
legal process brought with it.

What went unsaid was that lately the political tide had turned
against foreign business investment entities that had been welcomed by
the previous administration in Ghana. Inglima was basically requesting
that the DOJ work quickly, because time was growing short for me. All
the better if the DOJ would be able to see through the political situation
and issue a ruling that might save me from prison. Dimock made no
promises, but assured Inglima they'd give us a reaction to our proffer
based upon what they knew on their end.

Inglima and Femi Thomas then came to Ghana so I could help
them prepare the proffer presentation to make to Dimock and his team.
When we were finished, they left for Washington, D.C. All I could do
was to wait for a response. After the DOJ finished making an initial
assessment, they would summon me to D.C. to answer questions. I
could only pray the Ghana A.G. would let me out of the country to go
to Washington when that time came.

In the meantime, I had oil consortium work to tend to. I was nervous about the upcoming interview with the FBI and DOJ and looked
forward to the distraction business would provide for me during the next
few weeks. It was a particularly busy period of time. We were getting
ready to start production on Jubilee Field, and the consortium partners

were starting to have meeting after meeting. One crucial partnership meeting was scheduled for a Wednesday vote in London. As a partner in the consortium, it was crucial that I be at the meeting.

There were no restrictions against my traveling outside of Ghana during the Attorney General's legal proceedings; however I was still required to inform the authorities if I had foreign travel plans. Previously, anytime I had to travel outside of Ghana, my lawyer would tell them I needed to go, and it had been no problem.

This time, it was a problem.

On Monday, the week of my departure, the CID called and requested that I go in for another interrogation that Wednesday. I told them I couldn't. I had a meeting in London. I suggested another day.

That day wouldn't work, they said, because the investigator was attending a funeral. I suggested another investigator who had questioned me on previous occasions.

He can't, they replied, because he was on Parliament business. The CID suggested I postpone my travel plans. I told them that was impossible; the partnership meeting was scheduled and I had to be there. I suggested we do it later that day or wait until I come back from London. They replied that they couldn't do that.

"You have to be here," they stated.

"I have responded to every request you've made of me," I replied. "You've had free access to me for an entire year. Every time you call me in, I'm there. I'm not going to run away from this. I've been in and out of the country and I always return. I see no reason why I can't postpone."

"You have to be here."

"I'm here now. Ask me whatever you want."

"No. How about tomorrow?"

"I can't. I'm traveling tomorrow."

They wouldn't budge. It was as if once the 25 charges had been publicly revealed, the CID wanted to exercise a new level of control over me. I told them I'd talk to them later, and I phoned my law firm in Washington, D.C. They asked me if I planned to return to Ghana. I told them that I was.

"Then go," they advised me.

Against the demands of the CID, I departed, per my schedule, for London. My schedule was to fly from Accra to London and then back to Accra. Kosmos had paid for my round-trip airfare, because as part of our agreement, they had to cover my expenses until first oil.

After my London meeting, I was informed that the CID and Attorney General Mould-Iddrisu were very angry with me because I had not gone to the interrogation. I was afraid that if I returned to Accra, they would drum up charges against me that I had jumped bail; then they'd arrest me and imprison me. So I decided I could not go back to Accra.

Without telling them why, I called Kosmos and asked them to re-route my return ticket to Houston instead of Accra.

They refused.

I told them that the reason was because my life could be in danger, that I could be jailed the minute I landed in Accra.

They still refused to help me, explaining to me that I didn't work for them any longer.

I countered that, as part of our partnership contract, they were required to provide me with roundtrip airfare anytime I attended a business meeting, and that they would be reimbursed for such expenses when my share of the field was sold or otherwise monetized. I explained that there was nothing different this time, except that I did not want the return leg of the trip to be in Ghana.

They still refused.

I was stranded in London. So I called some friends and family members and purchased a one-way ticket from London to Houston.

Then Kosmos called me. They told me that they could not help me because it would be a red flag to the U.S. DOJ that Kosmos might be helping me avoid investigation by the authorities.

It was yet another instance where people I thought were my friends and partners had abandoned me at my lowest point. Kosmos seemed to be perfecting these needlessly hurtful business decisions to an art where I was concerned. My life and freedom were in peril. I was deeply hurt. To save their own skin, they didn't want to merely change my return to another city. I was constantly learning the hard way with Kosmos that bravery and loyalty were not their strong suit.

I traveled to the U.S. and took care of some business and family matters in Houston. In the meantime, back in Ghana, the CID had a field day with my departure for London. The news media erupted. Headlines blared, *"GEORGE OWUSU ON THE RUN!"* Newspapers reported that the FBI was chasing me and that I had "jumped bail."

As usual, newspapers were making stories up as they went along, without even trying to talk to me to get the facts right. To be fair, there were the news outlets that put in a decent effort at reporting the facts, such as *The New Crusading Guide* and the *Daily Guide*. But others, such as the *Ghana Eye* and my nemesis *The Enquirer*, treated facts and truth as anathema to their business plan and political bent. Information was being fed to these government-sponsored newspapers, generally supplied to them by the CID.

The investigation had been going on for over a year by then. Reporters were running out of stories to come up with, so they were grabbing at wisps of anything to sensationalize and make the story look good for their side.

The CID's theatrics were in full swing, as well. After I had not appeared for the interrogation meeting they had refused to reschedule, they filed a motion with the court that I be "produced" before a magistrate to prove I hadn't fled the jurisdiction. Then I was informed that they had issued a BOLO (Be-On-the-LookOut) notice for me at the Kotoka International Airport in Accra and all points of entry into Ghana, with instructions that I was to be "arrested on sight."

As I was about to leave Houston for Ghana, an associate warned me not to come.

"They are going to publicly humiliate you," my friend told me. "You'll be arrested at the airport, picture taken for the newspapers, paraded before a judge, have your inquiry bail revoked for leaving the country without permission, and taken straight to jail. Don't come."

The A.G. and CID's plan was to embarrass me, take my picture in handcuffs at the airport, and paint me as a fleeing criminal that they'd been clever enough to capture after he had tried to run. My friend advised me to stay in Texas for awhile to allow the situation in Ghana to cool down a little.

But I had never been officially restricted from leaving Ghana, and I had done my best to reschedule the CID interrogation before I left. When they had refused to accommodate my schedule, I had let them know that I had to go and that I'd see them on my return. I had been going above and beyond to deal with this travesty against me since late 2008. To add more pressure on me, my nephew Ransford, who had signed the 100,000 *cedi* Police Inquiry Bail on my behalf, was sent a court summons to produce me before the judge or pay the bill himself.

A half an hour after my return to Accra, I was resting in the hotel room Ransford had rented for me.

The morning of the hearing, I appeared in the courtroom, fresh as a daisy and looking appropriately puzzled at the proceedings, as if I'd had no clue why I had been accused of having fled Ghana. The state attorney arrived late. He did a double-take at me as if he was seeing a ghost standing there calmly. No police handcuffs. No cops hovering nearby.

"I understand this matter is about the disappearance of a defendant on a Police Inquiry Bail," the judge said, looking at the government lawyer. "Is Mr. Owusu present?"

"Yes, my lord," I responded. "I am here."

Those three words killed the suspicion of my having fled the jurisdiction. Outmaneuvered, the Attorney General's lawyer then made a verbal motion asking the judge to issue a bench bond requiring that I seek explicit court permission if I wanted to leave Ghana in the future.

The judge responded, "You asked for him to be produced in this courtroom today. He has voluntarily complied. Why should we limit his movement now?"

The lawyer started to answer. The judge waved her off.

"Look, this man has not been found guilty of anything. He has not been proven in a court of law to be a criminal. He has never left the country and refused to return to face any charges. He has been cooperating with you. I am not going to place any unwarranted imposition on him."

The motion was denied. *Hallelujah!* I thought, relieved that the judge hadn't allowed political winds or the rabid press to sway her. *God is great!* Each small victory like that was like a knife pulled out of me instead of being shoved in deeper. Small as they were in the bigger picture, I had learned to appreciate them.

That same week, news headlines claimed that I had been "bailed out of jail by a 17 year old boy," as they referred to my nephew Ransford. There was no "bailing out of jail" system in Ghana, nor was Ransford a boy. He was nearly 30.

I issued a release to the news media, stating that I was "not on the run and had not fled." I added that the CID had been informed of my whereabouts, as always.

None of it did any good.

February started with a news headline that claimed, "EO-Kosmos Rip-Off Exposed!—Royalties To Ghana Lowered In Favour Of Kosmos-EO." The story stated, "GNPC sources say the Kosmos-EO agreement was so bad that, it haunted the corporation throughout the subsequent agreements."

Whenever I read stories like those, I had to wonder, If the deal was "so bad," why did the GNPC negotiate it that way? Why did the Cabinet approve it? Why did the Parliamentary Select Committee on Energy approve it? Why did the full Parliament approve it?

February was no different than nearly every month for the past year, with battling headlines vying to get their political point of view across in the "news." A strongly worded commentary appeared, stating that America should withdraw all monetary aid to Ghana unless the government allowed the Kosmos Energy sale to ExxonMobil to go through. It was more proof that little Ghana had become a major pawn in the international political war to acquire resources to quench the world's thirst for energy . . .

"GHANA'S DUBIOUS NEW PARTNER"

"[American] Dollars aren't simply being delivered to corrupt regimes, helping keep them in power with nothing expected in return. Instead aid money is increasingly tied to serious reforms the countries must embrace to enhance the rule of law, enforce contracts, attract foreign capital and stamp out corruption. But recent actions taken by the government of Ghana deserve deeper scrutiny from Washington. What's unfolding on the ground in West Africa threatens to waste hundreds of millions of American taxpayer-funded aid dollars and undo hard-won reforms. It also threatens to supercharge China's continued rise in the region, at the expense of U.S. geopolitical and business interests.

"But this month Ghana's energy minister, Joe Oteng-Adjei, sent a letter to the Texas-based firm saying the proposed acquisition [of Kosmos by ExxonMobil] would not receive the government's consent. Instead Ghana 's state-run energy firm would be the only entity allowed to buy the Kosmos stake. While the minister promised the Ghana National Petroleum Co. would pay a 'fair market value' for the asset, that value would certainly be sent plummeting if there was only one bidder. What explains this bizarre move by the Ghanaian government? China signed an 'Agreement on Economic and Technical Cooperation' with Ghana at the end of 2009 and wants the Kosmos assets for its state-owned China National Offshore Oil Co.

"This development in Ghana is part of a larger pattern. China is now the second-largest consumer of oil after the United States, and the regime in Beijing is keen on securing access to energy supplies. It has been very active in Africa in recent years, even going so far as to hire former President George W. Bush's brother Neil to lobby for Chinese energy interests.

"While much of Ghana's progress can be traced to the sound macroeconomic policies adopted under former President John Kufuor, the country has also been helped by hundreds of millions of dollars of development aid extended it by the U.S. through the Millennium Challenge Corp. This program rewards recipients for reforming their laws and business practices to encourage investment and growth. And it has worked in Ghana—until the Chinese started moving in. Now the Ghanaians threaten to undo years of progress and make a mockery of millions of American taxpayers' dollars in the process."

—Dr. J. Peter Pham, February 26, 2010[98]

That sharp (though flawed) rap across the Ghanaian government's knuckles was joined by a two-part story that ran on consecutive days in the *Wall St. Journal*. The first part was more of a double slap across Ghana's face . . .

---

[98] Dr. J. Peter Pham, Senior Fellow at the Africa Project at the National Committee on American Foreign Policy in New York and Vice President of the Association for the Study of the Middle East and Africa, in a Feb. 26, 2010, commentary titled "Ghana's Dubious New Partner." Source: A Feb. 26, 2010 press release from Tony Bullock, Sr. V.P. of Ogilvy Government Relations, Washington, D.C.

"WHY AFRICA IS POOR—GHANA BEATS UP ON ITS BIGGEST FOREIGN INVESTORS"

"President Obama headlined his first trip to sub-Saharan Africa last July with a stop in Ghana. Speaking to the parliament in Accra, Mr. Obama praised the country's growth and its example that 'development depends on good governance.' Eight months later, Ghana's government is turning the nation into a cautionary tale for foreign investors.

"Exhibit A is the case of Kosmos Energy, a U.S. company based in Texas, which has lately seen capricious government meddling in a deal to sell a $4 billion stake in a Ghanaian oil field to ExxonMobil Corp. Ghanaian Energy Minister Joe Oteng-Adjei suggested in a letter to Exxon reviewed by Journal reporter Will Connors that the government would 'support the strategic intent and efforts of [Ghana National Petroleum] to acquire Kosmos's Ghana assets at a fair market value.' By 'fair market value,' Mr. Oteng-Adjei means fire-sale prices. . . . the desired affect was achieved. The strategy lets the government disavow its intention to directly intervene in deals while potentially scaring away potential buyers and making it possible for the government to buy the oil fields cheaply, possibly reselling them to a third party.

"That's the kind of official thuggery more frequently associated with the likes of Nigeria, where the vast oil and gas resources have driven corruption and exploitation while the people continue to live in poverty. . . . Other foreign investors are also getting the Kosmos treatment. . . After getting a license for offshore exploration in November 2008, the Norwegian oil company Aker was told this year that its development license was invalid, though the agreement had been unanimously approved by Ghana's parliament.'

"Attracting foreign investment has been a pillar of Ghana's development strategy, with the government pitching itself as the 'Gateway to West Africa.' Spooking new investors by repudiating contracts will rapidly ruin the country's prospects for long-term development. The Obama Administration has so far been silent on the shadows now haunting the country it heralded as a source of hope and leadership in Africa."

—*Wall St. Journal*, February 27, 2010[99]

The pressure was on Ghana from all sides to do the right thing. The *Wall St. Journal* didn't let up. Their beatdown of both the emerging oil player and America's President continued the following day . . .

"WHY AFRICA IS POOR II—GHANA TALKS NICE WHILE STRONG-ARMING FOREIGN INVESTORS"

"Ghana hasn't been a model citizen when dealing with foreign investors lately, but to hear the country tell it, more U.S. companies should be jumping in to develop its nascent oil resources. . . Ghanaian ambassador Daniel Ohene Agyekum said the country's stability makes it fertile ground for foreign capital and dismissed problems with investors as an 'irritant.' That might not be the first word that comes to mind for Texas-based Kosmos Energy. In recent months, the company's plans to sell a $4 billion stake in a Ghanaian oil field to Exxon Mobil degenerated into a spectacle of official thuggery as government ministers threatened to block the deal.

" . . . Ghana Minister for Information John Tia Akologu admonished that government meddling in the Kosmos/Exxon deal was merely evidence that Ghana 'insists that all investors operate lawfully.' The government still hasn't cleared the deal. The fiasco has become an embarrassment for the Obama Administration . . . While reviewing funding for foreign aid grants, U.S. lawmakers

---

[99] The *Wall St. Journal*, in a Feb. 27, 2010, article titled "Why Africa is Poor—Ghana Beats Up On it's Biggest Foreign Investors." Also see: http://www.wsj.com/articles/SB10001424052748704804204575069511746613890

have also questioned the practice of giving hundreds of millions of
dollars to a country in the habit of menacing U.S. businesses that
invest there . . . House Foreign Operations Chairman Nita Lowey
noted that 'we're seeing business as usual, corruption as usual,
and we're not seeing the lifting up of people in the country to make
this really different.'

"Ambassador Agyekum said . . . that foreign investment is
the key to Ghana's successful development. This would be more
credible if the country showed it believes in property rights and the
rule of law."

—The *Wall St. Journal*, Feb. 28, 2010[100]

None of these news stories were helping my case. The anti-Kosmos
pieces only seemed to harden Mills' resolve not to cave to whatever
America or the NPP were pushing. And China was grinning on the
sidelines, ready to massage out America's slaps against Ghana with a lot
of hard cash.

The *Wall St. Journal* stories and others like them were trying to tell
Ghana how to treat foreign investors who were taking money out of U.S.
and European markets or other monetary instruments and investing in
something that had eluded Ghana for over a hundred years: oil. The
message was that the best way to get rid of companies that were putting
money into your country would be to bully those companies around.
They would leave, all right. And your citizens would lose hope of any
possibility of rising up to a better socioeconomic stratum. Instead, the
message said, these investors should be treated fairly and made to feel
comfortable in that country, within the bounds of law and propriety, of
course. U.S. law and propriety, that is.

The *Journal* was attempting to admonish the Mills government, and
it was warning other investors who might want to come into emerging

---

[100] The *Wall St. Journal*, in a Feb. 28, 2010, article titled "Why Africa is Poor II—Ghana Talks
Nice While Strong-Arming Foreign Investors "

economies like Ghana that there would be some serious pitfalls along the way. However, I suspected that, had the situation been reversed, with a foreign company coming to Dallas and sharing proprietary data with which to solicit a bid for the oil field, the American partners would have put up the same stink Ghana was putting up with Kosmos.

What went unstated, however, and became obvious when the GNPC also began inviting bidders for the asset, was that the Ghanaian government wanted to be the only entity allowed to buy the Kosmos share, so they could then have the option of turning around and selling it to the Chinese (or any other party of their choosing) and carve out a quick extra billion in the deal for Ghana. What Ghana wanted was to become a middleman, rather than a gracious host country to foreign investors who were bringing in hundreds of millions of dollars worth of business and providing countless opportunities and thousands of jobs.

Nevertheless, what ExxonMobil and Kosmos and President Obama didn't seem to understand, with all their complaining and saber rattling at Ghana's refusal to bless the "irrevocable" $4 billion deal to sell Kosmos' share to ExxonMobil, was that President Mills was the guy in charge of the Government. That should have been obvious to everyone as soon as Ghana said *no*. A brewing legal war may have been an international lawyer's dream gig, yet, where things now stood was simple: any acquisition of the Kosmos percentage would require approval from the Government of Ghana. Period. Because any foreign company that blatantly disregarded the host country's wishes—whether those wishes were contractually relevant or not—would be escorted to the border.

I learned to ignore the news attacks, as well. Their *us-against-them* dueling stories would go on for as long as there were human beings who disagreed with one another's point of view.

Throughout February, the news droned relentlessly on, with each newspaper or television program examining every new morsel of information about the EO Group, George Owusu, and the Kosmos Energy saga, through the particular political lens of each individual news source.

CHAPTER

30

GRIM FAIRY TALES

Around late January to early February of 2010, Inglima and Thomas went to Washington, D.C. and made a two-hour proffer presentation to Nathan Dimock and his team of prosecutors and FBI agents at the Department Of Justice.

Inglima presented the history and background of how the transaction initially came about, the interests involved, the different percentages, and what it all meant. They laid out my case with a detailed timeline explaining the counterintuitive nature of the Ghana Attorney General's flawed argument. Ghana's case was that I had essentially been able to see into the future and knew exactly where the oil was, and that I had made a payment or promise of a future payment to a sitting President (who also supposedly happened to know where the oil had been all along) who then used his influence to pressure approval from the necessary managers, engineers, technicians, GNPC executives, the Ghana government, and the elected Parliament to give me the rights to the oil block—all at a price the government had approved . . . but which now the new government didn't like. A fairy tale worthy of the Brothers Grimm.

The DOJ and FBI had a few questions.

"How do we know there isn't going to be some money going to Kufuor later?" they wanted to know.

"There is no evidence of that having been discussed or set up," Inglima countered. "Why would anyone be paying the former President for something that he had no role in? The granting of the license was decided at a sub-minister level by technical people in the GNPC. Not by higher-ups. Certainly not a President."

Inglima took them through the myriad forms and paperwork and documents that had been generated during the entire application and approval process in 2003 and 2004.

"There's no substance behind any of Ghana's claims," Inglima stressed.

Dimock expressed interest in why Inglima kept referring to the CID questionings of me in Ghana as "interrogations."

Inglima explained that it was because that was essentially what the "interview" sessions of me were, repetitive questions asked again and again, session after session, for hours at a time, as if they were trying to break a suspect.

"As the sessions have gone on," Inglima said, "they've gotten more and more aggressive and interrogative in their technique."

Especially aggressive were the interrogations being led by Duke Amaniampong, the mysterious lawyer from San Francisco. Amaniampong was the man mentioned in the January 7, 2010, edition of the *Financial Times of London*[101] and had also been mentioned in the January 12, 2010, edition of *The New Crusading Guide* newspaper as a "protégé of Tsatsu Tsikata"[102] (who himself had also been mentioned in the *Financial Times of London* story). According to a story in *The New Crusading Guide* on January 16, 2010, Tsikata was the "former GNPC top shot in collaboration with AG [Betty Mould-Iddrisu, who had] contracted one Duke Amaniampong, a Ghanaian Lawyer resident in the US, to embark on a 'fishing expedition' which has turned out to be a 'wild goose chase.'"[103]

In effect, Amaniampong was serving as a defacto agent in the Attorney General's efforts to nail me. What expertise or credentials he brought to the process or what qualifications he had as an interrogator were never made clear. During the CID interrogation sessions of me that Amaniampong attended on behalf of A.G. Iddrisu, he personally asked me questions.

Dimock said he had heard from the Kosmos lawyers at Fulbright about some of what was happening in Ghana, and it concerned him. He made no assurance that any of the information Inglima shared would be off the record, and issued a proffer letter stating that the U.S. government would not directly use the information in a court proceeding.

Inglima again stressed his concerns about the repetitious and unending nature of the Ghana inquiry and interrogations of me, and repeated that he was hesitant to engage with the DOJ if they weren't prepared to make their own decisions as quickly and proactively as possible about what to do.

Dimock told Inglima that his presentation was persuasive.

---

[101] *Financial Times of London*, in a Jan. 7, 2010, story by William Wallis, Martin Arnold and Brooke Masters titled "Corruption Probe Into Sale of Ghana Oil Block." See: http://panafricannews.blogspot.com/2010/01/corruption-probe-into-sale-of-ghana-oil.html

[102] *The New Crusading Guide*, in a Jan. 12, 2010, story titled "Yet Another Wild Goose Chase – KOSMOS/EO PROBE FIASCO UNDERWAY" (p.3).

[103] *The New Crusading Guide*, in a Jan. 16, 2010, story titled "The Wild Goose Chase Is Almost Over: EO-Kosmos Probe Heading For An Anti-climax!"

"I want to see George Owusu," he told Inglima. "I'd like to interview him directly."

Inglima, cautiously trying to feel Dimock out, responded, "If you're going to trail behind the Ghana Investigations, that would make no sense to us."

Dimock assured him that the DOJ would come to a conclusion as quickly as possible after interviewing me.

"We'll go to Ghana or we can do it here," Dimock added.

I had been left to twist in the wind during the incessant CID investigations over the past year, basically under house arrest, unable to leave the country without Attorney General Mould-Iddrisu's blessing. When I did have to leave Ghana on business, Inglima's concern was that, as the Ghanaian government moved forward with actually prosecuting me, the A.G. might use one of those trips as a pretext for arresting me on charges of fleeing to avoid prosecution, and thereby set up a future expropriation of my share in the WCTP oil block.

"We want to do the interview here in D.C.," Inglima told Dimock. "We want to be out of the glare and manipulations in Ghana. But we'll need a proactive response. If Justice takes a wait-and-see attitude after meeting with George, then there's no benefit to George coming back here to do this interview."

Dimock made no promises, but assured Inglima, "Any DOJ decision would not be dependent on the Ghana decision. It would be independent, based on our own investigation."

They scheduled an interview with me for the third week of February. After the meeting, Inglima called and told me the meeting had ended on a note of guarded optimism. He said he read Dimock's assurance of independence as the DOJ's acceptance of the truth. All we could do now would be to hope that my meeting with the prosecutors and agents might possibly be an accelerant toward ending the Ghana investigation permanently. But the clock was ticking down, because 25 criminal counts were hovering over my head.

My next challenge was to get to the U.S. for the meeting. I was convinced Betty Mould-Iddrisu would never let me out of Ghana while her prosecution of me was getting underway, even though there was still no specific requirement that I receive permission to travel outside the country. I asked my lawyer, Addo Atuah, to contact the CID and request clearance for me to travel to the U.S. The CID refused. Atuah wrote a letter to the CID and explained to them that I needed to go to the U.S. on urgent business. The request was denied.

We contacted the U.S. Ambassador to Ghana, who contacted Minister of Justice Betty Mould-Iddrisu. She granted me permission immediately. I was a little puzzled. Was I being set up? Were Inglima's fears correct, that I was going to be arrested at the airport on my way to the U.S., with the police claiming I was fleeing to avoid prosecution? These were paranoid times for me. Anything was possible in Ghana, whether you were innocent or not.

My sources later contacted me and told me why Mould-Iddrisu had let me go so easily: when she was informed that the FBI wanted to question me, she was thrilled, and reportedly "danced in her office" with joy at the news because her sources had indicated that the U.S. government had certain plans for me. Her requests for America's DOJ to intervene in the prosecution of a crooked American who had violated the FCPA had finally been answered. The FBI was going to arrest me. Even some of the Ghanaian community in Houston was going after me in the news media as viciously as my detractors in Ghana.

I felt like an African piñata. No telling how many more blows I could take before I cracked.

CHAPTER

31

THE BREAKDOWN

For a person to voluntarily subject himself to an inquiry by the United States DOJ and the FBI, he had to be a little desperate. I wasn't desperate, but I was willing to go, even if it meant there might be a chance I might be charged by the DOJ with violation of the FCPA. Because I knew I had done absolutely nothing wrong.

I had been in America for more than three decades. I was a good U.S. citizen. I looked forward to telling my story to somebody who might actually listen to it with an open mind.

I was relieved that I wasn't in Ghana with the CID interrogators, but being the object of inquiry in the Justice Department was nerve-wracking. I don't remember being more anxious in my life.

The FBI questioned me for eight hours. We covered *everything*. I spoke candidly. I told them the truth. The FBI agents were straightforward. They didn't interrogate me, they simply asked me questions. It was straight Q&A. They indicated no bias one way or the other during the interview (as opposed to how I was treated by law enforcement authorities in Ghana). They pressed me about things that tied into some of the theories and concerns brought up by Anadarko, Kosmos, Mould-Iddrisu, the CID, and others.

They had the hardest time with things like EO Group receiving a 3.5% share of WCTP and that $250,000 payment we received from Kosmos.

"Why 3.5%?"

My answer was easy: "What's three and a half percent of zero?"

They got it immediately. There never was a guarantee we'd find anything in WCTP. It was a speculative venture that might have gone bust. Also, that was the percentage I had been hammered down to by Kosmos in our negotiation (from the 15% I'd had under my Ennex agreement with John Craven), and it came out of their share anyway. It was a non-issue.

"So, why $250,000?"

Another easy question.

"Why not?" I grinned. "I wanted a million dollars. I wanted five million. But I was happy to have $250,000 for all of my work instead of zero, and that's where we settled."

Even Kosmos knew that half of $250,000 was a tiny gift to have paid me for all I had done for them. And 3.5% was never going to break the Kosmos bank.

I explained to the agents and lawyers that somewhere inside the minds of the Kosmos executives and lawyers, considering my track record with them, there had to be some seed of understanding of how extremely fortunate they had been to be involved in Jubilee Field. I had taken them by the hand to the necessary ministries and patiently walked them through a complex licensing process for the WCTP block.

Knowing the people, the bureaucrats, the technicians, the ministry officials and managers, and establishing within them a trust in me and in Kosmos, and satisfying the many requirements all along the way as we worked through the process had made the achievement of our success that much easier.

Then, with the change of government, to the politicians bent on proving former President Kufuor wrong, I had become the easiest target. In spite of the fact that the EO Group/Kosmos Energy/GNPC/Government of Ghana Petroleum Agreement of July 22, 2004 had passed every legally required step and process, was in full compliance with the 1992 Constitution and the 1984 Petroleum Exploration and Production Law, and had the full approval of the GNPC top management and board of directors as well as the blessing of Ghana's Parliament.

Yet, through it all—the endless news media slander, the repeated CID and other police agency interrogations, the intense scrutiny by the Attorney General and her sending the U.S. Department of Justice the CID interrogation files on me, my own partners investigating me again and again, and Kosmos firing me without cause—I had remained steadfast, hardworking, and honest.

I gave the FBI every bit of information they requested, answered every question, and explained my actions and motives covering the better part of a decade in connection with anything having to do with Jubilee Field. We covered *everything*.

When I had first read Attorney General Mould-Iddrisu's 25 counts a few weeks before I had gone to the FBI, I was just as shocked at the list as Betty Mould-Iddrisu had been angry that it had been leaked to the press.

The list was breathtaking in length and scope. Money laundering. Forgery of official documents. Causing hundreds of millions of dollars of financial loss to the state. Making false statements. On and on. After my first quick read-through of the charges, my heart was racing and I was alternating between fainting and blowing up in anger.

Of the 25 charges listed, at first glance, the first four, related to my allegedly "Causing a Financial Loss to GNPC of $1.55 billion in May of 2004," were frightening. But as I dug into the allegations, I realized the A.G. had a huge problem with her claim: where did all those hundreds of millions, which I allegedly lost for the government, come from in the first place? In May of 2004, right after the government had negotiated what they felt was a good petroleum agreement for Ghana, we hadn't yet discovered or even produced one single barrel of oil to sell for fifty bucks, much less a billion dollars.

I wondered how Betty Mould-Iddrisu could lead a judge or jury through the money trail when there was no money, never had been, and no guarantee that it would be in the future. All she could point to were offers being made to purchase Kosmos' share in Jubilee Field several years after 2004—and none of those offers had even borne fruit, not a penny had exchanged hands, and the GNPC had never put forth an offer. And none of that had anything to do with me. The U.S. Department of Justice had grasped that logic immediately: they understood that there was no known commercial quantity in the WCTP in the beginning, because the oil venture was completely speculative. And any talk of estimates of the potential monetary value of the block had arisen only *after* we had made our big oil discovery.

The next two counts I analyzed involved the May 2004 "Money Laundering" allegation. That was also a scary accusation—of the type usually connected with drug dealers. But the fact was, I hadn't taken any cash and "laundered" it. The $175,000 was a simple bank wire transfer in connection with the $250,000 time and expense reimbursement paid to Bawuah-Edusei and I, and was readily traceable. The money had gone from the Kosmos bank account in America to my bank account in Ghana, and then half of it went on to Bawuah-Edusei. How was that "money laundering" when the passage of the money, all the way from point A to point B to point C, was well documented?

Nevertheless, that charge was nothing more than sensationalized political window dressing.

Next were the seven counts of "Forgery," which were directly related to the seven charges after those ("Making a False Statement" and "Deceit of Public Officer"). The most serious of these charges, that I had forged my partner's signature on the EO Group business registration form when we set the company up in Ghana, was possibly the single most potentially damaging charge against me. We knew Attorney General Mould-Iddrisu had contacted the Registrar General of Ghana, inquiring as to the repercussions of a company registered by means of an illegal act. Could the government cancel EO Group's business registration, and would that cause all of its subsequent activities to be invalid? Could the oil block be taken from us? Mould-Iddrisu was going for the fruit of the poison tree: if the signature on the company's founding document was fake, then the company was fake, and everything that flowed from it was illegitimate—including our ownership share in Jubilee Field, the most important oil discovery in Africa in over a decade.

However, even this allegation was easy to deal with: Bawuah-Edusei asserted by sworn statement that, as a busy physician in the United States, there were times when he simply couldn't travel to Ghana to deal with business matters, and with me in Ghana full-time, it was more efficient for him to authorize me to take all actions necessary to conduct the business of the partnership, including setting up the official company in Ghana, as well as signing any and all appropriate forms and documents on his behalf. There was no fraud and no attempt to copy his signature. I merely wrote (not signed) his name on a form, with permission from him and at his request. There was no crime; only efficiency and expediency. It was done all the time in the business world. *The New Crusading Guide* newspaper had even gotten hold of a copy of the document granting me signatory power for Bawuah-Edusei and printed it in its January 16, 2010 issue.[104]

Yet, in spite of our having Bawuah-Edusei's permission for writing his name, we took the extra precaution of hiring a legal expert in Ghanaian law to determine our chances of prevailing on that issue in a court of law. The essence of his two-page opinion stated the following:

> *"Mr. Owusu merely wrote the initials and surname of Dr. Edusei on the form. He did not attempt to copy, imitate or mimic Dr. Edusei's signature. In the light of these two facts, it is my opinion that it will be impossible to get Mr. Owusu convicted for forgery. . . . if what Mr. Owusu did amounted to forgery, would that be enough to justify seizing the assets of the company? According to Section 16 of the Criminal Offences Act (1960), what Mr. Owusu did will only amount to an intention to defraud if it can be proved that he did it with the intention to gain something of monetary value at the expense of Dr. Edusei. The facts I have examined do not support that conclusion. Mr. Owusu did not gain at the expense of Dr. Edusei."*

The good news was that even if a jury went against all laws and judged the offense to be forgery, the maximum fine was two months imprisonment or a fine of $2,000 or both, and the error would be ordered to be fixed. However, neither the company nor its assets could be seized nor the registration invalidated. Thus, even a guilty verdict of forgery would check any potential attempt by the A.G. to nullify registration of the company. The stiffest penalty that could be imposed against me would be two months in prison. And I'd been put through a lot worse than that by the government.

When I came to the next two charges, "Failure to Call an Annual Meeting" and "Failure to Circulate a P&L for 2003," I stopped and re-read the charges, thinking my eyes were playing tricks on me. No board meeting and no Profit and Loss statement? *Really?* Those were

---

[104] Ibid.

high crimes? I didn't even bother to analyze those charges.

After going through the 25 charges, I looked back over the allegations, and wondered, *Where's the big one everyone had been talking about incessantly for over a year, bribery of a public official, violation of America's FCPA law?* It wasn't there. Because it never happened.

That was it. The 25 charges boiled down to . . . nothing at all. I relaxed. I took a breath. I realized this wasn't an uphill battle after all. At worst, a negotiated settlement with the A.G.'s office, probably consisting of a small fine. At best, an across the board win with a jury. That is, if Betty Mould-Iddrisu was imprudent enough to put the charges before a jury at all.

As my sessions with the FBI and DOJ began to wind down, I started to relax. At the end of the final period of questioning, the agents were puzzled as to why I had come to the FBI at all. They could find nothing on me. No evidence of criminal activity, no wrongdoing.

When the official inquiry was over, I was asked, off the record, if I had ever been involved in a personal relationship with Betty Mould-Iddrisu.

"I've never even met her," I replied, puzzled by the question.

Through my lawyer, they gave me all of the documents that A.G. Mould-Iddrisu had sent to them after the CID had searched my office, and that was that.

I headed back to Ghana, wondering why Mould-Iddrisu had been so happy to let me go to the U.S. *What's waiting for me in Ghana this time?* I wondered in Houston as I boarded the plane back for Accra.

When Betty Mould-Iddrisu was told that I had arrived back in Ghana and that the FBI had questioned me, released me, and had declined to arrest me, she went apoplectic. She contacted the FBI and requested that they provide her with a copy of their file on me. The FBI refused.

The New Crusading Guide newspaper kept up the pressure on

Mould-Iddrisu with a front page headline story subtitled, "Charges Of Willfully Causing Financial Loss of $1.4bn To The State, Criminal & Illegal Acquisition Of Stake In Jubilee Oil Field, Etc., Dissipate Into Thin Air!"[105]

Attorney General Mould-Iddrisu had built up her case against me and had hinted at such grave accusations during the previous year that it almost seemed as if I must have at least committed murder. Yet, when the public read the charges to see what horrid things the Attorney General was claiming I had done, people were surprised. *That's it?* summed up the reaction of the public. Less than an uproar, the public's response was one of chuckling embarrassment for the A.G. herself; she was being looked at like she had lost her marbles.

After the CID had so relentlessly investigated me for more than one solid year, after Mould-Iddrisu had so carefully crafted the charges, after she had instructed the Director of Public Prosecutions to meticulously prepare the 25 counts against me, and after the press had boldly published the leaked charges for the world to see, Betty didn't file them. She didn't order me into court. Didn't have me remanded to the custody of law enforcement. She waited. Whether by plan or by the fierce reaction of the public and the news media to the charges she was supposed to file against me, she did nothing.

Based solely on the facts, Ghana's Minister of Justice had made the right decision not to file charges against me. With Anadarko's law firm exonerating me, the U.S. DOJ refusing to bring charges of an FCPA violation against me, the FBI washing their hands off it, and insiders in Mills' own government working against her by leaking documents to the press, Mould-Iddrisu's decision appeared to be calculated to save herself from public humiliation if she had lost a trial after blowing so much smoke and making threats and accusations for an entire year. Add in the steady drumbeat of public sentiment, much of which was now focusing

---

[105] Ibid.

on wanting the government to stop spending time and resources on efforts that did nothing to lift them up during an international economic collapse, and a news media that seemed torn right down the middle as to my innocence, and you had the perfect storm for an acquittal or, at the very worst, deadlock.

Mould-Iddrisu did the right thing in not filing. Sometimes the political decision also happened to be the right decision. And, perhaps she sensed the tide was turning.

I wasn't out of the woods yet. But I had almost reached the top of the mountain. Or the bottom of the gorge, depending on how I chose to look at things. And things were still looking pretty dismal.

With Mould-Iddrisu still lurking, with the CID an ever-present ghoul at her beck and call, and with access to my money cut off and no way to earn a living in Ghana, my wife and I moved back to Houston. I had lived in Ghana from 2004 to 2010. Most of my assets, my bank accounts, everything, were in Ghana. I didn't have much left in America. But now, I had nothing in Ghana.

CHAPTER

32

RAY OF HOPE

In May of 2010, the turret-moored Floating Production Storage and Offloading (FPSO) vessel was completed. Built by a Japan-based general contractor called Mitsui Ocean Development & Engineering Company (MODEC), it was the size of several football fields and cost $750 million to build.

The ship was christened FPSO *Kwame Nkrumah MV21* . . . ironically, the name of the man who had initiated the government's Preventive Detention Act over 50 years earlier. It was a program that had led to the destruction and scattering of my family when I was a child of ten. The name had now come back full circle, representing the rebuilding of the Owusu family name even greater than ever before. My father was now indelibly connected to the tumultuous and fascinating history of Ghana.

The Jubilee Field consortium partners were scheduled to go to the Jurong Shipyard in Singapore to inaugurate the ship before it was to be towed in June to its location in Jubilee Field and prepared for linking to the various production wells on the ocean floor beneath it.

Travel to Singapore would be difficult for me. Not only because the CID was still keeping tabs on my whereabouts, but because my bank accounts were still frozen. Not to mention that I had no income and no money to travel to Singapore for the ceremony.

I called Kosmos and asked for a ticket to Singapore. They refused. They didn't want to be seen by the Government of Ghana as helping me out. Besides, they reminded me, they'd already fired me. I reminded them that I was still a partner. They said, "Then pay your own way." I reminded them that our agreement was that they carry my expenses until first oil; and inauguration of the production vessel was part of my expenses. They still didn't want to pay my way. I told them it wasn't money out of their pocket, because contractually EO Group was required to reimburse them once production began. We went back and forth. Finally, they agreed, and bought me a ticket to Singapore.

When I got to Singapore for the big ceremony, the first thing I noticed was that all of the partners except for EO Group were furnished with luxury cars with drivers. I hitched a ride on the media bus. Life was hard for a pariah from Ghana in 2010, co-owner and initiating discoverer of one of the greatest oil finds in West Africa. The way I was being treated was horrible.

Arriving with the press corps, I got to the venue earlier than my fellow Jubilee owners and looked for my chair at the ceremonial grounds. Every company involved in Jubilee Field had reserved seating. Tullow had a group of chairs. Anadarko did. Kosmos. GNPC, of course. Even Sabre Oil did, though they declined to attend the ceremony. But there were no seats for EO Group.

I found some of the organizers and asked, "Hey, what's going on here—where's my seat?"

(Source: Author Records) The FPSO Kwame Nkrumah MV21

"Who are you?"

"I'm George Owusu."

"Okay. And how can I help you, Mr. Owusu?"

"I'm a partner in the consortium. Where are the seats for EO Group?"

If it was a bus in 1950s in America's south, he would have pointed to the back.

Mariama Issakah, who worked for Tullow and who knew me and my contribution to the event, was unhappy with how I was being treated and within minutes chairs were shuffled around and seating was arranged for me.

But it was embarrassing to have had to ask. Not embarrassing for me, but for my so-called partners.

The ceremony was no better. At the conference, a top representative from each company was to give a short talk. Each of them had prepared speeches. The Anadarko executive spoke, Tullow's exec addressed the gathering. Kosmos had their man talk. My name was nowhere on the schedule.

The genesis of the project, the one person whose history with Jubilee Field predated that of every person in the front row of the ceremony by nearly two years and one of the reasons these happy, smiling people were gathered that day to be honored and to give thanks for the new jobs that had been created and for the opportunity Ghana had been presented with, to lift the nation from poverty to Player, was nowhere on the schedule.

Near the end of the speeches, I was approached by someone from MODEC[106] who leaned in to me, almost as an afterthought, and asked me if I would like to say a brief word. I already felt enough like an unwanted burden. I said a big "NO."

From the moment Anadarko had reported me to the U.S. DOJ, to the first time the CID interrogated me a couple of weeks after that, to the day a few months later when Kosmos fired me as Country Manager, my partners (other than the Tullow executives) had treated me with nearly open contempt. I had never been dishonest with any of them. Never rude or disrespectful or dismissive or unhelpful. I was always eager to assist, ready to encourage, glad to add my 20 years of petroleum industry management experience to the collective effort and goal of the partnership. Yet, what they really wanted of me, once I had led them in through the doors of opportunity, was to simply go away.

It was beyond dismal. It was shameful. Pride could have gotten the better of me. There were times when it tried. But it wasn't pride or ego that gripped me that day as I sat and watched each of my partners go up to the dais, one after another, and tell the assembled guests and dignitaries and energy industry leaders about how proud they were of their involvement in one of Africa's greatest oil discoveries of the 21st century. It was a profound sadness.

"Partner" meant *equal, co-worker, collaborator*. Team member. If

---

[106] The Japan-based general contractor that had built our Kwame Nkrumah FPSO.

this was my partners' public embodiment of *partnership*, then it was a wonder these firms were able to function at all. Their leaders' methods of operating represented a great opportunity for better people than them to move in, take over, and build far greater companies.

I was learning.

And the cavalry was on the way.

On June 2, 2010, I received a letter. Addressed to my lawyer, Phil Inglima, it was written by Charles E. Duross, Acting Deputy Chief, U.S. DOJ, Criminal Division. It was short and to the point . . .

U.S. Department of Justice

Criminal Division

Charles E. Duross
(202) 353-7691 Direct Dial
charles.duross@usdoj.gov

Fraud Section
1400 New York Avenue, NW
Washington, D.C. 20005

June 2, 2010

VIA FEDERAL EXPRESS
& ELECTRONIC MAIL

Philip T. Inglima, Esq.
Crowell & Moring LLP
1001 Pennsylvania Avenue, NW
Washington, D.C. 20004

Plato Cacheris, Esq.
Trout Cacheris PLLC
1350 Connecticut Avenue, N.W.
Suite 300
Washington, D.C. 20036

Re: *E.O. Group, George Owusu, and Dr. Kwame Edusei*

Dear Gentlemen:

As you know, the Department of Justice (the "Department") received an allegation from Anadarko Petroleum Corporation of a possible violation of the Foreign Corrupt Practices Act of 1977, 15 U.S.C. §§ 78dd-2, *et seq.*, by the E.O. Group and its principals, including your clients, George Owusu and Dr. Kwame Edusei, and Kosmos Energy LLC in connection with securing licensing, exploration, and production agreements relating to petroleum blocks located in the territorial waters of the Republic of Ghana.

On behalf of your clients, you have provided certain information to the Department and made your clients available to the Department for an interview. Based upon our investigation and the information that has been made available to us to date, we presently do not intend to take any enforcement action against E.O Group or its principals, including Mr. Owusu and Dr. Edusei.

Very truly yours,

REDACTED

CHARLES E. DUROSS
ACTING DEPUTY CHIEF

cc: N. Nathan Dimock, Esq.

United States Department of Justice Investigation Resolution, 2010

I could have cried with joy.

The following week, *The New Crusading Guide* published a front page story titled "MILLS' 'MESSY OIL POLITICS' HITS HARD ROCK—KOSMOS, EO GROUP CLEARED," which stated that the "US Department of Justice (DoJ) finds no evidence to support Anadarko's allegation of violation of Foreign Corrupt Practices Act (FCPA)!" The story added that after the press had leaked the 25 charges against me on January 13, 2010, Attorney General Mould-Iddrisu had "openly lamented the loss (theft?) of the Charge Sheet from her office, and hinted of investigation into how the Charge Sheet disappeared . . ."[107]

The next day, the *Daily Guide* newspaper followed up with a commentary on the DOJ decision . . .

"EO GROUP VINDICATED"

"The United States Justice Department has cleared the EO Group and its two principals George Yaw Owusu and Kwame Bawuah-Edusei of all violations of Foreign Corrupt Practice Act (FCPA) in their acquisition of the West Cape Three Points Block in Ghana on July 22, 2004. This decision was reached after extensive investigations launched following allegations leveled by one of EO partners Anadarko Petroleum of Houston, Texas, yielded no evidence of FCPA violations.

". . . the new NDC government in Ghana also started its own investigations and used the state security agency to ransack the offices and homes of the EO partners collecting all documents, computer motherboards, bank records . . . As if that was not enough, the EO partners have also been subjected to intimidating and biased interrogation by state security agents, many of whom were politically appointed. . . . no Ghanaian company in our nation's history has ever endured such extensive, demeaning, humiliating

---

[107] *The New Crusading Guide*, in a June 6, 2010, story titled "Mills' 'Messy Oil Politics' Hits Hard Rock – Kosmos, EO Group Cleared"; front page banner (story p.3).

and invasive scrutiny based on such unfounded allegations.

"Unfortunately, despite the outstanding accomplishment by EO Group by inducing otherwise unwilling investors to come and take risk in Ghana which has now resulted in the formation of a vibrant oil and gas industry, there are some who are still seeking to destroy its good works. [The] discovery of commercial quantities of oil in Ghana cannot be mentioned without the due recognition of the role played by members of EO Group. The Group and its principals have indeed earned its rightful place in history for the transformational role in Ghana's history.

"Ironically, those spearheading this political persecuting are themselves running over each other to fully control Ghana's oil and gas for their selfish interest while depriving the risk takers of their due rewards. . . . now that the investigations have concluded, and EO Group is exonerated, the Ghana government . . . must accept it, do the right thing, and conclude its own investigation of Ghana's heroes."

—*Daily Guide*, June 10, 2010[108]

It had been a long time since a Ghanaian news report had referred to me as a "hero."

The fact that prosecutors from the United States DOJ and agents from the FBI had brought considerable resources to bear in coming to a conclusion that there was no basis for prosecution of me, was monumental, a potential game-changer. The decision was, effectively, commercial immunity. It was the U.S. government's way of saying, "Hands off George Owusu; we're not doing anything more on this." There had been no favoritism at play in coming to their conclusion. But I believe there was suspicion about Anadarko's motives in having formally

---

[108] *Daily Guide*, in a June 10, 2010, story titled "EO Group Vindicated" (p.2). See: http://www.ghanaweb.com/GhanaHomePage/NewsArchive/artikel.php?ID=1 837696

accused me to the American authorities of having violated the FCPA.

Anyone who had an interest in my being prosecuted by the DOJ was not happy with the letter from the most powerful investigative law enforcement entity in the world saying I'd done nothing wrong. A lot of money had been riding on my being incapacitated by the authorities.

The Duross letter was fuel for my efforts to convince my detractors to back down. My lawyer sent a copy of the letter to Betty Mould-Iddrisu.

When the U.S. government said I had done no wrong, I hoped for a phone call from Brian Maxted, apologizing for having fired me for believing whatever Betty Mould-Iddrisu had told him after his eight million pages of investigation documents had revealed that I'd committed no crimes. I never got that call.

A business commentary story in March titled "VANCO OIL FIND—ANOTHER EO HANDIWORK"[109] had painstakingly laid out the facts detailing EO Group's key involvement in the first major discovery of oil in Ghana and the long history of Ghana's lack of ability to find commercial oil before my return to my country. "Ghanaians are slated to be swimming in oil soon," the story began. It went on to tell how the EO Group/Kosmos discovery of the WCTP find had, "substantially reduced the risk formerly associated to the Tano Basin as [an] 'exploration graveyard'," and it gave a nod to my early efforts in helping Gene Van Dyke obtain a foothold in the lucrative Gulf of Guinea offshore in Ghana.

At last, credit was being given where credit was due. And my detractors were starting to fall by the wayside.

---

[109] Ibrahim Tanko, in a March 2, 2010, commentary published by the Diaspora Business Council titled "Vanco Oil Find – Another EO Handiwork." See: http://www.modernghana.com/news/266071/1/vanco-oil-find-another-eo-handiwork.html

"VANCO OIL FIND—ANOTHER EO HANDIWORK"

". . . in a few months, when oil-producing countries are mentioned, Ghana's name would be right there with the Angolas, the Nigerias, the Equatorial Guineas . . . As refreshing as that sounds, contextualizing these new discoveries behind all these African countries against Ghana's leadership reputation on the continent suggests a growth regression that cannot elate anyone. More so if you consider the fact that the one private sector entity most responsible for our current oil fortunes is also the most vilified company in our nation's history. Did you know that Vanco was led to Ghana by the duo who eventually became the EO Group?"

—Ibrahim Tanko, Diaspora Business Council, March 2, 2010[110]

As good as things appeared to be turning for me after the DOJ made their ruling, by July of 2010, the news seemed to be worse for Anadarko Petroleum. Eighteen months earlier the company had set all of the dominoes tumbling by reporting me to the DOJ, which had led to the Ghanaian A.G. launching her investigation of me, which had led to the CID interrogations of me, which had led to Brian Maxted firing me, which had led to banks shunning me. All of which had been churning up a relentless news media assault against me.

Now, Anadarko was paying—in a different way altogether. An analysis of the impact of the explosion of the Deepwater Horizon rig in the Gulf of Mexico three months earlier, published by the National Coordinator for an NGO called the Osagyefo Network for Rural Development (OSNERD), revealed that "BP has billed Anadarko more than $272 million for its share of cleanup and response costs." The report stated that, "assuming Anadarko is held liable for its 25% ownership in the well, the company may need to pay around $7.3 billion in the next few years," a figure that included "the company's potential share of cleaning up the spill, its contribution to the $20 billion claims

---

[110] Ibid.

fund announced by BP and the US government, and potential fines and penalties."[111]

Through July and August of 2010, things were becoming complicated for others involved in Jubilee Field activities, as well . . .

"ALARM BLOWS OVER FPSO KWAME NKRUMAH CONTRACT—TSIKATA 'GRABS' $5M DEAL . . . BUT IFC & WORLD BANK SUSPECT 'KULULU' & INITIATE 'FORENSIC PROBE' INTO HOW MODEC AWARDED CONTRACT TO HIS COMPANY (SOG) IN JUNE 2008!"
—*The New Crusading Guide*, July 26, 2010[112]

"ENDANGERING OUR COLLECTIVE INTERESTS . . . TSIKATA'S 'CORRUPT' ACTS DELAY OIL! . . . WORLD BANK LAUNCHES INVESTIGATIONS"
—*Daily Searchlight*, July 28, 2010[113]

However, while I appreciated the news media leaving me alone for awhile, I knew they were far from finished with me.

---

[111] Stephen Yeboah, National Coordinator for the NGO Osagyefo Network for Rural Development (OSNERD). See: http://www.ghanaweb.com/GhanaHomePage/NewsArchive/artikel.php?ID=185868

[112] *The New Crusading Guide*, in a July 26, 2010, story titled "Alarm Blows Over FPSO Kwame Nkrumah Contract – TSIKATA 'GRABS' $5m DEAL"; front page banner (story p.3).

[113] *Daily Searchlight*, in a July 28, 2010, story by Betty Dadzie and Charles Quaye titled "Endangering Our Collective Interests...TSIKATA'S 'CORRUPT' ACTS DELAY OIL!"; headline banner (story p.2).

CHAPTER

33

ANOTHER KICK IN THE TEETH

In September, Kosmos pulled the trigger on me. Again. This time, they fired the law firm they had hired for me, Crowell & Moring, by cutting off payment of their fees.

Phil Inglima protested because, although I had been cleared by the U.S. government, I was still under assault from the Ghanaian government and still required representation. Firm in their decision, Kosmos refused to reconsider, explaining that they were bleeding money from ongoing development costs of the Jubilee Field. Inglima reminded them that they had fired me without cause, on the word of the Ghanaian Attorney General who had accused me of committing crimes—charges that had been investigated and dismissed by the United States DOJ. Therefore, my firing had been questionable, at best. But what were we going to do, sue Kosmos in Ghana for unlawful termination? Even if that was a legal option in that country, I couldn't afford it.

"George," Inglima told me, "we are not going to abandon you. This isn't over. We will keep sending you bills, and one day we believe you will be able to pay them. But we just don't walk away from our clients. Right now, let's get you free and clear."

Talk about a prince among men. His belief in me only increased my belief in myself all the more. I knew that within any company—law firm or not—it was not a popular business approach to delay payment from a client with zero income while continuing to provide him with services. Inglima had just created a loyal friend and client for life.

As relieved as I was at Inglima's generosity, if I thought I had known pressure before, it was nothing compared to what I was now experiencing. A man needs to know he can pay his bills. I was taking blood pressure medicine like popcorn, pushing myself relentlessly forward like a machine, keeping all of the roiling emotions at bay inside me, and ignoring the voices in my head that were telling me to quit, to move back to America and put together a nice life in Houston like I had enjoyed for many years before I had gone to Ghana to get into this adrenaline pumping, evil, exhilarating, cruel business.

But cutting off my lawyer fees was only half of the new move Kosmos was making against me. The other half came during the last week of September 2010, when I was summoned to a meeting at Kosmos Energy's headquarters in Dallas, Texas. After a tedious preamble, the message they had for me was short and to the point. I was informed that, although I was a partner in the oil consortium and had taken Kosmos to Ghana and had been subsequently subjected to "all this trouble" (which, they added, "we know is not your fault"), they "have decided to make peace with the Government of Ghana."

Okay. So far, so good. It was no secret that the well had been poisoned, so to speak, with all of the negative press over the previous couple of years. And it was nice to hear that the GNPC and Kosmos were going to stop bickering and play nice. But then I was given the real reason I had been summoned.

"As of first oil," Brian Maxted told me, "we will be making cash calls."

Basically, he was saying, I was on my own. It would have felt the same if he had kicked me in the gut. He went on to explain that since the Government of Ghana wasn't giving any of the partners consent to sell their share in Jubilee Field, EO Group was worth nothing.

To meet the ongoing expenses, Tullow issues cash calls to correspond with expenditure associated with the field. EO Group's 3.5% equity interest in WCTP was a "carried interest." In other words, our agreement with Kosmos was that they would pay for all exploration and appraisal costs, and would carry EO Group's 3.5% share of development expenses, for which we would pay them back.

The question was, when did we have to pay them back? What contractually triggered payment due? Our agreement stated that if and when the partners were successful in finding oil, then all of EO's share of the past costs for development would have to be reimbursed to Kosmos *and* we would also have to begin paying our portion of costs moving forward.

Fair enough. We were in a business partnership together. We had to pay our share. The problem was, however, that the revenue that was going to come to EO Group would not be enough to pay for the arrearages, because of our particular *trigger*. I was about to learn the hard way about a potential downside to being carried by a partner: the "trigger," the particular event that would cause payment due for our past costs and for our share of the bill moving forward. Our trigger was "first oil." And it was going to kill us. Because first oil meant when the first drop of crude hit the bottom of the tanker, we were instantly going to be required to come up with 3.5% of the cost of paying for the salaries of hundreds of crew members and staff, tons of equipment, a floating production storage and offloading vessel and other ships, fuel, electricity, and all other related expenses. With estimates of the size of Jubilee Field ranging up to 1.8 billion barrels, and production slated at up to 120,000 barrels per day, it was going to be a huge production—easily two million dollars per day for a deep-water project like ours. EO Group's share of the tab would be significant every month.

The hard business lesson I was learning was that if your costs were going to be carried by a partner, be mindful of the trigger that causes the carry to stop. For example, if we had been required to start paying our share of costs as soon as the oil began selling on the market and the partners would all start earning cash, then that would have eliminated our problem. But when you're still pumping and exploring for oil during production and you have no income, you are running up a massive daily deficit before the oil even begins selling.

Our free ride was going to stop the instant the first oil hit the tanker, which was scheduled to happen sometime in late 2010. From then on, we would have to pay our share of development and production costs. And I didn't have a dime to my name. I owed friends, relatives, family members and acquaintances money that I had borrowed to live on after I'd been fired by Kosmos. Even the couple of thousand dollars Bawuah-Edusei sent me from Washington didn't last long.

When EO and Kosmos had negotiated our agreement back in 2004, this wasn't seen as a problem, because we had assumed that EO would be able to get funding to continue in the project and pay our way. What couldn't have been foreseen, however, was that lies would continue to be stirred up about me, that I would be publicly accused of bribing a President, that Ghana's A.G. would go after me, that my own consortium partner Anadarko Petroleum would report me to the U.S. government, that the CID would investigate me relentlessly, that Kosmos would turn on me as soon as Jim Musselman was gone, and that the Government of Ghana would level 25 criminal counts against me . . . all of which would make it impossible for me to borrow a dime.

We were scheduled to start production by late November. In two months, I would start owing a million dollars a month. Give or take a hundred thousand or so. As a businessman and as a partner, I could understand that. We each had to fight our own battles. Mine had just been made a bit more difficult than those of my partners. And often by my partners.

Compared to other oil companies, Kosmos was a small player in the industry and had virtually no capital of their own. But they had the financial backing of private equity firms Blackstone Capital Partners and Warburg Pincus, which, combined, managed worldwide investments valued at more than US$100 billion. Kosmos was not hurting. Not by a long shot.

But I was hurting.

Kosmos had helped make sure of it.

EO Group had just sixty days of remaining carried interest from Kosmos until first oil and first cash call. I was on my own.

I left Dallas thinking, *What do I do now?* For five years I had been on a team, fighting a joint battle with partners I had introduced to Ghana and WCTP.

Now it was every man for himself.

34

TICK TOCK—*BANG*

I was in deep trouble. It wasn't the first time in my life I had been shoved into a corner with a metaphorical gun to my head. But I refused to be robbed. It was just another problem to be figured out. From way back in 2000, when Presidential candidate John Kufuor had come to Houston and challenged the Ghanaians in Houston to find oil in Ghana, solving problems had become my métier.

The meeting with Kosmos in Dallas lit a fire under me. It was time for a whole new shift in strategy. If Kosmos had made peace with the Ghana government, maybe it was time for me to build some bridges, too.

I had moved to the United States a couple of months earlier, after becoming tired of the threats, tired of the accusations, tired of the A.G.

constantly telling the news media she was investigating me, was going to charge me, prosecute me, expose me, jail me, ruin me. Throughout the entire barrage against me and EO Group, I had given no public defense, no explanations to the news media, nothing. I had kept quiet, on the advice of legal counsel, because I had been told I was going to be arrested any day. But my leaving Ghana had given rise to the idea, in the mind of the public and the pundits, that I must have been guilty because I had "fled."

Eventually, however, a man has to stop fearing the attacks of the powers that be, and take a stand. Either they take me to court and put this all before a judge and see what comes of it, or back off and stop the threats and harassment. It was time to return to Ghana and dance to the music.

When I moved back to Ghana in late 2010, I brought unassailable ammunition with me: the letter from Acting Deputy Chief Charles Duross, of the U.S. Department of Justice. I was now ready to go on the counteroffensive, to vindicate myself, and to restore my reputation.

Talking to the news media in person was something I had been hesitant about doing when I'd had the specter of the U.S. DOJ hanging over me. But now that they had refused to get involved in Attorney General Mould-Idrissu's persecution of me, and with her seemingly putting prosecution of me on hold, it was important for me to go on the offensive and allow the press to interview me. They had already outed Tsatsu Tsikata as the one who had been pulling strings behind the scenes. Maybe they were also ready to listen to my side of the story without prejudice or political pressure.

Now that the U.S. government had spoken, and the newspapers were looking in other directions (albeit still on the story that had started with my arrival in Ghana in 2004), I was determined to tell my side of all that had been said about me and done to me for two solid years. I set up appointments to visit reporters, including those who had written unsavory things about me, to recount the facts and to try to sway them with the simple truth.

By this time, my friend and associate Joseph Owusu had moved to Ghana, and was working for Hess. I brainstormed with Joseph. Almost everyone who had benefited from the initial WCTP opportunity that had birthed Jubilee Field (people who had once treated me like a hero) had either turned against me or had gone silent or neutral. But my counteroffensive against the slanderous words spoken about me and the libelous statements written about me during the past 20 months, as well as my angry reactions and defensive posture at being attacked on so many different fronts, had done nothing to nudge public perception over to my side. Why? Could it have been that by expressing anger with the newspapers and media, my defensive stance (which was more of a righteous indignation) made me appear guilty to some?

Part of the perception of the public about me and EO Group boiled down to one idea: that we were the front for a former President to whom we were funneling money or were planning on doing so when the oil income started rolling in. That perception was everywhere in Ghana. And nobody had heard EO Group's side of the story directly from me.

Perception was the hurdle I had to overcome. A picture had been painted of me as a shady character who had weaseled his way into a sweet deal by underhanded means. If I could change the negative atmosphere created against me by the Government and the actions of my own partners, then perhaps the banks might reconsider, and help with our first oil obligations. But it was about more than money. It was about *truth*. It was about protecting my reputation. It was time to counterpunch, to get the truth out.

It was time to find out what Ghana was really made of. It was time to go on the road, to make the rounds of industry leaders, decision-makers, government officials, legitimate journalists. I would tell them the plain, simple, honest truth. The rest would be up to them. It was a strategic decision, of course, but a necessary one. If we could change perception by informing corporate and political decision-makers, nudge the narrative a bit into the green, and positively impact news stories, then we might be able to go to the banks for a loan against our asset and be able to post what we owed during production.

First, I went to Ato Ahwoi, the Chairman of the GNPC who had replaced Sekyere-Abankwa, and said, man to man, let's talk. Let me tell you the facts. He listened. I showed him the GNPC document that had broken down each of the Petroleum Agreement percentage details of every oil company that had signed an agreement with Ghana from 1997 through 2008. Surprisingly, Chairman Ahwoi had never seen the document, which was in his own department's files. His demeanor began to change as he read it and realized that indeed EO Group had not received a sweetheart deal and that there were other oil company deals that had been even better than ours.

The meeting with Chairman Ahwoi encouraged me. I then went to the President of the Ghana Bar Association, to Deputy Minister of Energy Armah-Kofi Buah, to Moderator of the Presbyterian Church, Kwasi Botchwey, to Vice President Mahama, to the newspapers. I went to anybody who would listen to me. I looked in their eyes and I talked. I laid out the course of events from 2002 to 2010 in meticulous detail. I was on a crusade to clear my name.

I spoke to people like Nana Butler, a professional in resource procurement and logistics who was connected to the government. I explained everything to him, from beginning to end.

"That's the story?" he stated when I had finished.

"That's it," I said.

"We'd been made to believe that you guys are just a bunch of bad guys."

I had my work cut out for me.

Between Joseph and other friends of mine, we went everywhere, talked to everyone. We talked to friends and loved ones who might be able to help us get an appointment to talk to people in positions of influence. We talked to politicians and bureaucrats. Anyone who would listen to us, hear our case, intervene.

I told them that EO Group owed millions of dollars and that if I didn't get a loan as quickly as possible, everything was lost. Forfeiture of EO Group's shares would allow Kosmos and the other partners to get EO Group's share, free and clear. I gave them an earful, telling Minister Oteng-Adjei that if the government was willing to let all the work I had done on behalf of Ghana go down the drain, that they and their children would suffer for it.

Not all members of the media were happy about me showing back up in Ghana and going to bat on my own behalf. On September 14, 2010, *The Enquirer* newspaper, displaying their keen skill at not allowing facts to interfere with their reporting, repeated old news stories ad nauseam. Showing a jaunty sense of humor in making criminal accusations against me, they ran a front page headline story . . .

"INVESTIGATORS CLOSE IN ON EO GROUP—GEORGE OWUSU ON THE RUN!"

"As the Criminal Investigations Department (CID) and Attorney General close in on the circumstances under which . . . criminality came to characterize the dealings between the EO Group-Kosmos Energy in their operations in Ghana, a key suspect in the plot . . . has jumped bail and is suspected to be hiding in the United States of America. Mr. Owusu, who was on a $100,000 surety bail failed to report himself to the police CID on August 31, 2010 prompting a police enquiry into his whereabouts. George Owusu's lawyer was said to have told police that he could not locate the whereabouts of his client whilst the one who stood surety also told police that he could not trace steps of Mr. Owusu.

"It was there that it dawned on the dumbfounded police that Mr. Owusu had jumped bail. Mr. Owusu's bail hearing has been

scheduled for September 16, 2010. If by that time he has still not
been located by the police, an arrest warrant may be issued by the
court. It is not clear why Owusu decided to jump bail . . . George
Owusu's alleged absconding has heightened suspicions in some
circles that he must certainly have something to hide . . ."

—GhanaWeb.com, September 14, 2010[114]

Most Ghanaians understood that *The Enquirer* was not a legitimate
"newspaper" and that they took their marching orders from certain politicians lurking in the shadows, but enough was enough. It was time
to punch back. The next day, EO Group issued a press release titled
"George Owusu Is Not on the Run." In it, we took the discredited publisher of *The Enquirer* to task for printing a litany of lies about me, and
stated that I had not jumped bail, as had been erroneously published.
We added:

> "Rather, he has been fully co-operative with Ghanaian authori-
> ties, and has conducted no less than thirteen interviews with them.
> He has continuously maintained contact with Ghana authorities,
> either directly or through his counsel. The lawyers involved know
> where he is or how to reach him at all appropriate times.
>
> "The fact is that increased activities by all partners, includ-
> ing EO Group, leading up to first oil, have necessitated a series
> of meetings mostly overseas that George Owusu has to attend.
> These meetings are at times separated by a couple of days and
> on different continents. This makes it financially imprudent to
> always return home to Ghana after meetings . . . In fact, at the
> time of issuing this statement, Mr. Owusu is at one such meeting
> in London. Mr. Owusu formally informed Ghanaian authorities

[114] Online news website GhanaWeb.com in a Sept. 14, 2010, article citing an Enquirer story
titled "Investigators Close in On EO Group." See: See: http://ghanaweb.com/GhanaHomePage/
NewsArchive/artikel.php?ID=190351

about these developments and the need to attend these meetings before he left the country. The investigating committee is aware that it is Mr. Owusu's intention to return to Ghana to confer further with the Ghanaian authorities.

"The EO Group's activities leading to Ghana's first commercial quantity oil discovery were all transparent and legal. The United States Department of Justice has so discovered and consequently exonerated the EO Group, and there is no basis for the Ghanaian authorities to reach any other conclusion. Thus, given the EO Group's interest to see a speedy resolution to this matter, it would make no sense for one of its partners to delay unnecessarily this inevitable and overdue outcome.

"In the meantime, it serves the interest of Ghana and Ghanaians for all to desist from peddling falsehoods. The EO Group hereby reserves its rights to pursue any legal recourse available to it under Ghana's laws."

Yet, two days after we issued our press release, *The Enquirer* was back at it with another story, this time asserting that my lawyer had "appeared at the Cocoa Affairs court 6 in Accra," and "promised that he will produce his client on the adjourned date." The tale went on to repeat the lie that "Mr. Owusu has violated his bail terms by refusing to report himself to the police," and added, "It is not clear why Owusu decided to jump bail . . . "[115]

Obviously, the U.S. decision had not pleased everyone.

I refused to give up. Correcting the libelous assertions of these so-called "newspapers" was an exercise I had become tediously familiar with over the past two years, like a teacher having to constantly correct

---

[115] Online news website GhanaWeb.com, in a Sept. 17, 2010, article citing an *Enquirer* story titled "Court Adjourns 'Runaway' George Owusu's Case." See: http://ghanaweb.com/GhanaHomePage/NewsArchive/artikel.php?ID=190544

an intellectually challenged student who couldn't seem to grasp that two plus two equals four.

Throughout October and November, we worked our way down the list. I spoke with corporate executives, lawyers, bureaucrats, newspaper editors. Some meetings lasted hours. I was thoroughly familiar with subjecting myself to litanies of questions. I answered everything they asked. The responses were mostly surprise that there was an intelligent, reasoned, logical answer to all they had been hearing in the news (or writings in the print media) during the past two years. Gradually, the word spread to the powers that be that there was another side of the story apart from the one that had been fed to them.

During the process, something interesting began to happen. We became energized. We realized that nearly everyone we sat down with had a complete misunderstanding of the facts. They had been buying into the media hype and political division because there was only one point of view being put out there, as we had decided not to speak to the news media until there was a resolution with the CID and Ghana's Attorney General and their prosecution of me. The more we sat down and talked with these officials and leaders and businessmen, the better I felt about things. Ultimately, this had a snowballing effect for the perception of the EO Group case.

Going on my "media truth tour" had been crucial in correcting the erroneous impression that had been created about EO Group and our involvement in the discovery of Jubilee Field. It was also an important precursor to going to the banks and financing sources to try to get a loan before Jubilee production began and bills started coming due.

Our next step was to meet with bankers. We went to JP Morgan and Goldman Sachs. We made our case to anyone who would listen. A banker at Goldman Sachs took an interest in our case. She immediately grasped that EO Group was presenting her with a solid bet.

"If I had the money," she told us, "I would invest in you."

But Goldman wouldn't let her, she explained, because of all the negative news about EO Group. It was a relief to finally start feeling encouragement and hope flooding through me.

Yet, to my surprise, even with all the interest from insiders and outsiders, Americans, Chinese, Brits, Indians, and Koreans who wanted to buy a piece of Jubilee, nobody would touch me. Banks and investors tend not to finance people branded as criminals.

I was not a criminal, of course, but from January of 2009 through 2010, the Ghanaian government had been investigating me with an unrelenting fury, leveling 25 criminal charges against me, freezing my bank accounts, feeding negative reports to news reporters. Then my partners began digging into everything I had done, every penny I had received and spent, and every conversation I'd had during the past decade. Between my "partners," the media, and the Ghanaian Government, my name had been utterly trashed. All toward the goal of trying to prevent me from getting what I had earned. It was like having a winning lottery ticket that the store clerk refused to cash because he was upset that I had won the lottery—and then accusing me of forging the winning ticket.

The *Washington Times* story and several others that had estimated the value of EO Group's share of Jubilee Field at "as much as $200 million," had apparently made little impact on bankers, because my efforts with the banks proved futile. Every bank we had approached had said "no" to a loan against our equity. Some didn't even take a meeting with us. It seemed like no matter what I said, the fact that respected international publications such as the *Wall Street Journal*, the *Financial Times of London*, the *Washington Post*, and the Ghanaian media had been leveling charges, making toxic insinuations and publicly chastising EO Group for two straight years was too high of a hurdle to overcome.

Finding a loan against our stake in Jubilee Field so we could cover our portion of costs was its own very big incentive. But there was another clause in our agreement that added an extra kick: EO Group would forfeit *all* of our shares to the other partners if we were unable to pay our portion of ongoing production costs. Everything I had would go to all of those who had been trying to take it from me for almost two years. Unless I came up with my share to defray the costs.

Basic math had told me that, using ExxonMobil's multibillion dollar valuation of Jubilee Field in their attempt to buy out Kosmos, it should have been no problem obtaining a loan against EO Group's share. In fact, one of my consortium partners, Tullow Oil, had received with "ease" the equivalent of nearly $2 billion from investors in connection with Jubilee Field . . .

"TULLOW OIL RAISES £1BN"

"Tullow Oil . . . has raised £1 billion from shareholders, mainly to finance projects for the commercial production of oil. . . . Chief Executive of Tullow Oil, Mr. Aidan Heavey, expressed optimism about investor confidence in Ghana, saying that he saw no evidence that investor sentiment in Ghana had been dented.

"In apparent reference to the Kosmos/Ghana government's dispute which has generated speculation that the problem has impacted negatively on foreign investment in Ghana, Mr. Heavey said the dispute would not delay production of the first barrels of oil scheduled for the fourth quarter of this year. He said the proof of investor confidence in Ghana was reflected in the ease with which Tullow raised £1 billion pounds from shareholders in February of this year, most of which was meant to finance projects in Ghana."

—*Daily Graphic*, March 18, 2010[116]

It seemed I was more toxic than the Gulf of Mexico waters that Anadarko was having to help clean up. Even the Koreans, who had 20 oil and gas fields in 14 countries, including Libya, Nigeria, Peru, Vietnam, Russia, Canada, Indonesia, Yemen, and Kazakhstan, were

---

[116] *Daily Graphic*, in a March 18, 2010, story titled "Tullow Oil Raises £1bn" (p.2).

eager to put up money for a piece of Jubilee. On March 23, 2010, the *Daily Graphic* reported, "A delegation from the KNOC [Korean National Oil Corporation] led by its President and Chief Executive Officer, Mr. Young-Won Kang, made this known when he paid a courtesy call on the Minister of Energy, Dr. Joe Oteng-Adjei, at the Ministry. . . . Korea did not see its investment in Ghana as a short-term move but would remain committed to ensure that parts of its profits were reinvested in the development of its host country."[117]

The difference was that none of these players were going to banks for loans. They were going to shareholders and private equity funds to back them. The banks had already turned me down. I was the only player at the table who had no backers. I was so down on my luck, I was a walking country song. And with the rapport between Kosmos and me completely gone, I couldn't even throw myself at their mercy and ask them for a loan, even after CEO Brian Maxted had told *The Washington Times* in late March, "We have always viewed the possibilities of the project as a success story for everyone."[118]

Failing to get a loan to be able to start paying Kosmos at first oil cash call was putting us in a bad position. Soon, there would be a first oil celebration when the first drop of crude hit the steel floor of the FPSO Kwame Nkrumah. Soon, Kosmos would be sending us bills. The oil wouldn't be producing income for awhile, and some of the partners would be in negative cash flow until then, but they each had deep pockets or financial backers to get them over that hill. Even the GNPC would be able to carry their share once their carried interest came due, because foreign countries in need of black gold were lining up to "befriend" Ghana.

Only little EO Group had no one.

[117] *Daily Graphic*, in a March 23, 2010, story by Seth J. Bokpe titled "Korea Oil Company Expresses Interest In Jubilee Fields" (p.25).
[118] *The Washington Times*, in a March 26, 2010, story by Chuck Neubauer, quoting Kosmos CEO Brian Maxted.

It was bad enough that the market was ignoring EO Group because we had been so publicly vilified almost daily for nearly two years. What was worse was that our own partners had no incentive to help us, because if I was forced off the field and my shares forfeited, that would mean more for them—for *free*. My work of an entire decade would be gone. And it would be going to those who had been trying to get it from me since January of 2009.

First oil was a day I had dreamed about for years. It had now become a day that scared me to death. The clock was ticking down like Big Ben in my head.

I shut out the noise and focused on the words of Carthaginian General and statesman, Hannibal: "Aut viam inveniam aut faciam."

Either find a way, or make one.

CHAPTER

35

FIRST OIL

First oil hit the FPSO Kwame Nkrumah on Sunday, November 28, 2010. I called myself an oilman. And I was about to be treated like one.

I wanted to enjoy that day. I could have, too, if I had been able to focus on the fact that we wouldn't officially receive a cash call for a few days, and wouldn't be considered deadbeats for 30 days after that. But something even worse happened on November 28 that prevented my being able to enjoy that milestone in my life. Normal business practices allowed for a 30-day grace period to pay bills once they were received. Usually, I would have until December 28 to pay our share of the ongoing production bills. But there was that trigger clause in my deal with Kosmos that ended our carried interest at first oil and stipulated two other events: payment of our 1.75% share of ongoing daily production costs for Jubilee Field. Those numbers for EO Group alone would eventually total tens of millions of dollars.

There was no way I could enjoy first oil. Because the carry had stopped for me, and I had to start paying my way going forward. As of December 29, 2010, day 31 after production began, I would be in default. Forfeiture proceedings would begin at day 90 of default.

I was joyful that we had arrived at first oil. But my joy was bittersweet.

"GEORGE OWUSU'S TEARS OF JOY"

"The name of George Owusu, the man whose untiring efforts led to oil discovery in Ghana, was missing in yesterday's [first] oil launch. He and others were eclipsed by a concentrated dose of politics in a deliberate act of rewriting the history of Ghana's oil find. Before yesterday's event, Ghana had been prospecting for oil in large scale without success until EO Group, led by Mr Owusu, brought in Kosmos Group to drill oil at Cape Three Points in the Western Region, striking oil in commercial quantity over three years ago. . . . The sad news however is that Mr Owusu, who is currently the Chief Executive of EO Group, and other architects of the oil project, had been humiliated in the past, thereby denying them the fruits of their labour.

"In his emotional address to the press, when his company and other Jubilee partners met journalists in Accra ahead of yesterday's inauguration of first oil, he said Ghana could only reap the benefit of the oil if more George Owusus were created. 'These are the kind of people who will stay and invest in Ghana. Until government supports the local entrepreneurs, the foreign players in the oil sector will continue to have the lion's share,' he stated."

—GhanaWeb.com, December 16, 2010[119]

---

[119] The online news website GhanaWeb.com, in a Dec. 16, 2010, story titled "George Owusu's Tears Of Joy." See: http://www.ghanaweb.com/GhanaHomePage/business/artikel.php?ID=199625

I told journalists that our Jubilee partners, who were foreign oil investors, were not fools—they were in business for profits, first and foremost, and then send them back to their respective countries. According to the December 16, 2010, GhanaWeb story, even Ghana's vast gold reserves mostly benefited foreign investors, who took the majority of the money out of Ghana.[120]

Without realizing it, I had begun a precarious transition: from businessman to activist. When people, through no fault of their own, are on the verge of losing all they had worked so hard for, they tend to speak more freely and more fearlessly to those who need to hear the truth.

There was no time to wallow. I had to act like any normal businessman, put on my game face and act as if my world wasn't teetering on the edge of a cliff.

On November 30, 2010, I was invited to speak at the Jubilee First Oil Dialog at the La Palm Royal Beach Hotel in Accra. The conference, hosted by the Jubilee partners, discussed issues concerning Ghana's emerging oil industry. Attended by business leaders, the news media, and other interested parties, the conference included a Q&A session that deliberated on potential challenges in connection with development of Jubilee Field. I spoke on a topic close to my heart: the need to reserve some sectors of energy industry supply services for Ghanaian citizens, who represented a minority ownership in the country's resources and related infrastructure. Hundreds of workers in Ghana's oil field were from other countries. We were equally as capable, experienced, and educated as the foreign employees, companies and countries coming into Ghana to take resources out. It made sense that Ghanaians should share in more of the work and profits.

Dai Jones, President and General Manager of Tullow Oil Ghana, who was born in Ghana, echoed the sentiment, adding how important

---

[120] Ibid.

it was that we "manage the expectations and the misconception that Ghana would become an oil rich country once production starts." Jones warned that Jubilee Field "is just a step to developing an oil and gas industry, and just one oil field is not enough to get there."[121] But the truth was, with Tullow's latest discovery in the Tweneboa Field, the oil fields off the coast of Ghana were rich, vast, and hugely promising for the country—if the nation would decide not to give it away as Ghana had her gold resources to foreign firms. Ghanaian citizens should not be treated as latecomers to the feast found in their own backyard, but become true owners of the yard *and* the feast.

In their report on the First Oil Dialog, the *Daily Guide* newspaper stated that, "Preparedness of the indigenous people living in the catchment area of the oil find and of local industries/companies to provide services and products were some of the major challenges identified at the dialogue," but, the story added, government plans allowed for the training of only 200 Ghanaians in the oil industry. That simply wasn't enough.

Obviously, as the pressure mounted on me to come up with my share of Jubilee production costs, my mindset about the industry was undergoing a shift. Was I an oilman first, or was I Ghanaian first? I was a Ghanaian oilman. I was starting to question why it was important for the industry to take so much from the indigenous people, and why so few Ghanaians owned Ghana's own natural resources. Was I part of the problem in owning a piece of Jubilee? Or was I part of the solution by being one of only three Ghanaian citizens who did?

That was an internal debate that would have to be put on hold. I was too busy hunting for a white knight to step in and save EO Group from being shoved out of the nation's new oil industry altogether. Yet, I was one of the primary reasons such conferences were taking place in Ghana at all in the new millennium. I would continue to attend these

---

[121] *Daily Guide,* in a story titled "Jubilee First Oil Dialogue Held." See: http://www.modernghana. com/news/306369/1/jubilee-first-oil-dialogue-held.html

conferences as a Jubilee partner, whether Kosmos or Anadarko or even the Government wanted me to or not, because I refused to fade into the woodwork.

36

TAKE A PITTANCE ... AND GO HOME

During December, I borrowed, begged, and found the money to travel to meet with VIPs and Government officials who might take up my cause and help EO Group stay afloat. The press had proven somewhat willing to hear my side of the story. The banks had listened, but had been unable to make a loan structured to use our interest in an oil field as collateral.

I was making some progress with the possibility of Société General Bank coming to our aid. I walked into the bank with the bank's executive who had arrived from Switzerland, and knew of me through another of his colleagues. A Ghanaian bank manager immediately rushed towards the door and screamed *"Him?"* He was pointing at me.

Just before we could gather our thoughts to ask his concern, he continued "No, no—you don't want to do business with *him*."

This was one of the most embarrassing moments in the whole ordeal and how I learned how much of a cancer I had become in the local Ghanaian circles. And my meeting was cancelled without discussion.

It was over with the banks. Now it was time to see if movers and shakers would help us avoid being snuffed out. We were dying. We did not deserve to be killed. I was not the bad guy. In fact, EO Group had done something for which we should be lauded.

I wanted the government to clear my name publicly, to tell the world I was clean, so banks would help me.

"Let's not kill off the only Ghanaians among the consortium partners," I told them bluntly.

It was almost as if I was pitching the NDC party line. *Let Ghana control the fields.* But that shift had been forced upon me by my own partner, Kosmos Energy. I felt that they were not only disregarding what I had brought to their doorstep, but they were disrespecting and disparaging me personally. They were not acting as a partner, as fellow Texans, as oil industry team members. They were acting as adversaries of a Ghanaian man, as if now that they had gotten something valuable from me, it was time to drown me. That was not the way to do business. They had access to plenty of funds to come up with a creative solution to prevent EO Group from being shoved against a wall with a knife to our throat. Instead, they had issued cash calls, knowing we couldn't pay until oil began selling on the market, and knowing that our not being able to pay would put us in breach of contract, and knowing that *that* would trigger forfeiture of our ownership.

Then, Kosmos surprised me. They told me they would be willing to buy EO Group's share of the field. They calculated what we owed them, they estimated the interest rate they would have to pay to finance the purchase, they deducted other various fees and charges, and they offered to pay what they determined EO Group's share in Jubilee Field was worth: $18 million. Basically they were saying, *Take a tiny pittance and go home*—in spite of the fact that Kosmos was sitting on a find potentially worth more than $4 billion dollars and they stood to make hundreds of millions on it.

Rather than making an offer that would honor the founding member of the team that had discovered the richest oil field on the African continent in more than a decade, they were offering me virtually nothing. Protocols of business behavior didn't advocate partners stabbing one another in the back.

I understood Kosmos was simply operating from a purely business position. After all, they too were under tremendous stress. Still, I didn't enjoy being bullied by a firm I had helped to get its first major project.

Bawuah-Edusei thought we should take the money. Jim Barnes, who had been working on a delayed fee basis, strongly advised us to take the offer. When I stood my ground and refused the insulting $18 million offer, Barnes stepped aside. Barnes felt it would be very foolish for me to turn down the offer and clearly indicated that he was nearing the end of his desire to continue the fight. Bawuah-Edusei also felt it was time to accept the offer or we might end up with nothing. They asked Joseph Owusu to approach me to try to convince me to accept the $18 million.

I told them no.

I felt I had been forced into this war by foreign partners who didn't see things the way I did in Ghana. I simply couldn't take a paltry sum for an important resource that I had been fighting to help bring to life for years.

I pressed onward with my loyal and faithful friend, Joseph Owusu, and continued to seek potential buyers who understood the bigger picture. As always in these resource wars across developing nations, it was the citizens, and particularly the indigenous people, who were affected the most. Only by the grace of God was I now involved in something that had the possibility of lifting many of my fellow Ghanaians out of poverty—and that was worth fighting for.

As a December 15, 2010, story in the *National Geographic News* stated, "The Jubilee Field is expected to raise hundreds of millions of dollars a year in revenue for the government's coffers—money that could help this poor West African country improve people's lives by investing in education, health care, industry, and infrastructure."

Sure, Ghana wasn't exactly a poster child for managing resource revenues to the benefit of her citizens, but they'd barely experienced one decade as a true democracy. Which was probably why that same *National Geographic* story stated that many people were concerned that our oil discovery "could transform Ghana into a smaller-scale Nigeria, a nearby oil-rich country plagued by corruption, ethnic violence, and frequent spills—often tied to vandalism."[122]

Still, it would have to be up to Ghanaians like me to fight for what belonged to Ghanaians. All I could do was to hope that the Government would stop getting in the way of my efforts to do exactly that.

---

[122] *National Geographic News,* in a Dec. 15, 2010, story by Jeff Smith titled "New Oil—and a Huge Challenge—for Ghana." See: http://news.nationalgeographic.com/news/energy/2010/12/1012115-oil-ghana-environment-jubilee/

CHAPTER

37

Victors Rewrite History

On December 15, 2010, the First Oil Celebration was held in Ghana. The partners were flown from Accra, 120 miles west to Takoradi, our base of operations. From there, we were taken by helicopter to the FPSO for the inaugural ceremony. We then flew back to Takoradi for the celebration event, where several hundred people were assembled for the gala.

It was the same arrangement as in Singapore. Chairs for each corporate partner group of representatives. No chairs for EO Group.

I asked where I should sit. I was directed to a chair in the front row. I sat down.

An usher approached me and said, "No, no. I'm sorry, but you can't sit here. It's reserved."

In fact, the chair had been reserved for an executive from one of Kosmos' big financial backers (Blackstone or Warburg Pincus). But the problem was that the only vacant chair was all the way in the very back.

For being 61 years old, I was an extremely vigorous man. Fit, in great condition, healthy as an African bull elephant. But I was tired. I was weary of being shunted here, sent there, told to go, told I can't go, told they don't want me, told to get lost, told to stand, told to ride on the press bus, told to sit in the back. *I. Was. Tired.* I was not going to get up for a finance tourist visiting Ghana on behalf of Kosmos who hadn't put in a single day in the trenches like I had for the past several years.

"I'm not moving," I responded to the usher.

"Sir, it's reserv—"

"Over my dead body," I cut him off.

I wasn't asking for a red carpet; just to at least be recognized. No more courtesy than that. "Hey, there's George Owusu. Here, George, sit right here, sir." But when I came in and was totally ignored as if I didn't matter, didn't count, even though I was one of the main reasons this ceremony was taking place . . . that hurt.

The man looked at me. I didn't break his gaze.

I told him, "I am not moving an inch. If that means causing a commotion here, then fine. Call the police to arrest me. But I'm not moving."

Bring it on.

The ceremony was chilly that hot day in the oil port city of Takoradi, Ghana.

The relationship between Kosmos and me was already bad enough, so it didn't surprise me when they stopped mentioning my name on background during interviews with the national and international news media, and wrote my name entirely out of the history of Jubilee Field. It was as if Kosmos Energy had formed in mid-2003, received a pile of cash from their benefactors Blackstone and Pincus, wet a finger and stuck it in the air, and then trooped over to Ghana, found WCTP and

Jubilee Field, and got a fully approved Petroleum Agreement from the GNPC, all within 12 months. Without ever having so much as visited Ghana. As the victors often do, Kosmos had rewritten history.[123] I was just another African at the back of the bus.

One good thing came of the First Oil ceremony. When the seating arrangements had been settled, I happened to be near President Mills and the Minister of Energy. By then, my ire had reached the point where I could contain myself no longer.

I felt like I was reaching the end of the road. Between the Government of Ghana and Kosmos Energy, they were crushing me. I was not a criminal. I was, foremost of all of those people onstage with us that day, the one who truly deserved to be a part of the celebration.

As December wound down, we were approaching 30 days past due on the cash call, and hadn't posted a penny. I became frantic. I continued meeting with financial institutions around the world to pitch my dilemma and explain my unusual collateral. None were able to help.

I talked to any government executive and minister who would listen to me. I was angry at the politicians in Ghana, at the NDC Government, and management bureaucrats for going down this road to national embarrassment for allowing one of the only Ghanaians connected to Jubilee Field to be pushed out of the country's greatest achievement in the modern history of Ghana.

We were almost 30 days past due. At 60 days of nonpayment, our delinquency would go into forfeiture proceedings. We were looking at the obvious. Nobody would make us a loan, so we decided to try to sell EO Group outright. The problem with selling was that, although there were many potential buyers, the issue was that we had to go to the government to get approval to sell. The same Government that had been

---

[123] Even though the company's own founder and former CEO Jim Musselman acknowledged it in the movie "Big Men" (directed by Rachel Boynton), stating, "I came to Ghana because of George Owusu."

trying to put me in jail, and had refused approval for Kosmos to sell to ExxonMobil. There was no way I could go to the Government and ask them to help me out.

Still, I couldn't let that hurdle stop me from at least getting out there and soliciting offers. I hit the road again.

The owner of the telecommunications company called Airtel made an offer. That didn't work out.

I went to London to meet with a company called Renaissance Capital. That didn't work out.

One of the richest Indian men in the world wanted to buy EO out. We reached no deal.

Mattel Group, in London, wanted to buy. Their attempts failed.

I talked with Standard Bank. They said no.

I went to the International Finance Corporation. That didn't work.

I met with Sam Jonah, a wealthy Ghanaian who once oversaw the gold mining corporations in the country. We discussed the possibility of him making us a loan for a percentage of our shares to help us meet some of our cash obligations. That didn't work.

I called the Minister of Energy and appealed to him.

"You need to be careful with what you are doing," I told him. "Ghana had tried to produce oil since 1896 and was not successful. Through our effort, we were able to find commercial oil. This asset is for the whole country, it is not for me or EO Group. We are trying very hard to hold onto it. Are you going to sit down and deny us our share—the only share that will be coming to Ghanaians other than the GNPC's share—and most of it goes to the U.K. and the United States?"

My last meeting had been arranged by a friend who had contacts in Angola. It was Friday, December 24, 2010. Christmas Eve. Sonangol, the Angola National Oil Company, wanted to talk. I flew to Angola and met the Sonangol executives. They made us an offer of $200 million. The value of EO's share of Jubilee had been calculated at somewhere between $300 and $400 million. They wouldn't come up. I passed on the offer. Estimates of the top range of the value of the Jubilee Field and EO Group's percentage of those numbers were higher than $200 million.

Was it arrogance on my part to walk away from that much money? Was it foolishness? No. It was based on the fact that I had put my entire life, my heart, my mind, my soul into this venture for years, and I wanted to get the real value for it. When you're used to being strapped for cash, and you're down, and you're against a wall, and you are fighting for your very existence, and you have already gambled all you have on something you deeply believe in, and you have nothing left to lose, why not go for the best? I did not know for a *fact* that I could get a higher offer. I did not know where my confidence was coming from. Maybe I was naïve, maybe I was stupid, but for whatever reason, I didn't want anyone to take me for a ride. My back was against the wall, I knew I could fail, but something inside me told me that the world would not let me fail after all the work I had done. But the biggest reason of all was that I felt like the good Lord was behind me.

We hit 30 days past-due and were now heading to the point where most companies begin default proceedings—60 days of missed payments. As I flew home from Angola to Ghana that Christmas weekend, I calculated that I had only 30 days left.

Boy did I calculate wrong on that.

After 30 days of non-payments, Kosmos Energy served EO Group with notice that we were in default of our contractual agreement to pay back our carried interest plus arrearages. If we didn't start payments to them by February 28, 2011, we would be forced into forfeiture of our share in Jubilee Field. The letter was signed by Brian Maxted.

I became frantic.

I told Maxted, "Look, you're my partner. We've been in this together from the beginning. Now you're throwing me over the side. I'm going to lose everything."

Maxted[124] told me later that he felt that with the Mills Government in power, I was going to "have a problem" because I was a partner with Kosmos, and as long as I was associated with them, I was "going nowhere." He pointed out that the difference between Kosmos and me was that Kosmos had financial backers that would continue funding them, but I had nobody. So he was jettisoning me, he said, "to save our own [posterior]," and that putting me into default on this contract was, "like throwing somebody off the side of a ship in the middle of the Atlantic Ocean and believing it's the best thing you can do for him."[125]

In my opinion, it was an unfortunate and imprudent business decision by the Kosmos CEO. By refusing to continue to carry our interest in Jubilee, Maxted was effectively forcing Tullow and Anadarko into a difficult position: they could either shoulder our costs until we could find funding or a buyer, or until the field was monetized, or they could allow Kosmos to force EO Group into forfeiture and thus be robbed of our share of Jubilee Field. The latter move would pose an ethical dilemma fraught with political ramifications: it might not look well to either the U.S. or Ghanaian public for an American firm to force out the Ghanaian partner that had led them to the Ghanaian oil field in the first place. It would also be adding incredible insult to the earlier injury of having fired the partner who had previously been cleared by Anadarko's investigation, cleared by Tullow's investigation, and even cleared by Kosmos' own investigation.

Maxted told me later that I, "had no options," and that Kosmos couldn't help me, "because the DOJ investigation [was] going on and creating more red flags."[126] Yet, everyone involved was aware that the U.S. DOJ had completed and ruled on their investigation of me more than half a year earlier, officially stating on June 2, 2010, that I had not violated any American laws.[127]

---

[124] Brian Maxted, former CEO of Kosmos Energy, during an interview with authors George Owusu and M. Rutledge McCall, April 8, 2014.
[125] Ibid.
[126] Ibid.
[127] Ibid.

The victors indeed rewrite history.

We didn't know how quickly Kosmos was going to shut us down on the carried interest stipulation violation after we couldn't post our cash calls. But we desperately needed to post some capital. We had been carried up till this point. It was now past due time to chip in our share of production costs. There were commercial ways that could have been handled by Kosmos, for example, from a distribution setoff once oil was selling. But Kosmos wasn't interested in talking serious ways to help us out. They merely demanded, "Time to post."

Put up your millions, George. Now.

For EO Group, the game was finally over. Kosmos, billions. Owusu, zip.

That old familiar depression wrapped itself around me like a clammy blanket.

CHAPTER

38

NOTHING LEFT TO LOSE

The first week of the New Year, 2011, a wave of nostalgia overcame me as I read a newspaper article in the *Daily Guide* titled "George Owusu: The Oil Magician."[128] Musselman had officially retired only days earlier. The story took me back to the days in 2007, when we had first discovered Jubilee, back when I had been hailed as a national hero and later had the Order of Volta bestowed on me by the Government. The story, by Charles Takyi-Boadu, even had the photo of me, President John Kufuor and Jim Musselman, which showed me pouring the crude oil from the small bottle onto the plate being held by Mr. Kufuor. I smiled at the fond memory.

---

[128] *Daily Guide*, in a January 7, 2011, story by Charles Takyi-Boadu titled "George Owusu: The Oil Magician."

The story closed with a much appreciated line: "It is time for Ghanaians to celebrate their own because if not for the fighting spirit of the EO Group, the much talked-about oil may not have been discovered."

The story also corrected many misperceptions that had cropped up in the past couple of years about the first major oil discovery in Ghana, a historic event the details of which many people seem to have forgotten. I could only shake my head after reading the story. The oil business indeed had strange bedfellows. The following week, I borrowed some money to fly to London to meet with another potential buyer. That deal fell through, too.

On the shuttle between terminals at Heathrow Airport for my return to Ghana, I encountered GNPC Chairman Ahwoi. It was the second time I had seen him. But this time I was more insistent than earlier. I let loose on the man.

"We are the only Ghanaians in this whole consortium," I told the Chairman firmly. "The entire thing is owned by foreigners. Tullow, Anadarko, Kosmos—they're all American and European companies. I am the only African who owns a little piece of it, but because of all of your charges and the false accusations put out against me, it's been impossible for me to either sell or finance. Are you going to allow these foreigners to rip this from the hands of the Ghanaian who initiated it all in the first place?"

The time for political correctness was past. The Government of Ghana knew the score. They knew the end was near for me. What would the world think if Ghana allowed its only citizen involved in Jubilee Field to be stripped of the very asset he had initiated the discovery of? I hoped Chairman Ahwoi would get the political ramifications of the thought.

To my surprise and some chastisement, the Chairman responded calmly, "George, you are worrying too much. If I were you, I wouldn't worry so much."

His retort struck me as odd. He offered no explanation, and in the bustle and busyness of Heathrow, there was no time to ask him what he meant. Had I just been given a ray of hope?

Or was it a foreshadowing of my final doom.

After I returned to Ghana from my meeting in London, I phoned the Minister of Energy, Dr. Joe Oteng-Adjei, and spoke with him. Then I made an appointment to visit Ghana's Vice President, John Dramani Mahama. I was at the end of my rope.

I pled my case to Mahama in his office. I told him what he (and the entire country) had already been told, that the efforts of EO Group during the past seven years in Ghana had been clean and legitimate, that we were a business that had gotten the job done without ever cutting corners.

"We didn't pay anybody a bribe," I told him. "If we had paid any-body anything, you would have seen it. Because the Government has looked at all of my bank accounts and financial statements, and at re-cords from banks all around the country, including the U.S. And they found nothing. Your Government knows this. Mr. Mahama, we are only a few days from forfeiture. If someone does not intervene, we are going to lose everything."

The irony was not lost on me that I had for so long avoided the Government as much as possible, due to the legal assault against me by the Attorney General, and the interrogations of me by the CID throughout 2009 and 2010, yet there I was, appealing to the country's Vice President to intervene. I was only doing what any dedicated CEO would do to save his firm after all avenues had been exhausted.

I sensed that Mr. Mahama was sympathetic to my case. I pressed gingerly forward.

"In a handful of days, this whole thing is going to collapse," I said. "I think it's going to be shame on us, on the Government, on the country, that you were the sitting Vice President when the only Ghanaian who helped the country get an entire oil industry lost everything because the Government stood by and did nothing to help."

I could push a little because, to his credit, Vice President Mahama was very sympathetic. He was the only Government official who seemed to understand, both from a business standpoint and a political one, that it would be the right thing to try to assist EO Group. He was one of the few people in Government who had expressed a willingness to help me.

When I finished presenting my case, Mahama said something even more eye-opening than the odd remark the GNPC Chairman had made to me at Heathrow on my return from my meeting in London.

"But, George," the Vice President remarked, "Tullow is going to buy EO Group's share."

What?

He continued. "Yes. Tullow is going to buy. They just left my office. They're meeting with the Minister right now. They said they are going to buy."

Chairman Ahwoi's remark suddenly made sense.

Questions, curiosity—*hope*—flooded my mind. Why had I not been told? How long had this been in the works? If it was true, why had I been kept in the dark?

"Let me call the Minister of Energy," he said.

He picked up the phone and called the office of Minister Joe Oteng-Adjei. The line rang. And rang. No one answered.

"He's probably in the meeting with Tullow right now," Mr. Mahama said, hanging up the phone. "Why don't you go there?"

When I arrived at the Minister's office, the door was shut, indicating that he was in a closed-door meeting. I sat in the outer office for a long time, burning with curiosity, waiting for someone to come out.

After awhile, I treaded to the men's room. On my way, I noticed a window that seemed to be in the general area where the office of the Minister of Energy was located. As I passed by, I glanced in the window. Seated inside, talking with the Minister, I could see Paul McDade,

Chief Operating Officer of Tullow Oil, Ike Duker, President of Tullow Africa, and Dai Jones, President of Tullow Ghana. Tullow heavyweights. Something big was going on.

After I finished in the men's room, I went back and resumed my vigil by the Minister's door, nearly sick with anticipation. After awhile, the group came out. I stood. Paul McDade padded past me. He stopped and turned to face me.

"Hi, George," he said. "Can you meet us this evening at the Golden Tulip Hotel, say, around seven thirty?"

I told him I'd be there. The Tullow entourage left. I looked at the Minister, inquiringly.

"George," Minister Adjei said, pointing in the direction of the departing Tullow men, "those Tullow guys have some very important information for you. When you meet with them, listen and listen carefully. They may have some good news for you. Because it might help you."

It was cryptic. It didn't reassure me. Informally, I knew what was probably happening. But still, I wondered. Was this going to be another Kosmos type of offer, take a tiny pittance and go away?

And what did Adjei mean by, "good news for you, it might help you"? That could mean anything. *Good news: the oil business is through with you. Go back to Texas.* Is that what he meant?

I assured him I would listen to whatever they had to say to me. "By the way," I added, "Vice President Mahama is trying to get in touch with you."

"I've already spoken to the Vice President. *Don't worry.*"

I went straight home from the Minister's office, changed clothes, and headed to the Golden Tulip.

I got there an hour and a half early. My mind was racing. If this was American football, the clock would be at the two-minute warning. Then, forfeiture would take hold like a python and choke EO Group off. I was so nervous I could barely think. No matter what was going to happen that night, I realized one thing: my life as I had known it since

I had arrived back on the shores of my home country in 2003 was over. If a deal wasn't struck, I would go home to America, permanently. If we struck a deal, I would go home to America, relieved. And, hopefully, well-compensated for my adventure.

I waited. Two hours felt like two days. People came and went. People checked in and checked out. People went into the bar lounge sober and came back out not so sober. Paul McDade and Ike Duker walked in. We exchanged pleasantries and sat down.

"George," McDade said, getting right to business, "how would you feel if we buy EO Group?"

I could have fainted from relief. I shouted, "Hallelujah!"

I was beyond exuberant. Barring whatever they were about to offer for EO Group's share of Jubilee Field, Tullow Oil had always treated me fairly, like a business partner, with respect. They also had deep pockets of their own. They'd recently discovered the massive Tweneboa Field. They weren't suffering huge oil cleanup bills like Anadarko was with BP in the Gulf of Mexico. They had never kicked me around like Kosmos had. Tullow had been the good guys all along. More importantly, they always remembered who I was in relation to Ghana's emerging oil industry.

It felt right.

"If you're interested in discussing terms," McDade said, "come to London and we'll talk."

If I'm interested? Here I was, about to lose everything, and along comes Tullow, with the best news I had heard since that day in June of 2007 when I'd been told we had discovered a huge field of oil. We set March 4, 2011, for me to go to London to discuss a possible deal.

I had to assume, since the Tullow executives had been talking to Ghana's Vice President and the Minister of Energy, that some groundwork may have been laid. And the Minister's last words to me were a clear indication that whatever was about to be discussed may have earned at least a conditional agreement from the government of Ghana. *Don't worry.*

Things were finally progressing. Over the past year and a half I had been subjected to Kosmos firing me, 25 criminal charges prepared against me by Ghana's Attorney General, Kosmos cutting off my legal representation, the U.S. DOJ investigating me and then clearing me, and Kosmos putting my company into default. Now there was talk of a possible sale—to the most stable of my Jubilee consortium partners.

After the meeting was over, I called my business partner Bawuah-Edusei and broke the great news. He said he wouldn't be able to attend the negotiating session that March.

I assured him I would be fine; I'd been on my own in this venture for many years.

He warned me not to be cocky about things at this point, and to "accept whatever they offer."

I promised him I would take anything over $200 million.

CHAPTER

39

HARD BALL

By the time March 2011 arrived, I was broke had been out of a job for 18 months. Tullow agreed to provide my airfare to London and pay for my accommodations. And Joseph Owusu and my lawyer Jim Barnes flew from Houston to London to meet me for the initial round of discussions with Tullow. We three would comprise my basic negotiating team.

By the time I boarded the plane to London for the March 4 meeting, the winds seemed to be changing. Hope was in the air. Oil prices were at their highest since the 1990s. Betty Mould-Iddrisu had been replaced by Martin Amidu as the nation's Attorney General and Minister of Justice. I hadn't heard a word from Amidu's office and he hadn't formally filed the charges Mould-Iddrisu had so painstakingly prepared against me before she left office. Refreshingly neutral noises had been coming out of the CID about me; they hadn't called me in for another interrogation in quite awhile. My Ghanaian lawyer, Addo Atuah, had expressed encouragement that the heat on me, while not entirely cooled down, seemed to be fading.

Talks got off to a quick start. Tullow wanted to buy EO Group's 1.75% share of Jubilee Field. We wanted to sell. They laid out a rough idea of their terms. At first glance, the basics seemed fine to me, but it would take awhile to hash out the details. I had gone into the negotiation with my hands tied, because if Tullow had offered a few million and we said no and walked away, there was nothing else left for EO Group to do. I was at the mercy and fairness of the Tullow executives. But this Ash-Town boy wasn't going to roll over. I had put the best years of my working career in the petroleum industry into this discovery. It had always been worth fighting for.

One of the early considerations to get out of the way was that EO Group owed Kosmos Energy for our share of development expenses they had carried for us prior to first oil, plus our portion of cash calls afterward. By now, that totaled around $70 million, and Kosmos was filing a lawsuit to recover the money or force us to forfeit our stake in Jubilee.

When Joseph Owusu, Barnes and I first sat down to map out our strategy, we did some research. The sole question was, *how much is this share worth?* How would you determine the price of EO Group's portion of the block? BlackRock Capital had done some research on it and had come up with a number. An energy and mining research firm named Wood Mackenzie (WoodMac) had also done some research. WoodMac was responsible for a lot of research in the oil industry. Whatever they said was taken as gospel. We also had Tullow's annual report. Even though companies tend to put the best spin on figures in their annual reports, the numbers helped establish the outer edges of a reasonable range of value for EO Group's 3.5% ownership in the WCTP portion of Jubilee Field.

I was negotiating from a weakened position with an extremely high-value asset against a highly experienced, well-heeled, venerable opponent like Tullow Oil. I had to ignore the pressure of the clock, block out of my mind the impending forfeiture date, and keep in mind that Kosmos Energy was lurking on the sidelines, waiting for me to fail.

My main counter-party negotiators were Tullow's CFO and another man, and the numbers they were pushing for weren't working for me. They were off by just enough to make me balk. I dug in and played hardball—knowing the deal could be stopped at any time by Tullow. Discussions nearly went off the rails a couple of times as we battled to come up with a number we could all live with.

Joseph and I played our hand as if we had partners behind us and that outside counter offers were being proposed to us. What I really had behind me was commonsense business negotiating experience and Ash-town shrewdness: *Only sit down at a table you're willing to walk away from. Don't bully anyone. Do your best to make everyone feel they got a fair deal. Be reasonable but firm. Be fair but strong. Never fear.*

It was tense. It was exhilarating. It wore me out. Over the course of the negotiations, several numbers had been argued for. $195 million. $264 million. $325 million. Wood and Mackenzie had their numbers. Tullow had theirs. We had ours. I was convinced our share was worth $400 million. Things had been meandering somewhat in the right direction, but Tullow was balking.

I wrote down $345M on a slip of paper and handed it to Jim Barnes. He looked at it, turned it facedown and casually brushed it aside as if Tullow would only laugh at us. Joseph Owusu pointed out to Tullow that they had already publicly committed themselves to a value for Jubilee Field—a number that favored us.

"When did we do that?"

"It's in your annual report," Joseph said.

Pointing to their own numbers in the report, Joseph said, "You are the ones telling the market and your shareholders that this is what you value Jubilee Field."

Of course, we knew full well that annual reports contained elements akin to bragging to potential suitors about how beautiful your daughter is, but it was a convincing move that boxed them in. We were playing a dicey game, using everything possible to our advantage. We were at the mercy of Tullow Oil, but I played an all or nothing hand as if my entire life depended on it.

Because it did.

All we needed to do was to agree on one number. Then we could notify Kosmos and the other partners that we had come to an agreement to sell and were just hammering out the details. Theoretically, between business partners operating under commonsense business guidelines (*Don't be unreasonable to a partner who is working earnestly to solve a problem*), something like that would stop the clock while we finished negotiations.

We argued back and forth on a number. Tullow didn't like our number, and countered. We didn't like theirs, and countered. There was too much air between the two. We went back at it. We narrowed down the range, but still had no firm number. We couldn't conclude. We were at a stalemate. We had no price.

We sensed that Tullow was possibly, just maybe, prepared to go up on their number. They gave us a range. It was tepid, but . . . workable. And suddenly, it happened. I began to feel dizzy and felt an odd tightening sensation in my chest. My breathing grew short and labored. Tullow CEO Aidan Heavey called for an ambulance. I was rushed to the hospital in London.

We'd been so close to an equitable number that Joseph Owusu and Jim Barnes tried to press for a conclusion after I was taken away. But the momentum had dissipated. Talks were put on hold.

Meanwhile, Kosmos was making angry noises from the sidelines.

They wanted their past-due money and ongoing cash calls and there were rumors that they were threatening to take EO Group to court to enforce a mandated forfeiture of our shares over to them.

"EO GROUP FAILS TO REPAY $61.7M DEBT TO KOSMOS"

"Kosmos Energy has revealed that one of the Jubilee Partners at Ghana's oil fields, the EO Group owes it an amount of $61.7 million and it might have to go to court to claim the amount as the Ghanaian owned oil company has failed to repay the amount on schedule in December 2010.

"Kosmos Energy indicates that under what is termed as the EO Participation Agreement, it was entitled to reimbursement for the development capital expenditures paid for the EO Group's 3.5% share of costs.

"In a filing to the US Securities and Exchange Commission, Kosmos disclosed, 'EO Group was obligated to pay their share of costs under the West Cape Three Point (WCTP) Petroleum Agreement pursuant to the joint operating agreement for the WCTP Block... Each non-defaulting party must pay its proportionate share of the EO Group's default amounts and has done so... EO Group has also not reimbursed Kosmos Ghana for the $61.7 million in EO Development Costs and accordingly currently remains in default...'

"According to Kosmos, as a defaulting party under the WCTP JOA, the EO Group loses its right to sell its share of oil production which is instead sold by the non-defaulting parties to repay the default amounts paid by the non-defaulting parties. Kosmos meanwhile, threatens to send the EO Group to court if EO fails to pay debt."

—GhanaOnline.org, May 2011[129]

---

[129] Online news website GhanaOnline.org, in a May 2011 story by Emmanuel K. Dogbevi & Ekow Quandzie titled "EO GROUP FAILS TO REPAY $61.7M DEBT (*cont.*) TO KOSMOS."

At the hospital, doctors had gotten my heart rate and blood pressure under control and ordered me to get some rest and not to continue to push myself so hard. But that was like telling an African lion to eat vegetables.

The next day, Tullow sent an emissary to my hotel room to set up a meeting for the following day.

"Just you, Aidan and Ike Duker," I was told. "No lawyers. No one else. Just us."

I told them I'd be there.

The next morning, I arrived at the Tullow office and walked into the conference room. Heavey, Duker, and I talked. And talked.

Finally, Heavey said, "George, we'll give you $300 million."

We were almost there.

The biggest offer I had received prior to my discussions with Tullow was from Sonangol for $200 million. The Mattel group had matched that. I had said no to both. The biggest number Tullow had given me up to this point had been $265 million. But I had still not been satisfied. I had been pushing Tullow hard for $400 million, which I thought our share was easily worth. But I understood that they needed to come out of these negotiations with their heads up, and I didn't want to kill the deal.

But it could still use some sweetening.

"Three fifty," I responded.

Heavey had gone up from $265 to $300. I had come down from $400 to $350.

He looked at me. He looked at Duker.

"Well . . . that may be a problem with my Board of Directors," Heavey said.

Sometimes, I mused, *meeting halfway is the right thing to do.*

"Look," I said, "why don't you give us just a little bit more? Let's settle it now."

See: http://ghanaoilonline.org/2011/05/eo-group-fails-to-repay-61-7m-debt-to-kosmos/

"Three zero five."

It was almost exactly halfway between the amount he had gone up and the amount I had come down.

I smiled. "Done."

Nearly a third of a billion dollars. Not a bad day's work for my eight years on the continent. $305 million. An average of thirty-eight million dollars a year during the eight years I had been in the oil business in Ghana. And what felt like a century of hell to get there.

Now we needed to buy some time to get Kosmos off of our backs. Tullow agreed. They didn't want this to be a bigger war for us than it already was. Tullow informed the consortium partners that they were in the process of acquiring EO Group, and that we were now working out the details of the deal. They requested that the partners exempt EO Group from default, not preempt the deal, and that Kosmos suspend forfeiture proceedings against us. As soon as the purchase was completed, Tullow would pay all of EO Group's past-due costs, as well as ongoing production cash calls. This would stop the clock, give us space to continue forward, and prevent any of the other partners from stepping in and trying to take the deal away from Tullow.

The partners agreed, and sent us exemption letters, assuring us that they would not attempt to preempt the deal. Kosmos agreed to suspend further action, pending the outcome of negotiations.

It would take us several more weeks to hammer out the details, but we could finally breathe. The law firm McGuireWoods was brought in to write up the contract.

We were almost home.

CHAPTER

40

FINAL OFFER

Before we had even begun talking, Tullow had wisely laid tracks in preparation for officially entering negotiations with us. Considering the acrimony that existed between EO Group and the Government of Ghana, Tullow wanted to get certain approvals before moving forward. As a publicly traded company, they didn't want premature news or later snafus to affect their stock price. So, they concocted a clever strategy. First, they had approached Ghana's Vice President, John Mahama and let him know that they were going to try to purchase EO's stake in Jubilee. Mahama okayed it. Then they moved downstream to the Minister of Energy, Joe Adjei. He also consented (as overseer of the GNPC, his approval to proceed would give the GNPC no choice but to go along, had he chosen to inform the GNPC at that time).

With those two high-level approvals in place, Tullow had then approached potentially the biggest obstacle of all: Attorney General Martin Amidu. Even though Amidu was effectively outranked by the V.P., Tullow might not think it wise to offer to shell out potentially hundreds of millions of dollars for the purchase of EO Group if Ghana's A.G. was going to rehash old news to the media that Tullow was dealing with criminals who used fraudulent means to acquire the EO block. Or worse, that as the deal was in the process of being buttoned up, Amidu had decided to officially serve me with the 25 charges that his predecessor had prepared against me. The press frenzy alone would kill the deal.

Mahama and Adjei approved Tullow making an offer to buy EO Group. The A.G., however, while offering no objection to Tullow's request, didn't give his specific approval.

Tullow had solicited these Government approvals before approaching me because of all the political madness surrounding me and EO Group, and the manner in which Kosmos had handled the failed ExxonMobil attempt to buy into Jubilee. Going first to Government officials to feel them out, Tullow was smart. They showed respect toward the host country. Equally important, they had done their homework prior to approaching me, because they didn't know for sure how I would respond to their offer. As a publicly traded company, if Tullow Oil approached EO Group and told us they wanted to purchase our share in Jubilee, and for some reason could not consummate the deal, it would affect their stock price.

All the way through the process, Tullow Oil had followed a classic, smart business approach.

On May 14, 2011, we officially informed the Minister of Energy that we had reached an agreement to sell and that we were close to working out the specific terms. We then informed Kosmos, Anadarko, and Sabre, and requested that they agree in writing to the sale and officially waive their preemption rights. Ten days later, on May 24, they each waived their preemption rights irrevocably, allowing the sale to go forward unimpeded.

There were conditions attached:

1. The deal would not go forward without the final, written consent from Ghana's Minister of Energy.

2. The deal would not go forward without the final, written consent from the Chairman of the GNPC.

3. Tullow wanted assurance from the Government that if there were any future investigation of EO Group by Ghana's Attorney General, it would never impact the deal. That is, if someday the Government claimed to have come up with irrefutable evidence that Edusei or I had committed some criminal offense in connection with our initial acquisition of the WCTP block license, Tullow would not be left holding the bag after having spent over $300 million and find themselves pitched against the Government. Tullow wanted a clean bill of health from the Attorney General before they would consummate the deal.

4. The funds were to remain in escrow and out of the reach of EO Group until January 31, 2013. (I was left in the dark as to the motive behind this condition, but I would soon find out—and it would surprise me.)

Twenty months seemed like a long time to wait for transfer of funds after the close of the deal. But who was I to argue? Besides, I'd already been without a job or salary for over a year, and was hanging on all right. I could do this. Three hundred and five million? Oh yes, I could do this.

I agreed to everything.

I felt a strange numbness after we shook hands. It was almost anticlimactic, because the monster had been slain. It was no longer a big deal.

The news hit the wire almost instantly . . .

"TULLOW OIL BAILS OUT GHANA PIONEERS"

"Tullow has bought EO Group, one of its partners in a giant Ghanaian oil field, for $305m (£186m). . . . . . EO Group was founded by two Ghanaians, George Yaw Owusu and Kwame Bawuah-Edusei, who first attracted foreign investment into the African country's oil industry. . . . EO was last year cleared in a US Department of Justice investigation . . . . . . after another partner, Anadarko Petroleum, raised concerns about its compliance with the Foreign and Corrupt Practices Act. The Department of Justice said it did 'not intend to take any enforcement action against EO Group or its principals, including Mr Owusu and Dr Edusei, and have closed our inquiry into the matter.'"

—The *Telegraph*, May 26, 2011[130]

"TULLOW TO BUY EO GROUP'S INTERESTS OFFSHORE GHANA"

"Tullow has entered into a conditional agreement to acquire the interests of EO Group Limited (EO), consisting of its entire interests offshore Ghana, for a combined share and cash consideration of $305 million. Tullow will issue 10,137,196 ordinary shares of 10p each in the share capital of the Company to EO to satisfy approximately $216 million of the consideration. The balance, which will include certain working capital adjustments, will be paid

---

[130] *The Telegraph*, in a May 26, 2011, story by Rowena Mason titled "Tullow Oil Bails Out Ghana Pioneers"; see: http://www.telegraph.co.uk/finance/newsbysector/energy/oilandgas/8539713/Tullow-Oil-bails-out-Ghana-pioneers.html

in cash. The receipt of Tullow shares as part of the consideration gives EO the opportunity to retain an indirect interest in the upside potential of all of Tullow's Ghanaian assets.

"Aidan Heavey, Tullow's Chief Executive, commented, 'This acquisition represents an excellent opportunity to extend our interest in these high-quality assets in Ghana. . . . this purchase further demonstrates Tullow's long-term commitment to Ghana . . .'"

—Rigzone.com, May 26, 2011[131]

On May 30, 2011, Tullow Oil Ghana President Dai Jones and EO Group sent an official letter to the Minister Joe Oteng-Adjei stating that as of May 26, 2011, the parties had entered a sale and purchase agreement which set out the terms and conditions for the proposed sale by EO Group to Tullow Oil of all of EO Group's 3.5% interest in the West Cape Three Points block contract area and EO Group's corresponding interest in the Jubilee Field effective as of December 1, 2010. A portion of the consideration would be in cash and a portion in Tullow ordinary shares at an agreed price per share, to be deposited into a legally binding escrow mechanism, where they were to be held until January 31, 2013.

We reiterated that the conditions for the sale and purchase were that EO Group and Tullow would obtain the consent of the Ministry of Energy and the GNPC, and that the Government of the Republic of Ghana was to confirm that any investigation by the Attorney General's office or any other governmental entity in relation to EO Group would not prejudice the acquisition. The letter closed with a respectful request for the Minister's consent to the transaction contemplated by the parties, and set the deadline for receipt of such consents at June 30, 2011.

It was nearly over. Now, it was just a waiting game. I wondered vaguely what would happen if we didn't get those written consents. I would know within 30 days.

---

[131] Internet website Rigzone.com, in a May 26, 2011, online story titled "'Tullow to Buy EO Group's Interests Offshore Ghana." See: http://www.rigzone.com/news/article.asp?a_id=107506

During that time, I discovered why the escrow clause had been in-cluded, preventing EO Group from receiving the funds until January 31, 2013: that date happened to be eight weeks after the 2012 Presidential election was over, which would allow plenty of time for the results to be safely decided and a run-off election dealt with, if necessary. The escrow condition had been requested by the Government, because they did not want me to have access to enough money to potentially attempt to swing the election away from the NDC in retaliation for all they had put me through. I had to chuckle at that condition. After all the Government had put me through, there was little chance I would want to stay in Ghana at all, much less back a political campaign there.

Only EO Group would have to wait out the escrow period. Kosmos refused to give their final approval unless they were paid in advance. So they and our creditors, including lawyers, consultants, and other people who had assisted us along the way, were paid a combined total of nearly $100 million, with the remaining funds and Tullow stock being put into the escrow account.

We settled in to wait for the required consents. The waiting indeed was the hardest part. In Ghana, deadlines aren't always taken as gospel. In some circles, they were mere suggestions than requirement. I prayed that nothing would happen to destroy the deal. Because it wasn't official yet. And this was still Ghana. Land of perpetual uncertainty.

CHAPTER

41

THE BANK WIRE

At last, three weeks past our June 30 deadline, we were told by the Government of Ghana that we could expect to receive the consents on Friday, July 22, 2011.

We gathered that morning in the Tullow offices in London at nine o'clock for the expected announcement from the government representative.

Ten o'clock. No word.

Eleven o'clock. We were told that the A.G. had been called into the President's office and wasn't available just then.

Noon. Nothing.

We made calls to Ghana. We were told to sit tight; they would get back to us.

By two o'clock, not a word.

A bank wire transfer of the $62 million owed by EO to Kosmos would be the final act that officially closed the deal. But that couldn't happen until the Minister of Energy, the Chairman of the GNPC, and the Attorney General said yes.

Three-thirty in the afternoon, no phone call, no fax, no email, not even a text message.

My blood pressure flared.

We waited.

At a few minutes till four, we received the first consent, from the GNPC boss. I relaxed, a little. London was in the same time zone as Accra. People were still at work in Ghana. There was still hope.

Around four thirty, we were told by a source that the A.G. was upset with the deal and didn't want to sign off on it, so he had shut off his phone and left the office. That was going to jam the whole deal for us. Had the retired A.G., one of my staunchest nemeses for so long, gotten to him? Did some "unnamed, Deep Throat, highly-placed government inside source" come forth with alleged new "proof" of alleged crimes?

A few minutes later, I let out another sigh of relief as the official consent came in from the Minister of Energy.

One more to go. Then we could hit a button and $62 million would be instantly transferred into the Kosmos account and my Ghana adventure could end.

I prayed like never before.

We waited. It was like having six of the numbers for a seven number lotto ticket, with the final number yet to be called. Would the Attorney General relent and assure Tullow that the government planned no more action against EO Group, that the investigation was concluded, that there was no wrongdoing, and that we were free to go on about our business?

At nearly 5:00 PM, we realized that the A.G.'s letter was not coming.

The mood in the room was somber. The roller coaster had come to a stop.

Then Aidan Heavey stepped in, took the reins of leadership, and made an executive decision.

"We've examined the investigations," he said. "We know everything that has gone on with them. We know there's nothing there. We're the ones who put that condition in there about an okay from the A.G., but it isn't a requirement of the law in Ghana. We're going to waive it."

The button was hit. The money was transferred.[132] The deal was now officially concluded.

I had won.

George Owusu with the representatives of the Jubilee Partners boarding a flight to the FPSO for the First Oil celebration, 2010

---

[132] The bank was in Houston, Texas, five hours behind London, giving us plenty of time to initiate the transfer.

George Owusu with the late President Atta Mills and government officials cutting a cake in celebration of the First Oil, 2010

From Left to Right: Paul McDale, Dr. Kwame Bawuah-Edusei, George Owusu, Aiden Heavey (CEO of Tullow Oil), Ike Duker of Tullow Oil after Tullow acquired EO Group interest in the oil fields.

When the news was picked up by the non-industry press, detractors began to gush out of their holes. A well-known, former high-ranking executive with the GNPC had reportedly approached Tullow and complained bitterly that they had paid too much for EO Group and that we didn't deserve all that money.

Another rumor suggested that the chairman of the GNPC had gone to Tullow and convinced them to buy EO Group. Maybe that had been behind his comment to me at Heathrow airport in January ("If I were you, George, I wouldn't worry so much"). This was more than possible, because timing was everything. If indeed Tullow had been approached by a political figure, it had not been done on my behalf. During the time of my 2011 negotiations with Tullow, the 2012 Presidential election year was right around the corner and election rhetoric was already heating up.

It was standard business practice to take any legal, moral advantage of every reasonable opportunity to succeed. I did do a PR job to try to bring about the sale of EO's asset, all the way from my press tour to rehabilitate my damaged reputation, to my visiting Government officials to plead with them to understand my cause and how it could affect their political fortunes for good or for ill. I believe it could have struck a chord when I had railed at the Government officials back in December.

It was very likely that certain politicians were afraid of the political ramifications of trying to crush one of their own in a sea of foreigners taking natural resources from Ghana and selling them for their own profit.

My motives were equally selfish, though more noble: I had always strived to do something for my country, to help Ghana rise and shine. That was the original purpose of the EO Group in the first place. I also wanted not to be robbed of a decade of hard work in bringing a multibillion dollar industry to the country, starting from the day Presidential candidate John Kufuor challenged Houstonian oilmen to find oil in Ghana, all the way to the day Aidan Heavey and I shook hands on the deal to sell EO Group to Tullow Oil.

Tullow had played a brilliant hand. It was a triple win, for them, for EO Group, and for Ghana's public image.

But I'd had to go through hell to win the battle.

CHAPTER

42

VINDICATION: THE BEAT GOES ON

Once the sale of EO Group was announced and the government seemed to be backing off me, many of my supporters began coming forward.

In the June 30, 2011, edition of *The Chronicle* newspaper, former President John Kufuor expressed that he felt "disappointed when some elements within the NDC decided to persecute and spread false-hoods about Bawuah-Edusei and George Owusu, the two leaders of EO Group, who helped find oil for the country." It was nice to have the former President go to bat for me publicly. Kufuor added, "These people have brought so much into our country. I honoured them for their dedication to the cause of the nation. The moment they [the Mills government] started persecuting them, I felt very sad for the nation."[133]

Yet, as the news of the sale began to reach the media and the public, as often happened when someone achieved success accompanied by wealth, crazies came crawling out of the woodwork. Some to whine, some to renew old accusations of malevolent deeds by me, some to weave new conspiracy theories (this time involving the Mills government) and some to try to have the deal reversed. Simple jealousy was usually at the core of such grumbling, and by then I had developed thick skin and an ability to ignore the naysayers.

The media knew they would make a lot of money selling their stories, and they went at it with gusto. The theme that had continually been weaving through nearly every story where oil or EO Group or George Owusu was mentioned, was my allegedly "pending prosecution." A news story on June 20 stated that I would soon be "dragged into court on nine charges, including forgery, conspiracy to commit fraud and deceiving a public officer" and that Bawuah-Edusei was "at large" . . .

"OFFICIALS OF EO GROUP TO BE CHARGED"

"The Attorney General and Minister for Justice, Martin Amidu has confirmed to Citi News that officials of one of the Jubilee Partners, EO Group will soon be dragged to court. Although he declined to state when the officials will be charged, Mr. Amidu alleged that the EO Group has committed offenses which the police have been instructed to charge them on. . . . Mr. Amidu's comments confirm a report in the Monday June 20 edition of *The Enquirer* newspaper which claimed that the promoters of the EO Group will be slapped with some 9 charges. The charges include forgery, conspiracy to commit fraud and deceiving a public officer. . . . Mr. Amidu noted that the court would not be hindered from

---

[133] *The Chronicle*, in a June 30, 2011, story titled "WE PUT GHANA ON RECOVERY – Kufuor Speaks on Achievements"; front page banner (story p.3).

charging some EO officials even though a member of the group likely to face fraud charges is at large. '. . . when he is charged eventually the case would go to court,' he said."

—*The Enquirer*, June 20, 2011[134]

The story didn't explain why, if I was still on the verge of being "dragged into court," I hadn't been arrested while I had met with different Ghanaian Government officials in the months before, during, and after the recent Tullow negotiations.

In spite of the steady drumbeat against me, it was a great relief to soon be leaving behind some of the partner-related controversies of the oil business.

The best news headline that month was probably one that appeared in late July . . .

"EO GROUP 'LAUGHS LAST'—AFTER PROTRACTED SHADOW BOXING OVER MIRAGE"

"After months of unrelenting attempts by some elements in the ruling government to cause commercial and collateral damage to EO Group, the only Ghanaian partners in the Jubilee oil field, with planned prosecution of the group by the Attorney-General's office, reason has finally prevailed, thereby fine-tuning government's earlier posture on the issue. The twirl of controversies that surrounded EO Group's share in Jubilee Fields attracted major concerns from industry players, who argued vehemently that protracting the issue could gravely affect investment flows into the country's oil sector.

"The group was subjected to an incomprehensible campaign of character assassination, false allegations of misconduct, and abuse. However, the Ghanaian partners made a major stride

---

[134] *The Enquirer*, in a June 20, 2011, story titled "Officials of EO Group to be Charged." See: http://www.modernghana.com/news/335535/1/officials-of-eo-group-to-be-charged-ag.html

yesterday following the approval and conclusion of an agreement
with British firm Tullow Oil for acquisition of EO's stake in the
oilfield."

—*The New Crusading Guide*, July 26, 2011[135]

Meanwhile, over at *The Enquirer*, their latest comedy routine included a front page headline banner that read, "EO GROUP'S $15
MILLION SIN – Justice for Sale?" The newspaper proved once again
their expertise at reporting ancient rumors, dusted off and repackaged,
with some new jokes thrown in here and there. But this story contained an interesting new suggestion: Kosmos Energy had been let off
of Ghana's legal hook so they "could be used as a prosecution witness"
against EO Group, saving Kosmos from "collapsing."[136]

During the months of preparation for the drastic change my life
was soon to undergo, newspapers like *The Enquirer* seemed to be realizing that my days as their whipping boy were drawing to a close.
So they pumped out a last gasp, thinly rewritten rehash of a previous
story. Titled "EO GROUP CHARGES REMAIN . . . Gov't Resolved
To Prosecute Case," the tale claimed breathlessly, "The government
has no intention of dropping criminal charges against the EO Group,
highly placed sources within the corridors of power have disclosed to
The Enquirer. . . . the government took a firm stand after a marathon
meeting and resolved to deal decisively with the EO Group."[137] You
could almost hear the pleading desperation in the words as the writer
realized they were being printed in vain.

Throughout mid-2011, the news media cranked out their stories,

---

[135] *The New Crusading Guide*, in a July 26, 2011, story by Samuel Frempong, titled "EO GROUP
'LAUGHS LAST' – After Protracted Shadow Boxing Over Mirage"; front page banner (story
p.3). See: http://business.peacefmonline.com/news/201107/58898.php
[136] *The Enquirer*, in a July 26, 2011, story titled "EO GROUP'S $15 MILLION SIN – Justice
for Sale?"; front page banner (story p.4).
[137] *The Enquirer*, in a July 27, 2011, story by Godfred Opare Djan, titled "EO GROUP
CHARGES REMAIN...Gov't Resolved To Prosecute Case"; front page banner (story p.4).

theories and accusations, with some outlets simply reporting the facts as they were, others fabricating stories around slivers of truth, and still others missing the boat entirely. News of the sale was all over the television, the radio, newspapers, magazines, across Africa and around the world.

Anyone and everyone connected with EO Group and the oil industry in Ghana was under scrutiny after the sale. EO Group was accused of buying off the Mills government in order to get the sale approved—a 180-degree reversal of the media's earlier accusations that EO Group had bought off the previous government in order to get the exploration license in the first place.

After all the insinuations that the Mills Government had taken a bribe to let the deal go through, in late July of 2011 the media reported that the government had issued an official statement that it was aware of news reports suggesting that the Mills government had given up on its investigation of EO Group, and that in exchange, EO Group had paid the government several million dollars. Joe Adjei, Minister of Energy, strongly denied that the government had let EO Group off the hook in exchange for a payoff and explained that what had taken place was merely "the government's consent for Tullow Oil to enter into contractual arrangements with the EO Group for an eventual takeover of the latter's shares in the Jubilee Oil Field."[138] The Minister's statement then threw a warning at me: "The transaction did not in any way indemnify the EO Group from on-going criminal investigations which can lead to possible criminal prosecution."

Which meant that I was not out of the woods. It felt like I was back to square one all over again.

---

[138] Online news website ModernGhana.com in an Aug. 2, 2011, story titled "AFAG [Alliance For Accountable Governance] Commends Government on 'Amicable' EO Group-Tullow Shares Resolution." See: http://www.modernghana.com/news/343266/1/afag-commends-government-on-amicable-eo-group-tull.html

Though the sale had been completed and the EO Group episode of my life was starting to wind down, kicking around the *Prosecute EO or not?* ball had become the new political pastime in Ghana. In spite of the government approving the sale of EO Group to Tullow, thereby effectively admitting that EO Group's shares were legitimate and there was therefore no impediment preventing them from being legally sold, stories like those stood as constant reminders that I was still a political football. Ghana's rubber knife prosecutorial threat was being forever held to my throat, in spite of my having been repeatedly cleared or deemed not to have been involved in illegal activities, by several different investigative bodies, teams of lawyers, and even the U.S. government.

Some news reports suggested that if the deal actually had been approved by the government, then the hapless President Mills must have been tricked into signing off on it . . .

"DAGGERS DRAWN OVER EO GROUP'S SHARES"

"Deep-throat sources say the A-G insists that government should not consent to the sale because there is a prima facie case (justification) for prosecuting officials of EO Group for fraudulently acquiring the stake in the Jubilee project. . . . But he faces opposition from the Energy Minister who has publicly stated that government has consented for Tullow Oil to enter into contractual arrangements with the EO Group for an eventual takeover of EO's shares.

"Unconfirmed reports also say President John Evans Atta Mills endorsed the Energy Minister's position without consulting with the A-G. The President's action might not have been deliberate as the Energy Minister is said to have kept the decisions of an earlier meeting between the Vice President, the AG, and the Energy Minister on the subject (which ruled out reparation) away from the President."

—*Public Agenda*, August 5, 2011[139]

There were even news reporters who didn't seem to grasp how business worked.

On August 9, 2011, an online news organization released an article claiming "for a fact" that EO Group "never paid for the shares" we acquired in WCTP. Yet, the story never revealed that years ago the Government had accepted payment from, and issued a license to, EO Group and Ennex to explore the WCTP oil block in a deal that had been approved by Ghana's Parliament. It never mentioned my tireless years of work with other partners that had led to the discovery of the Jubilee Field (efforts that were never guaranteed to pay off). It didn't discuss the vast amount of money and hard work by EO, Kosmos, Tullow, and Anadarko to explore, discover, and develop the field. It never mentioned that EO Group's percentage of ownership was actually smaller than subsequent Ghana oil deals. It didn't reveal that the government of Ghana would receive many times more money from the find than EO Group ever would. And the writer failed to understand that EO Group's share had come, not from the government's portion, but from Kosmos Energy's.[140]

Some news organizations reported the facts. Others distorted them. And some just ignored them. Everybody had an agenda.

In war, the saying went, *truth is the first casualty*.

I had not been assured by any high government official that prosecution was off the table. Hanging over my head throughout the remainder of 2011 as I waited out the clock for the 2012 Presidential election to come, and then for escrow to close in early 2013, and then for the funds and Tullow stock to be transferred to EO Group, was the constant

---

[139] *Public Agenda*, in an Aug. 5, 2011, story titled "DAGGERS DRAWN OVER EO GROUP'S SHARES"; front page banner (story p.5).

[140] Online news website GhanaBusinessNews.com, in an Aug. 9, 2011, story by Ekow Quandzie, titled "Group Says Oil Companies Never Paid for Shares Acquired at Ghana Oil Fields." See: http://www.ghanabusinessnews.com/2011/08/09/group-says-oil-companies-never-paid-for-shares-acquired-at-ghana-oil-fields/

threat that I could still be grabbed, arrested, incarcerated and put on trial for those criminal counts against me.

Having a sword of Damocles hanging over me gave me an interesting mix of righteous indignation at all that had happened to me—and humility that I was at the mercy of a power greater than I. If I was to ever have lasting peace in my life, in my mind and in my heart, humility would have to overcome the resentment. It was a matter of choosing to express compassion and to feel empathy for others, even to those who would do me harm—as the Bible put it in Matthew 7:12, to "do to others what you would have them do to you."

I wanted to be viewed differently than how many Ghanaians had been viewing me for so long, but more importantly, I wanted to see people in a better light. That meant I would have to forgive. Everybody suffers heartache and disappointment at some point in their lives. We never know what people are going through that may cause them to treat us poorly. As the 1970s song by singer-songwriter Joe South went, "Walk a mile in my shoes. Before you abuse, criticize, and accuse, walk a mile in my shoes."[141]

All this negativity was a cancer.

I realized that, somewhere not too deep inside me, I was not unhappy to be exiting the oil business. It had served me well. My career had been one of exhilarating highs (cutting a deal to sell EO Group for almost one-third of a billion dollars), depressing lows (two dozen interrogation sessions with investigators, including those of my own business partners, being fired from a job I had both created and loved, and facing the U.S. DOJ and the FBI), and heart-pounding fear (the ARCO plant explosion in Channelview, Texas, on July 5, 1990), and on and on.

My career had begun with a literal bang. And my new one would begin with a rocket ride to new heights.

Not bad for a kid from Ash-Town.

---

[141] Joe South, "Walk a Mile in My Shoes"; Capitol Records (1970).

CHAPTER

43

REDEMPTION

"You get strong leaders only after a period of pain and hardship. You don't get them in a world of high prosperity."[142]

—Felix Zulauf

After the sale of EO Group to Tullow Oil, my next battle was with Ghana's Revenue Authority.

In Ghana, politics ran through everything. Because of envy, jealousy, vindictiveness, and anger that I had made a profit from my investment, some people decided that EO Group had to pay tax where tax was not

---

[142] As quoted in an August 2, 2010, interview of investor Felix Zulauf by Barry Ritholtz, economic and financial markets commentator, analyst and author. See: www.thebigpicture.com

due. Bureaucrats in the Revenue Authority were so concerned that I had made a lot of money that they became obsessed about finding a way to tax EO Group.

Petroleum operations in Ghana had their own set of tax rules and laws, as embodied by the Petroleum Income Tax Law. When this law was written, it was determined that in order to attract oil investors to the country, petroleum operations would not be taxed under the general tax code; a separate code was established for those.

First, the Revenue Authority attempted to charge me with breaking a tax law that didn't apply to the petroleum industry. When that failed, they sent a tax bill of $61 million, under the Natural Resource Tax. The WCTP petroleum agreement, as with all other agreements we signed with the Ghana government and approved by Parliament specifically stated that no tax shall be levied on petroleum operations other than what was stipulated in the Petroleum Income Tax Law.

The Natural Resource Tax was not in the petroleum income tax law. In all the Petroleum Agreements at the time there was a Stability Clause, which meant that even if Ghana passed a new law today, it could not be retroactive. The central issue was that when the Petroleum Income Tax Law was passed in Ghana, it stated that petroleum operations would have to operate under the Petroleum Income Tax Law and no other. They were saying that even though there was a general tax code and rates for the entire country, and everything else was taxed under that code, the Natural Resource Tax still applied in our case, and not the Petroleum Income Tax Law Parliament had passed. This interpretation was wrong.

I filed a protest of the $61 million tax assessment.

In the meantime, election rhetoric during the 2012 presidential race in Ghana was more heated than ever. By the last quarter of the year, it seemed it could go either way. For me, the election was a virtual nonevent. My mind was focused on other priorities. Thankfully, the news media was focused on the election and didn't pester me as much as usual. I traveled a lot, to meet with financial advisors, bankers and money gurus, in preparation for the official close of escrow of the EO/Tullow deal, and transfer of funds from the sale.

The year brought unexpected tragedy, as well. On July 24, 2012, 68-year-old President John Atta Mills passed away at a military hospital in Accra. Vice President John Dramani Mahama took office. Mahama was sworn in the same day, and would be on the ballot for the December elections.

His death prompted within me a certain amount of introspection and self-examination. I looked at all I had experienced and learned in the petroleum business, places where I had failed and where I had managed to succeed, what I should have done better, and what I would have done differently. In hindsight, I might have given President John Mills a bit more grace during the brief period of time he was the leader of Ghana during my tribulation had I only known his days were numbered.

On Christmas Eve of 2012, I received a Merry Christmas message from the Ghanaian Revenue Authority in the form of their decision on taxes due from EO Group: zero. The ruling was based on laws enacted to encourage oil investment many decades earlier, when Tsatsu Tsikata had been Chairman of the GNPC.

Who could have foretold that, many years before I even embarked on this journey, legislation and coincidences took place that would one day save me $61 million? Amazing.

At long last, January 31, 2013, arrived. EO Group's funds were released. It was ironic, however, that my Ghanaian bank accounts remained frozen. Not that I needed the money any longer. Yet, even if I wanted to, the Government made it impossible for me to invest money in the country without going about it by exercising certain financial gymnastics. Not that I wanted to be in Ghana much longer.

My trials in Ghana were finally winding down. My loyal friend,

Joseph Owusu, former Managing Director of EO Group, probably stated it best when he said, "When he was fighting this thing, George only had one thing in his corner. Truth. But now he has something else: he has money. If you want to mess with him now, you're going to have a big fight on your hands."

But I was not out to fight anybody. I had healing to do and a new life to build. It was a comfort to know that there would be no more investigations, no more threats of jail or prosecution, and no more public slander and false charges, not without having to face some of the best lawyers on the planet. What I wanted now was peace. I wanted to come and go as any other person had the right to: freely and without threats hanging over my head or having to constantly wonder what my partners were up to behind my back.

One of the biggest lessons I learned about the business component of my oil industry experience in Ghana was the importance of partnership. I learned that if partners don't work cooperatively, they are working at odds against one another. Any competitor who comes along can simply pick at a thread of that loosely woven fabric and unravel the whole cloth. Partners should always remain united, and never go behind one another's back without first going to the partner they are questioning. If the issue isn't resolved in that manner, then it must be brought to the other partners to address and resolve as a *team*, standing shoulder to shoulder, in truth and in confidence that the issue can be dealt with in a calm and reasonable way. If not, then initiate more stringent measures.

Being a partner in any venture is no different than being a team member of a sports club. You would never see soccer players on the same team deliberately tripping each other as they ran toward the goal, or reporting rumors of violations among their own teammates to league officials without evidence, or deliberately deceiving one another. Yet, that happened to me in Ghana with some of my team members. It was embarrassing to have partners fight against me, complain about me, and tear me down behind my back. It was childish, weak and unprofessional,

GHANA REVENUE AUTHORITY

In case of reply the
number and date of the
letter should be quoted

Our Ref. No. CG/GRA/COR/157/12
Your Ref. No.

Tel. No. 233-302-953407

P. O. Box 2202
Head Office, 4th Floor
Ministries Accra

24TH December, 2012

THE LOCAL MANAGER
EO GROUP LIMITED
GHANA OFFICE
P.O. BOX CT 123
CANTOMENTS-ACCRA

Dear Sir,

A close reading of Article 12 does not provide for the taxation of any consideration received as a result of any of the parties to the Petroleum Agreement assigning its interest in the WCTP. I would hold that on the authority of Article 12.1 of the Petroleum Agreement the assignment of EO Group's interest in the WCTP Block to Tullow Oil PLC does not give rise to any tax liability.

DATED THIS 24TH DAY OF DECEMBER 2012

GEORGE BLANKSON
COMMISSIONER-GENERAL

cc:

- The Hon. Minister, MoFEP

- Board Chairman, GRA

- Mr. Graham Martin
  Director
  Tullow Ghana Limited
  PMB CT 386
  Cantonments-Accra

Ghana Revenue Authority Decision on EO Group's Tax Liability, 2012

and it put me and my family in a very dangerous position.

We are all human, subject to the foibles and temptations that are common to man. Yet, we also have a choice in how to treat those with whom we partner.

As I prepared to depart Ghana in 2013, I looked around me at the people and organizations I had become acquainted with since 2004, and realized what a mixed bag our fortunes had become. President Mills was dead. Former A.G. Betty Mould-Iddrisu had resigned and would soon be involved in a financial scandal.[143]

The first year after EO Group had finalized the sale to Tullow Oil brought good news for some of the Jubilee partners. And not such good news for others . . .

EO Group had sold off at a handsome—albeit expensively-earned— profit. Sabre Oil too had gotten out of Jubilee Field, selling their 2.8% stake to PetroSA, South Africa's national oil company, for an undisclosed amount in September of 2012.[144] Unlike EO Group, for Sabre there were no tax disputes, no CID drama, no criminal accusations against them in the news media, and none of the headaches EO Group was forced to go through. EO Group had blazed the trail.

Tullow Oil had done very well by Jubilee Field. It was Tullow's largest single oil production involvement to date.

Kosmos Energy had resigned themselves to remaining in Ghana, ceased efforts to sell their stake after missing out on the potential multi-billion dollar payday through ExxonMobil, and listed on the New York Stock Exchange.

Yet, strangely, at the Kosmos headquarters in Dallas, Texas, very few

---

[143] Online website Citifmonline.com, in a June 29, 2015, story by Raymond Acquah, titled "Woyome Judgment Debt: Trial Judge 'erred,' Betty Mould was 'Ignorant'"; after Mould-Iddrisu sanctioned the payment of 51 million *cedis* to businessman Alfred Agbesi Woyome for financial engineering work he never did. See: http://citifmonline.com/2015/06/29/woyome/judgment-debt-trial-judge-erred-betty-mould-was-ignorant-report/

[144] Online website GhanaOilOnline.com, in a Sept. 24, 2012, story by Megan Wait, titled "Petrosa Acquires Stake in Ghana's Jubilee Oil Field." See: http://ghanaoilonline.org/2012/09/petrosa-acquires-stake-in-ghanas-jubilee-oil-field/

employees (if any) are aware that they owe their jobs to a black man from Kumasi, Ghana. I could find nowhere in the firm's corporate brochure or anywhere on their website or in their written history the name "George Owusu." I saw no framed portrait of George Owusu hanging in the Dallas Headquarters of Kosmos. I have been scrubbed from their history as if Kosmos Energy LLC had sprung whole from the earth on that propitious day in September of 2003 (before the company had even made a single dollar in Ghana), the day when I had tracked down James Musselman and made him an offer that would, within a decade, lead to making Kosmos Energy a multibillion dollar company whose interest in Jubilee Field had become—*by far*—the largest income-producing piece of the company's entire portfolio.

All in all, I had been fortunate to have had only a few powerful detractors during my ordeal. There had been many supporters along the way, though not all had been able to come forward publicly during the worst of it without bringing about probable harm to themselves. But good friends, hardworking, solid people whose belief in me never wavered, had been a constant source of support and encouragement, even when the power and might of the government of Ghana was bearing down on me.

Yet, to me, what was more important than the steadfast belief from all of these people was my name, my character, my reputation. Not even great wealth can replace a good name. As I had learned early in life from Proverbs 22:1 in the Bible, "A good name is more desirable than great riches; to be esteemed is better than silver or gold."

My name was intact before God.

Apparently, before Ghana, too. One of the best gifts I received after everything was done and behind me was a gift that my own country gave me: a letter from Ghana's Attorney General stating that I had been cleared of all charges and that the government would no longer pursue action against me. Appropriately, it was dated July 4, America's Independence Day. The letter would be framed next to the one I had received three years earlier from the United States DOJ, clearing me of all accusations brought against me by Anadarko Petroleum and the Attorney General of Ghana.

At last, my battle with the Warrior King was over.

It had been an exhilarating experience for me in Ghana (easy to say when you're treading away from the scene of persecution, where your would-be attackers lay sprawled on the ground, wondering how you had escaped their clutches). Although, had I not emerged unscathed physically and financially, my assessment might not be so generous.

Yet, there I was, once a boy from Kumasi, West Africa, who journeyed to the United States to try to make something of my life. I had supported my family. I had done the best I could to better myself under the guidance and admonition of the Lord. Along the way, came ironies. So many ironies. I loved my country. I thought I might have a chance to do all I could for the country before my time on this earth was done. So, after doing pretty well in the United States, in my middle age I moved back to my country to try to take just one more step upward, if it were possible.

And was it ever.

My actions had led to a massive oil discovery—the biggest discovery in West Africa in a decade, the first discovery of commercial oil in Ghana, a discovery worth billions of dollars. A discovery that thrust me and the entire country into the planetary resource war and set in motion a new political evolution of Ghana. As the government fought over the prize, instead of becoming more sophisticated as a political system, it got caught up in a struggle over control of vast riches. In the process, my own country and my own business partners treated me with such disdain that it drove me back to America, the land that had adopted me as a young man in my 20s and whose Government had treated me fairly, in contrast to the vicious persecution by the Government of Ghana.

In case of Reply the
number and date of this
letter should be quoted.

My Ref No. XA 414/13

Your Ref No.......................

Fax: 667609

E-mail: attorney-general @ Ghana.com

REPUBLIC OF GHANA

MINISTRY OF JUSTICE
P. O. Box MB. 60
Accra

4TH JULY 20.13.

July 3, 2013

Mr. Thomas Hughes, Esq.,
P. O. Box GP 968
Accra

Dear Mr. Hughes,

Re: Outcome of Investigation into the EO Group Limited, its Directors and Associates

Your letter dated May 6, 2013 on the above subject matter refers. We also acknowledge receipt of the previous correspondence referred to in your said letter from the former solicitors of your clients, OBK Law Firm of Accra, on the same subject matter and dated November 29, 2012.

As you may be aware, the Attorney General's Department and its allied investigative agencies commenced investigation into the operations of the EO Group and its directors relating to the possible commission of specific crimes, to wit, forgery of documents, deception of public officers in the process of bidding for oil contracts, causing financial loss to the state, money laundering, tax evasion and corruption of public officials. The investigation was initiated based upon a Mutual Legal Assistance request from the United States Department of Justice, which had commenced its own investigation into possible commission of corrupt practices under its Foreign Corrupt Practices Act against Kosmos Energy, an associate of the EO Group in the Jubilee Field Project.

Under Ghana's Mutual Legal Assistance regime, it was imperative for Ghana's Government to commence investigations with a view to assisting the United States authorities in their investigation into the possible commission of crimes by Kosmos Energy and its associates, including your client. These investigations took a long time to conduct and were concluded several months ago.

It is as a result of the length and complexity of the investigation that this Department has not been in a position to communicate the outcome or status of the investigation to your clients. However, this Department can confirm that no criminal enforcement action will be taken against your clients based upon the findings of the investigation. However, in the event that additional information or evidence is made available to this Department, the investigation may be reopened.

It is our hope that this satisfies your clients' request for clearance in relation to the investigation.

Hon. Dr. Dominic Akuritinga Ayine
Deputy Attorney General and Deputy Minister for Justice
For: Attorney General and Minister for Justice

Letter of Exoneration from the Ghana Ministry of Justice, 2013

Then came the irony of my vindication and the Government's statement of exoneration.

Through it all, I loved Ghana. She is my roots. My family's blood for generations is in her soil. I am the child of a mother and a father whose bones rest in her bosom. I belong to Ghana.

CHAPTER

44

GAME, SET, AND MATCH

There were many reasons why I was relieved to be out of the oil business. More free time was not one of them. If anything, I had less time, now that I began involving myself in philanthropic and other business ventures.

One of the first community projects I initiated in Ghana was the construction of a hospital in Akyawkrom, near Kumasi. On August 25, 2014, my wife and I broke ground on a new medical facility. Our plan was to get it up and running quickly by first establishing a clinic and then building up to a 100-bed hospital. With the healthcare crisis West Africa is experiencing these days (Ebola, malaria, AIDS, Guinea worm, and other diseases), I could think of no better use of my time and resources.

As for Ghana, there remain many hurdles to overcome in her quest to forge a new national identity. In some ways, the nation seems to be trying. In March of 2014, after five years of denying me access to my funds, the government ordered my accounts unfrozen. By then, I no longer needed the money, but having been unable to access or open accounts, get cash from a bank, or even obtain a Ghanaian debit card had been a burden during my years of persecution by the government.

Another irony that occurred after my battle to retain EO Group's 3.5% share in the WCTP discovery was that it became law in Ghana that foreign investors in the nation's petroleum sector had to have at least a 5% Ghanaian equity participation partner.[145]

Thousands of people have gotten jobs because of the nation's new oil industry. There are now dozens of new companies operating in Ghana that wouldn't have been there if we had not made the effort. Takoradi is now a booming city. Many new Ghanaian oil and gas companies have been set up. The skyline of Accra has dramatically changed, with countless construction cranes raising new high-rise buildings to the sky. These are all good starts.

However, sadly, Ghana is still a country where a citizen can wake up one morning and be told by the authorities that all of his assets have been frozen, and that there is little that person can do about it. It is the corruption, the bribery, the bitter, partisan, scorched-earth politics, the rampant envy and jealousy, mixed with arbitrary and unchecked governmental powers that make it possible for this to occur. Ghana is a nation where authorities can watch you build a hotel, and if a person in power doesn't like you or your politics or your friends, you can be ordered to raze the building to the ground on weak or nonexistent technical, legal, or bureaucratic grounds. Or on mere rumor. I saw it happen. Things like those can make a person think twice before investing in a country like that.

---

[145] This is more than the 3.5% EO Group held in the WCTP oil block—which the very party that enacted the new law had once bitterly complained was "too much."

George and Angelina Owusu at the Ground Breaking Ceremony for the Medical Campus in Akyawkrom Ghana, 2014

George Owusu with Dr. Robert Satcher, Orthopedic Surgeon and Astronaut at Akyawkrom Hospital construction site, 2014

1 Thorpe Road, Accra
P.O. Box GH 2674, Accra
Tel: +233-30-266 2395
+233-30-266 6902-8
+233-30-266 6174-8
Fax: +233-30-266 6417
E-mail: bogsecretary@bog.gov.gh

BANK OF GHANA

OUR REF: FSD/58/2014   **DATE:** 14th March, 2014
YOUR REF:

The Managing Director
Prudential Bank Ltd
Head Office
Accra

Dear Sir,

RE: DEFREEZING OF ACCOUNTS

The Executive Director of the Economic and Organised Crime Office (EOCO) has directed in his letter referenced EOCO/ED/INTEL/054/V.1/123 dated 3rd March, 2014 that the following subjects whose accounts had been frozen under the Serious Fraud Office Act 1993, (Act 466) be defrozen unconditionally. The subjects are:

1) Dr. Kwame Bawuah Edusei
2) George Yaw Owusu
3)
4)
5) EO Group Ltd
6) Kosmos Energy LLC
7) Kosmos Energy Ghana HC
8) Newbridge Hospitality Services Ltd
9) Equiva Services Ltd

Please take note of the above for strict compliance.

Yours faithfully,

AKU ORLEANS-LINDSAY (MRS)
FOR: HEAD
FINANCIAL STABILITY DEPT.

CC: The Executive Director
       Economic & Organised Crime Office
       Old Parliament House
       Accra.

Order to Release Freeze of Financial Accounts, from the Bank of Ghana. 2014

When I was younger and less experienced, I thought a little differently. When I would hear of a successful Ghanaian putting their money in a Swiss bank, I would think, "Why would you do that? Bring every dollar home so your countrymen can enjoy its benefits." I no longer think that way. Now I understand why they take their money and run before someone decides to mess with them just because they can.

People put their money in Swiss banks because there are no guarantees in Ghana. Laws are not taken seriously in the country and are not backed up consistently by the government. You learn to put your assets in places where there is law and order, where contracts are obeyed, where you don't have to go to arbitration or court to seek redress, where your money is safe from unlawful prying hands.

The United States is not perfect. The U.K. is not. Yet, compared to Ghana, they are Fort Knox. It is frustrating, because outside investments could do much good in Ghana. They would put many people to work. But there's no safety if the government can arbitrarily seize it out of anger or jealousy or spite or sheer craziness. In another part of the world, what I had done in Ghana would have earned me at least a parade, if not being asked to become Commissioner of some professional athletic league. In Ghana, it earned me persecution. Hopefully, that will all change.

The Jubilee oil discovery opened a whole new chapter in Ghanaian history. She is a far different nation than when I returned to the country to search for oil in 2003. In the space of 48 months, the country had gone from energetic, hopeful, vibrant, poor little Ghana, to *Player*. After our oil discovery was made, Ghana found herself caught up in the raging international war over natural resources. That, in turn, led to a political evolution in the country and sparked new levels of partisan bickering.

Immediately after our huge new oil discovery, the nation's narrative became all about great men and freedom and building up a nation's infrastructure and developing a viable economy. Yet, there was resistance to sharing wealth and giving working citizens an opportunity to join together in building a great society, making it difficult for a middle class to emerge. We faced the Nigerian "Big Man" paradigm. Indeed, until most African nations rid themselves of that tribalism mindset, they will continue to condemn their citizens to lives of endless poverty. The struggle for future Ghanaian governments is how to break the habits of centuries, how to resist the urge to see the populace as just one tribe or another, and how to bring the nation together as a united people for the good of her future generations.

It's time to come into the 21st century, Ghana. You could be great.

I serve as a living example to the youth of Ghana that whatever you set your heart, your mind, your steadfast efforts to, you *can* succeed. Let this book, this incredible saga, all that one of your own countrymen experienced in the modern history of our nation, be an encouragement to you: if I—a man raised in poverty and in the admonition and teaching of the good Lord—could do all of this and win . . . then certainly so can you. The keys are to never give up, never let people drag you down, and always choose to impart a spirit of honesty, curiosity, helpfulness, and patience in everything you do. And you will win.

I believe that all I experienced in my ordeal was God's ordained plan; otherwise, it would never have happened. On several occasions when things had gone to the brink, there was always an intervention. At any point during my entire experience, from back in 2001 and 2002 when Vanco had declined to allow me to join them as a part of their team in Ghana after all I had done in helping to pave the way to their receiving a license for a huge offshore block, to when Ennex dropped out at the last minute in 2003, all the way to the sale of EO Group's share in Jubilee Field ten years later, my forward momentum in Ghana's oil industry could have ground to a complete stop.

Yet, it didn't.

In 2003, I pushed ahead and looked for other exploration partners. When I first found Jim Musselman and he expressed initial interest, he too dropped out. Still, it didn't end. I continued pressing onward and a few weeks later I contacted him again and Kosmos came in.

Then came all of the horrid accusations against me and EO Group, the investigations of me, all the things the Ghanaian government did to me in their efforts to strip EO Group's share from us.

All of these things failed to stop my momentum, because Jubilee Field was simply meant to be. I just happened to have been one of the people God chose to bring it about. Why he chose me is anybody's guess. He could have used anyone. I do know this: there was always something at the back of my mind that told me all would end well. At the height of the craziness from 2009 to 2012, I felt an inner peace, knowing that I had done nothing wrong and that somehow the truth would come out and all would be fine.

Even after I had won this long and grueling battle, I remained a hardworking "regular guy." What had never been crushed out of me throughout the hardships this odyssey brought into my life, was my determination to remain upbeat, to encourage those I met, and to stay focused on the positive, no matter what was thrown at me. I owed that ability to my upbringing by a humble, itinerate preacher, my grandfather, Reverend Yaw Adu-Badu, who taught me the tenets of Christianity, the Golden Rule, and to honor and respect all people. His teachings remain with me to this day. During moments when my quest for "black gold" had left me with little to lean on, I always had his words to uplift my weary heart.

I am sometimes asked if it was all worth it. It took its toll on me and my family, and it was unfortunate that I had to go through so much to get to where I am today. Still, my answer is a resounding *yes*. I didn't have to go to Ghana. I could have stayed in America, where things are not as unstable. I may not have done something historic for the nation of my birth, but I would have led a peaceful, comfortable life. Yet, had I not tried, had I not made the effort and the sacrifices, I would never have had the opportunity to accomplish something for my country.

And to all those who stood against me, who tried to prevent me from reaping the benefits of my efforts, who tried to jail me, destroy my reputation and run me out of Ghana, I harbor no ill will. For, there is another old saying that I have found to be true. *Success is the best revenge.*

My parents, Opanin Yaw Owusu and Margaret Afia Mansa, would be proud.

AFTERWORD

Through the years, I have granted interviews to journalists, business groups (Global Affairs Council in Washington D.C. and World Affairs Council in Houston); Public reviews in New York, Chicago, Dallas and Houston; and at some of the leading universities around the world including Rice University, University of Oklahoma, University of Nebraska, Kwame Nkrumah University of Science & Technology, University of Ghana, and the University of Cape Coast.

I appreciate all the intellectual feedback and am grateful that some of the insights I have gained have been useful for perspectives on international business, especially in Africa, where there is enormous potential for economic growth.

Below are some of the central questions from these interviews.

In your opinion, do you see oil exploration in Ghana as a blessing or as a curse?

GYO: I think it has been a blessing. The benefits have been tremendous on many levels. We are witnessing an influx of investors into the country. For instance, by the time we brought Kosmos to Ghana in 2004, there were only Dana Petroleum and Devon Energy exploring for oil. Kosmos certainly de-risked the country in order for Ghana not to remain what many had called a graveyard for oil and gas companies. By 2008, there were 41 international companies applying for exploration licenses in Ghana.

There were news reports that you were a surrogate for government officials, and perhaps these individuals helped you to acquire the block. Is this true?

GYO: That is absolutely not true.
I have worked in the oil and gas industry for more than 20 years. I had also brought two separate companies to Ghana to evaluate the oil and gas opportunity before the Kosmos entry, and we went through the standard rigorous processes just like anyone else. One thing I know for sure is that we didn't cut any corners and everything we signed was transparent. It is worth noting also that, this was all after renowned industry experts were adamant that there was no oil in Ghana. We didn't receive any preferential favor.

At the onset, did you invest your own money into the Jubilee Field project?

GYO: Money and far more. When I decided to pursue this, I had to quit my job and my six-figure salary in the United States to chase an opportunity many experts called risky and dead. I left my family behind and took any savings I had so that I could pursue a dream I believed in. I borrowed money from friends to finance a gamble in an industry that often has a 10% success rate—at best.
That was the investment I made, I took a big gamble and it paid off.

Was Ghana government's 10% share in the Jubilee Field a fair deal?

GYO: Let me add an important detail here. There is a misperception that Ghana government (and by extension the Ghanaian people) got 10%. This is not true. The government received the following:
  • 5% in royalties,
  • 10% in participating interests,

- 3.5 % in paying interests,
- 35% income tax,
- and additional oil entitlement.

Altogether, the government of Ghana stood to gain between 50% and 55% of the venture; definitely not 10%. It is worth mentioning that even the 3.5% that the EO Group received came from Kosmos' share, and had nothing to do with what the country received.

Why did the EO Group get 3.5% of the earnings?

GYO: EO Group began this whole adventure as a partnership with Ennex. Not long after, oil prices plummeted to historic lows. Ennex then abandoned the opportunity and EO Group found ourselves with control of the rights to the entire field – 100%. It was probably one of the most difficult years in my professional career, but those are some of the unforeseen challenges that come with establishing any speculative business.

In the absence of the technology and financial capability, our search for a partner with the resources and the willingness to invest in Ghana is what led us to Kosmos in Dallas. There was understandably tremendous risk at stake, and they negotiated EO Group's share down from our original 15% to 3.5%

Is it fair to assert that Kosmos got a better deal than any other company in Ghana's oil exploration history?

GYO: Quite the opposite. I have always referred back to Ghana's Petroleum Agreements signed between 1997 to 2008, which are well documented. Hess' royalty payment stands out, in that it had been lower than all other companies that had signed similar contracts with Ghana. One thing to note, however, their Additional Paid Interest was half a percentage point higher than that of Kosmos, but that does not compensate for the 1% royalty loss to Ghana. So I have heard people make the case that it was actually Hess that had benefited most in Ghana's exploration agreements.

What is your relationship now with Kosmos, Tullow and Anadarko?

GYO: Since the EO Group sold our shares in the Jubilee Field, I do not have any contracts or any business related to the field's operation. I have friends in both Tullow and Kosmos, many of whom have been incredibly committed to Ghana's success. I am sure there will be an opportunity to work together in future.

I don't have any working business relationships with Anadarko Petroleum.

Do you have any ill feelings or resentment toward the people who levelled allegations against you for all those years?

GYO: Absolutely not. I walked away with the hope that everyone did their diligent work for the sake of the country. Despite the frustration I endured for several years, I met many who were very honorable and I became very impressed with their understanding of petroleum contracts and even the law in general. Even for the few who unfortunately chose to dwell on innuendos and rumors, I still do not take it personally at all. Truth always wins, and I go to sleep every night knowing I made an honest investment and did the best I could for Ghana, as well.

What do you see as some of the benefits that have come to Ghana since exploration activities began?

GYO: There is an entirely new oil and gas industry that the Jubilee Field exploration brought to the country. As a result, a lot of service companies have also come to Ghana to support the industry, and all this pays huge economic dividends to the country. There has also been astronomical growth in the country's Gross Domestic Product (GDP), a revival of a city like Sekondi-Takoradi that has become the oil and gas hub for the country, infrastructure developments and expansion of education and training in the oil sector.

Take a look at the skyline of Accra and the beautiful buildings seemingly springing out every day. I would bet the oil discovery and the huge economic advantage it brought to the country has a lot to do with it.

INDEX

ABOUT GEORGE YAW OWUSU

George Yaw Owusu is an environmental scientist who has worked in the petrochemical industry for 27 years.

He was a founding partner of EO Group, a company which partnered with Kosmos Energy to discover commercial quantities of oil in Ghana. He served as the country manager for Kosmos for several years. The discovery was featured in the documentary "Big Men" which was directed by Rachel Boynton and produced by the world-renowned actor Brad Pitt.

Owusu is also the founder of a private equity firm, Mansa Capital which engages in investment of private equity and debt in various projects in the United States and across West Africa.

Owusu and his wife Angelina are actively involved in philanthropic endeavors focused on healthcare, education and development in Ghana and in the United States through the George and Angelina Owusu Foundation

ABOUT M. RUTLEDGE McCALL

M. Rutledge McCall has ghostwritten and substantively edited scores of books for dozens of authors around the world. He has been featured on TV shows such as "NBC Today," BBC News, PBS, CNN News, "Larry King Live," KNBC News "Nightside Cover Story," PBS/KCET's "Life And Times: Thinkers, Shakers and Newsmakers," ABC News 9 Australia, and others.

His critically-acclaimed book, *Slipping Into Darkness*, was optioned for film by movie producer David O. Sacks, Co-Founder of PayPal.

McCall has served as CEO of an L.A.-based literary career consulting and management firm, and he has been a Senior Managing Editor in the book publishing business. He has also worked in the one-hour drama writers departments for most of the American TV networks and in production management for all of the major US film companies on some of the highest-grossing movies and top Nielsen-rated shows.

www.MRutledgeMcCall.com